"This book is a masterpiece. Gripping and whip-smart, *The Education of Millionaires* will forever revolutionize your thoughts on the connection between education, career success, and prosperity. Ellsberg is careful to avoid 'motivational fluff' and instead provides mind-blowingly sharp (and humorous) brass-tacks advice on how to profit handsomely by becoming a lifelong learner."

—Jenny Blake, author of *Life After College*

"If entrepreneurs were running schools, instead of bureaucrats, schools would be teaching a lot more of the skills and mind-sets found in this book. Since they're not, this book is a necessary antidote to a traditional college education."

—Scott Banister, founder of
IronPort Systems, Banister Capital

"This is the must read of the next era of education. This one book could be all the education you ever need to massively outperform even the Ivy League. The secrets contained are brilliant and simple to adopt."

—Cameron Herold, author of
Double Double, former COO of 1-800-GOT-JUNK?

"Just like the entrepreneurs he highlights in his book, Ellsberg challenges the conventional wisdom of what it takes to make it in this world. If you have an idea and the drive, nothing can stop you. And Ellsberg proves it."

—Simon Sinek, author of *Start with Why*

"You don't need a degree to live life on your own terms: you need economically valuable skills. Ellsberg's book is the blueprint for entrepreneurial education."

—Josh Kaufman, author of
The Personal MBA: Master the Art of Business

"Provocative and timely, Ellsberg lays bare what he sees as a giant hole in much of traditional education—a focus on 'academic' knowledge and a de-emphasis on the knowledge and skills necessary to actually succeed in life. Drawing from a wealth of interviews with successful entrepreneurs, he homes in on seven key success skills that help put you back in the driver's seat."

—Jonathan Fields, author of
Uncertainty: Turning Fear and Doubt into Fuel for Brilliance

"Ignore the stats, break the rules, devote yourself to something meaningful. You won't get that in an MBA program. But you'll get it from Ellsberg and his self-educated millionaires—and plenty of proof that true and sustained success can only be defined on your own terms."

—Danielle LaPorte, author of
The Fire Starter Sessions, creator of WhiteHotTruth.com

THE EDUCATION OF
MILLIONAIRES

It's Not What You Think
and It's Not Too Late

MICHAEL ELLSBERG

Portfolio / Penguin

PORTFOLIO / PENGUIN
Published by the Penguin Group
Penguin Group (USA) Inc., 375 Hudson Street,
New York, New York 10014, U.S.A.
Penguin Group (Canada), 90 Eglinton Avenue East, Suite 700,
Toronto, Ontario, Canada M4P 2Y3
(a division of Pearson Penguin Canada Inc.)
Penguin Books Ltd, 80 Strand, London WC2R 0RL, England
Penguin Ireland, 25 St Stephen's Green, Dublin 2, Ireland
(a division of Penguin Books Ltd)
Penguin Books Australia Ltd, 250 Camberwell Road, Camberwell,
Victoria 3124, Australia
(a division of Pearson Australia Group Pty Ltd)
Penguin Books India Pvt Ltd, 11 Community Centre, Panchsheel Park,
New Delhi – 110 017, India
Penguin Group (NZ), 67 Apollo Drive, Rosedale, Auckland 0632,
New Zealand (a division of Pearson New Zealand Ltd)
Penguin Books (South Africa) (Pty) Ltd, 24 Sturdee Avenue,
Rosebank, Johannesburg 2196, South Africa

Penguin Books Ltd, Registered Offices:
80 Strand, London WC2R 0RL, England

First published in 2011 by Portfolio / Penguin,
a member of Penguin Group (USA) Inc.

1   3   5   7   9   10   8   6   4   2

Library of Congress Cataloging-in-Publication Data

Ellsberg, Michael.
The education of millionaires : it's not what you think,
and it's not too late / Michael Ellsberg.
p.   cm.
Includes bibliographical references and index.
ISBN 978-1-59184-420-4
1. Success in business.   2. Practical reason.   I. Title.
HF5386.E435 2012
650.1—dc23
2011019060

Printed in the United States of America
Set in Melior Std
Designed by Sabrina Bowers

For my greatest teacher of all,

Jena.

Your journey of self-education inspired this book.

CONTENTS

"[A] whale-ship was my Yale College and my Harvard."

—Ishmael in *Moby-Dick*

*(Read in colleges across the land;
written by a high school dropout)*

GET ARTICLES, RECOMMENDATIONS, TIPS, AND INVITATIONS TO FREE CLASSES— JOIN MY PRIVATE E-MAIL LIST

Send an e-mail to privatelist@ellsberg.com, with "private list" in the subject heading, and I'll put you on my e-mail list, regularly sending you all the goodies described above. I'll also e-mail you, as a thank-you for purchasing this book, these two free PDF reports related to my book:

- *The Dropout Revolution: Why Today's Savviest Kids Are Forsaking Debt and Educating Themselves*—In this free PDF report you will learn why many kids today are choosing to avoid student loans and to educate themselves. Featuring interviews with some of today's hottest young entrepreneurs and rising stars, this report is sure to inspire you, challenge you, and make you think. This book also has my detailed responses to nearly every objection I could imagine a reader having about the message of my book, such as "But college graduates earn more!" and "But you need a college degree to get a good job!"

- *Self-Education in Health and Relationships*—In this free PDF report, learn how to educate yourself to succeed in relationships and health. We all know that happiness depends on more than just money and career. Learn how to educate yourself for success in *all* areas of your life that matter to you, including your personal health and relationships.

I send only quality content I've written myself to my e-mail list, zero spam, and I never ever give your information to anyone else. You can remove yourself at any time with one click.

Once again, to get immediate access to everything described above for free, just send an e-mail to privatelist@ellsberg.com with "private list" in the subject header.

THE EDUCATION OF
MILLIONAIRES

THE CRAIGSLIST TEST OF THE VALUE OF A BA

(or, Why Practical Intelligence Almost Always Beats Academic Intelligence)

You've been fed a lie. The lie is that if you study hard in school, get good grades, get into a good college, and get a degree, then your success in life is guaranteed.

This might have been true fifty years ago. But it is no longer true today.

If you want to succeed now, then you must also educate yourself in the real-world skills, capabilities, and mind-sets that will get you ahead outside of the classroom. This is true whether you've been to college or not.

This book shows you the way.

A thirty-seven-year-old Harvard MBA and a twentysomething college dropout, the latter a few credits shy of a film and theater degree from USC, are sitting across from each other in a job interview. The MBA is wearing a crisply pressed three-piece suit with a yellow tie. The twentysomething is wearing jeans and a pullover sweatshirt, with no shirt underneath. The twentysomething is unshaven, and the state of his hair suggests that not much grooming had occurred between his departure from bed that morning and this interview.

The interview is going very, very poorly. The interviewer is entirely unimpressed with the academic background the interviewee brings to the table, and feels the interviewee doesn't have enough experience to provide tangible value in the chaotic environment of a real-world start-up.

Bryan Franklin, the dropout theater major, decided to hire someone else that day for the $10-an-hour administrative and data entry job he had posted on Craigslist a few days before.

Bryan had started a sound design business in college and got too caught up in building and running the business to finish his degree. Eventually, over three hundred feature films were edited or mixed at his studio, including *Gladiator, The Last Samurai,* and *Artificial Intelligence.* Bootstrapping the business from the ground up and never once taking on investor money, he eventually sold it in 2000, after Dody Dorn was nominated for an Oscar for editing the film *Memento,* which she cut at the studio. The sale of the company "bought me a house on Lombard Street in San Francisco," as Bryan put it with a smile.

Now in early 2002, he was on his third self-made, self-funded, profitable business, and he needed an assistant, so he posted an ad on Craigslist, Bryan told me. "Within twenty-four hours, I had two hundred responses. Most of them had BAs, but there were also many masters', several with JDs who had passed the bar, a few PhDs, and around six MBAs. The Harvard MBA got me curious. I put him on a shortlist. He was one of the ten or so I interviewed.

"He came to my house in a three-piece suit. I was talking to him about the website he was going to be doing data entry for at ten dollars an hour, and he was stuck in a very 1999 mentality about the Web. I don't *think* he said the word 'IPO,' but I'm pretty sure he said the word 'liquidity' at some point in the interview.

"And I'm like, 'Look, I'm looking for data entry and customer service. I want to make sure that when a customer calls, they feel taken care of.'

"And he said, 'Well, you know, I think that we need to be strategic about which relationships we can leverage . . .' And that's kind of how the interview went. At one point he started saying, 'So, there's obviously several disparate paths involved and different priorities, so one of the things I'd do in my first week is build a priority matrix, so that we could reference . . .' And I just had this picture in my mind of him building his priority matrix while I was doing all the work.

"I ended up hiring a young African American woman. She was a high school dropout, but she had a great work ethic and lots of street smarts. She ended up doing a terrific job over three years. She got several raises, and at one point was managing three people."

There are, of course, many wonderful things you can learn in college, which have absolutely nothing to do with career and financial success. You can expand your mind, sharpen your critical thinking skills, get exposed to new ideas and perspectives, revel in the intellectual and cultural legacy of the world's greatest thinkers. These are all worthy pursuits.

But the idea that *simply* focusing on these kinds of things, and getting a BA attesting to the fact that you have done them, guarantees you will be successful in life is going the way of company pensions, job security, and careers consisting of a single employer for forty years. More and more people—including people who haven't even graduated college yet—are waking up to the reality that the old career and success advice is no longer adequate. We need to start taking some new advice.

Let's say, in a tough market, you'd rather be Bryan Franklin than the Harvard MBA. In other words, you want to optimize your chances in life of being the one *posting* job ads during a recession instead of the one begging for the job. Let's say you want to be the one hiring (either as an entrepreneur or as a leader within an organization), not the one out on the street looking for work.

If this were your goal—to maximize the chances of your professional success under any economic circumstances—then what would you need to start learning?

That is the central question this book answers. I'll be answering this one question, in detail, for the next several hundred pages.

But let's take a first pass at answering it right here.

Why was Bryan the one hiring that day, despite having no college credential, and why was the man with the Harvard MBA the one seeking the job?

I don't know the MBA personally, so I can only make educated guesses about his plight. But Bryan's story I know quite well, as he's a close friend. He had by that time spent a decade of his life in passionate pursuit of learning things that would make him successful—sales, marketing, leadership, management, finance, and accounting—within the context of owning real-world businesses, with his own money at stake. In other words, Bryan had focused his self-education outside of class on what some researchers call "practical intelligence"—how to get things done effectively in the real world, a.k.a. street smarts.

The other man, the Harvard MBA, had presumably studied the same material about marketing, sales, management, leadership, accounting, and finance. But my guess is, he did so primarily in an abstract, theoretical way. To get through such hallowed educational grounds, the focus of his education was probably on academic intelligence—how to do well on tests—not on get-it-done-now real-world practical intelligence.

Both men were highly educated, but one man's education consisted—I am guessing—primarily of *theory*, which is the stuff most readily on tap in colleges and universities. The other man's education (and it was self-education, not obtained in a formal classroom) consisted primarily of *practice*. One man's education was bureaucratic, formal, and by the books; the other man's education was gained on the front lines, often on the brink of personal disaster. One man was educated in the most prestigious institution in the land, the other in the school of hard business knocks. One man had focused on book smarts, the other on street smarts.

Which kind of smarts do you think wins in an economic downturn? Which wins when the economy picks up again?

In the eternal debate between practical intelligence and academic intelligence, street smarts and book smarts, there's little ambiguity about which side parents, relatives, teachers, media pundits, and politicians push us toward when we're kids.

In the famous scene from *The Graduate*, Dustin Hoffman's character Benjamin, a newly minted BA, receives some unsolicited career advice from a family friend at a graduation party around the family pool. "I want to say one word to you. Just one word. . . . Are you listening?" the family friend asks.

Benjamin nods yes.

"Plastics."

If we had to boil down to just one word the career and success advice we give our own young people, that word would be "education." Or, if we had fourteen words, it would be: "Study hard in high school, get into a good college, and get your BA."

Yet, like "plastics" in *The Graduate*, this advice is starting to feel more and more hollow, stale, and outdated. If you want to know the value these days of having a BA certifying your academic intelligence—the value of the *single thing* we repeat to our young people again and again they should get, at great cost in time and money, in order to be successful—you need only place an odd-jobs employment ad on Craigslist.

I myself have placed many employment ads on the site over the years, for small odd jobs, moving and packing boxes, cleaning out garages, hauling junk piles. As in Bryan's example, I can confirm: *there is literally no job too shitty or low-paying* for which you won't get a *river* of BAs desperately asking you for the work.

These degree-bearing applicants have attained the very thing society, their parents, their teachers, and everyone else around them told them they needed to attain in order to be successful—a credential certifying their achievement in academic intelligence. And yet, in Bryan's case, the comparatively tame recession of the early 2000s had hundreds of these BAs, MAs, JDs, PhDs, and MBAs lining up for a $10-an-hour shit job posted by a scruffy young business owner without a college degree.

Is this really the best life advice we can give young people? As with "plastics" in *The Graduate*, shouldn't we ask ourselves if our advice couldn't use a bit of updating and refining?

▮ DO YOU WANT TO CHASE DEGREES, OR DO YOU WANT TO CHASE SUCCESS?

For people in the industrialized world, middle-class and above, the primary focus of our waking lives between the ages of six and twenty-two is—to a first approximation—grades. To a second approximation, the agenda also includes narrowly defined extracurricular activities, such as sports and music and volunteering, which look good on college applications and entry-level resumes. But if you ask, what is the primary thing parents, teachers, politicians, and society want us to focus on during sixteen years, roughly between the ages of six and twenty-two, the answer is plain and simple: get good grades.

Have you ever stopped to ponder how utterly *bizarre* this state of affairs is? How in the world did we all get so convinced that *academic rigor* constituted a prerequisite, necessary, and sufficient training for *success in life*? How did we all get convinced that this one end merited devoting sixteen of the best years of our lives toward it? That we should spend almost our entire youth—potentially some of the most creative, enthusiastic, energetic, and *fun* years of our lives—in pursuit of little numbers and letters certifying our academic intelligence?

Sir Ken Robinson, author of *The Element: How Finding Your Passion Changes Everything*, has pondered this puzzling question a lot. In a video talk in the famous TED (Technology Entertainment and Design) series, entitled "Ken Robinson Says Schools Kill Creativity" (which became one of TED.com's most downloaded talks ever), Sir Ken says: "If you were to visit education, as an alien, and say 'What's it for, public education?' I think you'd have to conclude—if you look at the output, who really succeeds by this, who does everything that they should, who gets all the brownie points, who are the winners—I think you'd have to conclude the whole purpose of public education throughout the world is to produce university professors. Isn't it? They're the people who come out the top. . . . And I like university professors, but you know, we shouldn't hold them up as the high-water mark of all human achievement. They're just a form of life, another form of life."[1]

Libertarian critic of our current educational system Charles Murray makes the point another way: "We should look at the kind of work that goes into acquiring a liberal education at the college level in the same way that we look at the grueling apprenticeship that goes into becoming a master chef: something that understandably attracts only a limited number of people."[2]

These critics are saying, essentially: training to become a college professor and academic scholar is fine for those who truly wish to do so. But if you've already gone through college, you are now the product of a system and cultural norm that holds that, in order to prepare for success in life, you must spend sixteen years of your life essentially training toward an ideal of academic perfection.

If you haven't noticed already, this is a silly system. It's silly for a very simple reason. For most fields you'd want to enter—aside from, say, research science—beyond basic levels of academic intelligence, developing additional academic intelligence will have virtually no impact on your life prospects and success. Developing your practical intelligence will have *far more* impact on the quality and success of your life.

In a core section of his book *Outliers: The Story of Success*, for example, Malcolm Gladwell argues meticulously that, above a certain IQ (around 120, which is considered "above average/bright," but not even "moderately gifted"[3]), additional IQ points have little correlation to real-world success. Ditto for grades—beyond a middling level of academic achievement, there is little evidence that grades (the center point of our waking lives for almost the entire sixteen years of our educational track) bear any causal relationship at all to real-world results, success, achievement, or satisfaction in life.[4]

In one segment, Gladwell compares the lives of two men born with exceptionally high IQs, Chris Langan, known as "the smartest man in America," with an IQ over 200, and Robert Oppenheimer, scientific director of the Manhattan Project. The brilliance of their minds is comparable, yet one of these men (Oppenheimer) had a profound impact on world history, and another (Langan) has had very little, despite repeated attempts to get his work published.

What is the difference between these two men? According to Gladwell, the main difference is that, in addition to his rocket-high IQ, Oppenheimer also possessed exceptional practical intelligence in navigating his way through the people who could influence his success in the world, "things like knowing what to say to whom, knowing when to say it, and knowing how to say it for maximum effect." Langan in turn possessed little of this kind of intelligence, and thus was never able to gain much of a toehold in the world of practical achievement.

In his book, Gladwell shows that once a person has demonstrated passable logical, analytic, and academic skills, other factors have *much* more influence on real-world results—specifically, creativity, innovative thinking, and practical and social intelligence. To the extent that we develop these aptitudes in our lives, we tend to do so out in the real world, not in formal institutions.[5]

This book is your guide for developing practical success skills in the real world. I focus on seven key skills that will be crucial if you want to succeed in your work and career. These practical skills are not meant to be a replacement for college. Indeed, a classic college education—in its most elite conception—is not meant to teach practical skills at all. That's not its purpose. You can learn many wonderful things in college. You can be exposed to new ideas, broaden your perspective on life, learn critical thinking skills, and immerse yourself in the great intellectual and cultural treasures of the human mind and spirit.

But, even if you've already gone through college, one thing I'm certain wasn't on the curriculum in school was how to translate these abstract, academic teachings into *real-world results* in your own life. Yet, this additional education around practical skills is not optional. Learning the skills in this book well is a *necessary* addition to a college education, if you want to achieve more success in your work and life. This book shows you the way.

I will turn to the seven key skills in a moment. But first, let me tell you a little about who I am and why I decided to write this book.

■ MY SHOCKING REALIZATION

Around two years ago, at the age of thirty-two, I came to a shocking realization.

Not one penny of how I earned my income was even *slightly* related to anything I ever studied or learned in college.

I was bringing in a very solid income as a direct-response copywriter, on a freelance schedule that many of my friends with paychecks and bosses envied (never at my desk before 10:30 A.M., lots of time for Rollerblading in Prospect Park, Brooklyn, in the middle of sunny weekdays). One could say I learned writing in college, but it is more accurate to say that I had to *unlearn* the turgid, academic style of writing favored in college, in order to write anything that moved product or made money for me or anyone else.

What's more, I wasn't making solid money (somewhere around $75,000 as a freelance copywriter, plus additional money coming in from my own book writing, which pushed me over $100,000) simply because I had become good at writing copy. I was earning money because I had become good at *marketing* and *selling* my copywriting services. There are boatloads of good freelancers who are broke, simply because they don't know how to market and sell their services. Think I learned any marketing or sales at Brown University? Rather, I spent my time writing papers decrying the capitalist system in which marketing and sales take place (and most of those papers came back with an A on them).

Beyond career, for the first time in my life, I was also having the feeling of being successful in my personal life. I had just gotten engaged to Jena and was enjoying a loving, stable, fulfilling relationship with her. This was after about a decade (my entire twenties) of being a total mess in relationships. It didn't just happen by accident that I was now enjoying a great relationship; I *learned* how to be a better partner, by investing in a zillion workshops and reading a zillion books on the topic, until something started to shift.

I was also enjoying vibrant day-to-day health for the first time since college. Years of partying (starting in college), combined with poor eating habits, began to take their toll in my twenties, as I began seeing a gauntlet of doctors and specialists for symptoms of depression, constant low energy, and mood swings. I didn't get better until I started paying a lot more attention to my diet and lifestyle. After doing that, I began to feel energized and vibrant on a consistent basis for the first time since I was a kid.

In other words, for the first time as an adult, I was absolutely loving my life. My professional and personal life were exactly where I wanted them to be. Yet, as I took stock of my life in this moment, I realized: the fact that I had done well in college—even the fact that I had gone to college in the first place—had absolutely nothing to do with my adult happiness, fulfillment, success, or contribution to others. Zero. Zip.

I had learned a lot about how to live as a successful, happy adult. Yet nearly all that learning had been self-education in practical matters, out in the real world in my twenties, outside the bounds of a classroom.

This got me thinking: *What would education for a successful life look like?* You can define a "success" any way you want— wealth; career; family; spirituality; sense of meaning and purpose; vibrant health; service and contribution to community, nation, and humanity—or any combination thereof. What would an education look like that was laser-targeted *only* toward achieving these real-world results, and zealously cut out all bullshit not directly related to living a happy, successful life and making a powerful contribution to the lives of the people around you?

Certainly, this education would look nothing like anything taught on current college campuses, or anywhere inside our nation's entire educational system. If you wanted to take this course of study, you'd have to do so on your own, outside of college, as your own teacher, because this course doesn't exist anywhere within the halls of academia.

So I decided to write this book, in which I pose these simple questions: What do you actually need to learn in order to live a successful life? How and where can you learn it?

While there are many ways I could have gone about answering these questions, I decided to answer them by interviewing and learning from successful people, like Bryan Franklin, who did not finish college.

I first got the idea to take this tack after entering into a serious relationship with Jena, who is now my wife. Jena, a year younger than I, did not complete college. Yet during her twenties, she amassed far more wealth than I did, despite the differential in our educational credentials pointing solidly in my favor. What did Jena learn during her self-education about making her way in the world that I did not learn during my college education?

Around 90 percent of the people I interviewed and feature in this book are literal millionaires, and several are even billionaires. Some are famous, many are not. I've also chosen to include, for around 10 percent of my interviewees, people like Jena, who are not millionaires (yet!), but who are clearly on their way, who exemplify the spirit and lessons of this book, and who are accomplishing amazing things in the world, via the strategies described in this book.

For the record, I'm not a millionaire myself, and I did complete college (Brown, class of '99). I'm *not* an example of the self-educated millionaires I write about in this book. But I've learned a tremendous amount from them. I write extensively about the changes I've experienced in my life applying the skills and lessons I've learned from them, so you can see how these skills apply to all people, not just those who are already millionaires, and not just those who didn't complete their formal education.

All of the millionaires and successful people I interviewed for this book said "no thanks" to the current educational model. And with their self-education, they have built businesses, amassed fortunes, helped others live better lives, and even changed the world.

These are the people we're going to be learning from in this book. They have much to teach us about how we can educate ourselves in the practical skills we need, in order to be successful in a rapidly evolving, shape-shifting, and self-reinventing economy. They are going to teach us how we can get, for ourselves, "The Education of Millionaires": the real-world skills that these millionaires studied and learned in order to get where they are in life.

What they have to teach applies to you no matter what age you are and whether or not you've been to college already. Lifelong learning and professional development are necessities in the current career environment; this book is your guide to self-education for success in the twenty-first century.

The people in this book also have much to teach us about what kinds of practical life skills and career-oriented content your children should be learning if our educational system is to take the new realities of this twenty-first-century digitized, globalized, flat-world economy seriously—an economy in which every traditional assumption is being turned on its head, shaken up, and called into question, including traditional assumptions about education.

We Americans are obsessed with success, and we readily snap up books promising insight into the lives of successful people and how to emulate them. Yet, up until now, there have been few voices making this obvious point about success (normally only spoken about in hush-hush tones, as if it were a dirty secret): despite sixteen years or more of schooling, most of what you'll need to learn to be successful you'll have to learn on your own, outside of school, whether you go to college or not.

I am passionately pro-education. There are few things I care more about than reading and learning constantly.

Yet, the lives of the people profiled in this book show conclusively that *education* is most certainly not the same thing as *academic excellence*. We've conflated them, at great cost to ourselves, our children, our economy, and our culture. And, while education is always necessary for success, pursuing academic excellence is not in all cases. As Mark Twain said: "I have never let my schooling interfere with my education."[6] (Twain dropped out of elementary school at age eleven to become a printer's apprentice.)

The driving theme of the stories in this book is that, even though you may learn many wonderful things in college, your success and happiness in life will have little to do with what you study there or the letters after your name once you graduate. It has to do with your drive, your initiative, your persistence, your ability to make a contribution to other people's lives, your ability to come up with good ideas and pitch them to others effectively, your charisma, your ability to navigate gracefully through social and business networks (what some researchers call "practical intelligence"), and a total, unwavering belief in your own eventual triumph, throughout all the ups and downs, no matter what the naysayers tell you.

While you may learn many valuable things in college, you won't learn *these* things there—yet they are *crucial* for your success in business and in life. Whether you're a high school dropout or a graduate of Harvard Law School, you must learn and develop these skills, attitudes, and habits if you want to excel at what you do. In this new economy, the biggest factor in your success will not be abstract, academic learning but whether you develop the real-life success skills evinced by the people on these pages, and how early you do.

This is a book about practical education. Street smarts. It's about what you have to learn in order to be successful in life and how you can go about learning it on your own, outside of traditional schooling. It is about the skills, habits, and mind-sets *you* need to make an impact on the world and find happiness and success doing so.

If you've already gone to college, you still probably want to make a bigger mark on the world than the one you're currently making. Even if you're a doctor or a lawyer—and you literally could not practice your profession *without* having graduated from college and graduate school—these real-world success skills are every bit as relevant to you for accelerating your career. And they definitely weren't on the curriculum at law school or medical school.

If you haven't started college yet—or if you're in college and wondering what you should do there and whether you should stay—then this book will also be an important read. If you do choose to go to college, or to stay there if you're already there, this book can help you get the most out of your college experience by helping you to avoid a lot of the BS you're likely going to encounter and to pay more attention to learning things that will actually be valuable to your achieving your dreams later in life.

This is the book I wish I had when I was sixteen, seventeen, or eighteen. If I'd had it then, I would have saved a lot of misery, stress, and drudgery in the rest of my education. I would have been more focused and clear on my path.

It also would have been useful to me as soon as I graduated college. If I'd read this book when I was twenty-two, I may not have spent a good part of my twenties wandering aimlessly.

In fact, this is the book I want *now*, at age thirty-four, well into

my career. It didn't yet exist, so I wrote it. I'm definitely still learning, with more appetite than I've ever had before.

If I can give just one person the value from the book I wish I'd
received at the age of seventeen, eighteen, twenty-two, or later, the
whole endeavor of writing it will have been worthwhile.

■ OUR CURRENT EDUCATIONAL SYSTEM IS A TYPEWRITER (WOULD YOU LIKE A WI-FI-CONNECTED LAPTOP INSTEAD?)

The already-questionable connection between *academic excellence*
and *preparation for success in life and career* became all the more
questionable during the time I was writing this book, as the Great
Recession of 2008–10 unfolded. As I was writing, a rash of articles
came out in a number of major publications in which Americans
expressed rage about their inability to earn sufficient money, given
their expensive academic education. The bargain used to be: give
up four years of your life (or more for graduate school), incur hundreds of thousands of dollars in tuition, debt, and forgone earnings
during the years you study, and when you graduate you'll be set for
life earnings-wise.

People who entered into this bargain four or five years ago are
beginning to realize that only half the bargain has held up: the
half in which they spend four years, incur up to $100,000 in debt,
and forgo earnings they would have gained in the workforce during their years of study. The other half of the bargain, in which
they were virtually guaranteed a job with a great salary upon graduation, has vanished.

An article in the *New York Times*, called "No Longer Their
Golden Ticket," covered the tidal wave of recent law school graduates, often carrying hundreds of thousands of dollars in student
debt, who can't find jobs. For those who were lucky enough to find
or retain employment during the recent colossal shakeout in the
legal profession, "it is harder to maintain that sense of esteem now
that your contract work is being farmed out to low-cost lawyers in
Bangalore, and your client who is splitting up with her spouse can
handle it herself with a $31.99 do-it-yourself divorce kit from Of-
fice Depot."[7]

Beyond the grim scene for recently minted JDs, MBAs, MAs, and PhDs, the picture was no brighter for fresh college graduates. We now live in an age when it is likely that the person pouring you your coffee at the café in the morning has spent four years studying literature, or even business and marketing, in a degree-granting institution. That person is likely to be carrying tens of thousands of dollars in student debt, and more in credit card debt accrued in college, for the privilege of having studied to pour you your coffee with such literary and business acumen.

A *New York Times* article entitled "Jobs Wanted, Any Jobs at All" describes Katie and Kerry Barry, twins who were then seventeen months past their Rutgers graduation, as living in "an unwelcome continuum of mass rejection." The twins had collectively applied to 150 jobs: "a magazine for diabetics, a Web site about board games and a commercial for green tea-flavored gum; fact-checking at Scholastic Books, copy editing for the celebrity baby section of People.com, road-tripping for College Sports Television. They did not get any of these. More than a year has lapsed without so much as an interview. Apparently, even a canned response was impossible in New York."[8]

While the recent bust times will have hopefully passed by the time this book comes out, more and more people of all ages are beginning to question traditional assumptions about how to make a mark in the world. Throughout most of the last century, large bureaucratic organizations dominated the path of social mobility, from school age to retirement. If you wanted to be successful and have an impact, you studied hard in high school, got into a good college, got an entry-level job at a large corporate or government bureaucracy, and rose through the ranks of middle management.

It is now widely understood that the latter portion of this timeline—getting an entry-level job and rising through the ranks of middle management at a large bureaucracy—is no longer the best way to do things, for two reasons.

First, job security is dead, as anyone who has had a job recently knows. You're going to have many different jobs, employers, and even careers in your life. So where you get your first, entry-level one—the single thing that a BA credential really helps with—becomes less and less relevant. Building a portfolio of real-world results and impacts you've created, over time, becomes more and more relevant.

Second, the Internet, cell phones, and virtually free long-distance calling have created new opportunities for flexible, self-created, independent careers; this trend has been helped along by the gathering storms of millions of hungry, highly educated young men and women in India, China, Eastern Europe, the Philippines, and elsewhere, happy to do the work that entry-level Organization Men would have done in years past, for a fraction of the cost. This emerging competition has encouraged many people in the West to "think outside the organization" to create careers for themselves that can't be outsourced, offshored, or automated.

More and more Americans of all ages are waking up to the reality that you don't need a nine-to-five job to be a valuable, contributing member of society and to create wealth for yourself and others. Millions of small-business owners, entrepreneurs, computer programmers, graphic designers, independent consultants, writers, and freelancers make valuable contributions to society (creating four out of ten new jobs in the economy), outside the realm of working for a boss nine to five (or eight to eight).

Until the last decade, the kinds of opportunities that got you ahead in the world—medicine, law, engineering, or rising up through the ranks of a large corporation—were all guarded by "gate-keepers" who checked your formal credentials vigorously before letting you in.

There were very few other ways to get ahead. The zeitgeist is changing, however. While the classic professions still require credentials, for young people today these professions are no longer the *only* (and certainly not the hottest) avenues toward social advancement, economic opportunity, and making a difference in the world.

A new breed of American is arising, and they are creating a new breed of opportunity. For them, the American Dream still includes a wonderful family life, a home, and financial security. But it does not include waking up each day and going to work for a boss. They want to work for themselves, creating value for other people on *their* terms—perhaps on a Wi-Fi-connected laptop from a mobile location.

These people, young and old, read books like *The Four-Hour Workweek: Escape 9–5, Live Anywhere, and Join the New Rich* by Tim Ferriss, *Escape from Cubicle Nation: From Corporate Prisoner to Thriving Entrepreneur* by Pamela Slim, and *Career Renegade: How to Make a Great Living Doing What You Love* by Jonathan Fields.

Daniel Pink, in *Free Agent Nation: The Future of Working for Yourself*, his 2001 book prophesying the current tidal wave of microentrepreneurialism, small business, and self-employment, calls them "self-employed knowledge workers, proprietors of home-based businesses . . . freelancers and e-lancers, independent contractors and independent professionals, micropreneurs and infopreneurs, part-time consultants . . . on-call troubleshooters, and full-time soloists."[9]

These new kinds of opportunities, open to anyone who wants to pursue them, without any formal, traditional, or academic qualifications necessary to compete, have arisen largely because of technology. As Pink points out in *Free Agent Nation*, there was a time in our nation's history, before the Industrial Revolution, when most people were self-employed—that is, "the butcher, the baker, the candlestick maker." In these times, writes Pink, mass self-employment made sense because "most of the things people needed to earn their living they could buy easily and keep at home." However, writes Pink, "it was only when these things— the means of production, to use Karl Marx's famous phrase— became extremely expensive . . . that large organizations began to dominate. . . . Capital and labor, once so intertwined the distinction scarcely mattered, became separate entities. Capitalists owned the equipment. Laborers earned their money by receiving a sliver of the enormous rewards those giant machines produced."[10]

Pink argues that in the last decade, in one area of the economy— called "knowledge work"—a shift has occurred as massive and with implications as far-reaching as those during the shift from an agrarian to an industrial society. For knowledge workers in the developed world, the tools of their trade have become so ridiculously cheap that the "means of production" have once again become affordable to individual workers. These workers no longer have to depend on bosses or large organizations to furnish them with the means of production. They can quit the factory-style organizations and become "butchers, bakers, and candlestick makers" once again—that is, digitally connected entrepreneurs and solo-preneurs.

Pink calls it "Digital Marxism: In an age of inexpensive computers, wireless handheld devices, and ubiquitous low-cost connections to a global communications network, workers can now own the means of production."[11] And increasingly, more and more of them (especially younger ones who have grown up with the Internet) are deciding to take their means of production, strike out on their own with their copy of *The Four-Hour Workweek* in their laptop bag, and flip a big, bad massive bird to their former employers.

And here's something else these self-employed people, small-business owners, and micropreneurs are starting to realize more and more: for them, formal educational credentials are irrelevant to the new economic reality they are operating in.

In this new reality, no one gives a damn where you went to college or what your formal credentials are, so long as you do great work. I'm not saying we're all the way there yet. But it's clearly the way we're headed. As science fiction writer William Gibson said, "The future is here—it's just not evenly distributed."

Education is still necessary to learn how to do the great work that gets you paid. But these days, almost all of the education that ends up actually earning you money ends up being self-education in practical intelligence and skills, acquired outside of the bounds of traditional educational institutions.

I asked Bryan if he felt he learned more starting up his businesses during and after school than he did during school. "Oh, my God. There's no question," he answered. "It would be the difference between a very well-planned seven-course meal done by one of the world's top nutritionists, and compare that in nutritional value to a gumdrop."

Let's say you want to eat the seven-course meal done by one of the world's top nutritionists, rather than the gumdrop.

This book provides you with a guide for acquiring key success skills you are very unlikely to learn in college. These are the real-world skills the self-educated millionaires I interviewed in my book all focused on learning, instead of abstract academic skills.

The typical college education consists of thirty-two courses—four courses a semester for eight semesters. The courses in *The Education of Millionaires* consists of seven key areas of lifelong self-study. These courses can and should be followed in addition to (before, during, and after) your traditional formal schooling in a classroom. But these aren't like normal college courses. Here are some key differences.

Normal college courses are . . .	Courses in The Education of Millionaires are . . .
Abstract. While these courses can be interesting, edifying, and enlightening, very little of the content bears any useful relationship to confronting your goals, dreams, problems, and challenges in life outside of the class.	**Practical.** Course content is directly related to helping you tackle challenges, achieve goals, solve problems, and reach for your dreams in your career and personal life beyond the course.
Focused on Your Achievement in the Course. In a typical college course, grading becomes the focus of the course, with little attention paid to how the object of the grading relates to your life outside of the course. If my Marxist and postmodernist professors were to turn the barrel of their lingo away from capitalism and instead point it at their own noses, they'd say the grades had become "reified" and turned into a "fetish," a "simulacrum" of reality. And who wants that?	**Focused on Your Achievement in Your Life.** There are no grades in these courses. Your "grade" is the results you get in your actual life. If you get the job you want, you're doing well in the course. If your small business starts making tons of money, you just passed the test with flying colors. If your dream guy or girl says "yes" to a date (or a proposal of marriage), you just got an A. Your success is your results and achievement in the real world. Period. There are no formalized, abstract evaluations of the material.
Evaluated by Bystanders with Nothing at Stake. Your college professor may have exacting, thoughtful, careful standards on how she tests you, grades you, and evaluates you in the course. But ultimately, she's not the one who's going to hire you. She's not the one who's going to buy your product. She's not the one who's going to pull out her wallet and invest in your idea. She's not the one who's going to say yes to a date. (Well, actually, I have some stories about that one . . .) Her opinions about how you should develop are like the opinions about military tactics offered among the gentlemen and women who watched Civil War battles from hilltop picnics.	**Evaluated by People in the Real World.** Since your "grades" are simply your results in the real world, your progress is being evaluated by people who've got skin in the game—who've got something to lose if you fuck it up. You're getting feedback in your course progress all the time by customers, employers, social connections, and loved ones. The feedback you get is vastly more meaningful.

Normal college courses are . . .	*Courses in* The Education of Millionaires *are . . .*
Bound by Four Months. In the context of a lifetime, four-month courses are to real learning as Big Macs wolfed in the car between appointments are to fine dining. You can learn a lot in four months, but anything truly worth learning takes a lifetime to master. So why do we cram most of our higher learning into a four-year period consisting of these four-month courses, and then select for that four-year period an age range when many people seem more concerned with guzzling shots and learning what condoms and beer bongs are good for?	***Bound by the Cradle and the Grave.*** *(This book just points the way; it is not the way itself.)* Welcome to the new lifelong learning. You don't "graduate" from any of these courses. But also, you're not stuck to cramming all of your "higher learning" into four years between ages eighteen and twenty-two. You get to enjoy the pleasure and fruits of study and learning throughout your life, at a realistic, comfortable pace, without having to cram for finals, give up career earnings while you study, or take out student loans. Take the pointers I give you as jump-off points—but ultimately, you're going to have to find most of your learning materials and teachers for these courses *on your own*, during the rest of your life.

OK, drumroll please. Here they are, the courses in *The Education of Millionaires.*

SUCCESS SKILL #1: How to Make Your Work Meaningful and Your Meaning Work (or, How to Make a Difference in the World Without Going Broke)

SUCCESS SKILL #2: How to Find Great Mentors and Teachers, Connect with Powerful and Influential People, and Build a World-Class Network

SUCCESS SKILL #3: What Every Successful Person Needs to Know About Marketing, and How to Teach Yourself

SUCCESS SKILL #4: What Every Successful Person Needs to Know About Sales, and How to Teach Yourself

SUCCESS SKILL #5: How to Invest for Success (The Art of Bootstrapping)

SUCCESS SKILL #6: Build the Brand of You (or, To Hell with Resumes!)

SUCCESS SKILL #7: The Entrepreneurial Mind-set versus the Employee Mind-set: Become the Author of Your Own Life

These seven courses, which correspond to the seven core chapters of the book, focus primarily on skills related to success in career, money, work, and business. Of course, for a truly integrated sense of success, in the fullest sense of the word, we all need to learn many practical personal skills as well. These include skills such as how to find and maintain a wonderful, loving relationship, how to sustain vibrant health, and how to navigate our spiritual beliefs in a world that seems to get more chaotic every day. It is possible to be a financial millionaire and an emotional and spiritual pauper. All the money in the world provides little comfort if we are lonely, sick, or forlorn of love.

But I will leave those personal success skills (crucial as they are) for another book. Since this is a business book, I am focusing here on skills related to success in the realms of career, money, work, and business. The seven success skills I explore here are of course not exhaustive, even in the realm of career and financial success. But they go a long way.

My format in the chapter devoted to each of these skills is quite simple. First, I provide some stories of successful self-educated people who learned and applied these skills, to great effect, in their own lives. Then, I give some examples of how I applied the same skills in my own life and the results I got. (I would never recommend to you something I hadn't battle-tested in my own life.) Then, based on the experience of my interviewees, as well as my own experience, I give some practical tips about how to go about learning and applying that chapter's skill in your own life.

Welcome to your own journey of self-education.

We're about to dive headlong into the success skills. But before we take the plunge, I want to offer two minor disclaimers, in the interest of full disclosure and transparency.

■ DISCLAIMER #1:
MY VIEWS ARE MY OWN! (AND PROBABLY NOT SHARED BY ALL OF MY INTERVIEWEES)

I should make something absolutely, beyond-a-shadow-of-a-doubt clear: my opinions, controversial as some of them may be, are mine and mine alone; they are not necessarily shared by the people I interview or feature.

My interviewees all chose to share their amazing stories of self-made success for this book, for the benefit of us all. They chose to share these stories because they all believe that no matter where you are in your life, no matter what your age or your life circumstances, you can strive to achieve more in life, to make a greater impact, to aim for higher dreams.

This book would not exist without the generous participation of the many, many experts and self-educated people I interviewed. My interviewees are a diverse, brilliant, and cantankerous bunch, with a wide range of opinions on many topics, as well as a wide range of backgrounds. I am profoundly grateful for their participation, and am proud that I am able to share their cutting-edge insights and their moving stories.

I'm certain, however, that some of my interviewees will outright disagree with some of my own views, as well as some of the views expressed by other interviewees featured in this book. Thus, I want to emphasize that there is a gulf of difference between my interviewees, having agreed to share their personal stories here, and their agreeing with everything or anything anyone else (including me) says in this book.

The interviewees I feature in this book are responsible only for their own views, clearly delineated by quotation marks, and for my general paraphrases of their views, both of which I have submitted to them to check for accuracy. (I edited all interviews for flow, readability, and space.) I repeat: interviewees' participation in this book should *not* be taken as endorsement for any other aspect of this book other than their own views in quotation marks.

I give a hearty thank-you to *all* my interviewees for their participation in this book.

■ DISCLAIMER #2:
I INTERVIEW SEVERAL CLOSE FRIENDS AND BUSINESS CONNECTIONS

The vast majority of the people I interviewed in this book were strangers to me before I interviewed them. However, several of my key interviews come from people who are very close to me. For example, I interview my wife, Jena. Another major source, Eben Pagan, is engaged to my close friend Annie Lalla, and I played a large part in introducing them.

Bryan Franklin, whom you met in the Introduction and about whom I write more in the coming pages, is one of my best friends. He officiated at my wedding ceremony. And I've done business with him in the past, both as a client and a vendor, and probably will again in the future. (Another company I mention in one of the stories, the Institute for Integrative Nutrition, was a copywriting client of mine in the past, though is not at present.) Whenever I have a personal or business relationship with anyone else mentioned in this book, I will disclose that.

(One other thing: if over the course of interviews I've talked to someone enough that I would address them by their first name in conversation, I decided to use their first name here in the text; otherwise I use their last name to refer to them.)

In no case did I receive any financial or other specified benefit for featuring anyone in this book. No pay for play, ever.

(OK, enough caveats. Let the fun begin . . .)

HOW TO MAKE YOUR WORK MEANINGFUL AND YOUR MEANING WORK

(or, How to Make a Difference in the World Without Going Broke)

A twenty-one-year-old singer, songwriter, and guitarist named David found himself in a hospital in Paris one night, being treated for malnutrition, in 1967. The reason he was malnourished was that he was not making a lot of money and couldn't afford proper foods, as he played gigs at bars, nightclubs, and dances across France and Spain.

No gig tonight, no eat tomorrow.

Two years before, he was in his sixth form in Cambridge, England (equivalent to the last two years of high school in the United States). David simply stopped going to his A-levels, the series of exams that determine university entrance in the UK. All he really cared about was rock music, and he dove fully into it, playing in local bands and eventually living by his wits, gig to gig, in France and Spain. Had you seen him in that moment in Paris, sickly in the hospital at age twenty-one, lacking funds to feed himself properly, you might not have thought he had made a good choice leaving his A-levels, or that he had any decent prospects in life.

And while that judgment may be correct for most starving artists, in the case of this particular artist—who was starving not just figuratively but literally—such a judgment would be as off the mark as you could get.

David returned to the UK, and later that year, a drummer he knew named Nick Mason asked him to join a little band they were putting together called Pink Floyd. The band went on to sell over 200 million copies of its albums over the next forty-plus years. *The Dark Side of the Moon*, the band's most famous album, has sold upward of 45 million copies worldwide and ranks among the greatest-selling, most critically acclaimed, and most influential albums of all time. As lead guitarist, lead vocalist, and songwriter for the band that produced so many hits for over forty years, David Gilmour (http://www.davidgilmour.com) is easily one of the most important musicians in the history of rock.

I count myself as a fan. I thank David personally for providing the soundtrack to so many blissful nights in university, philosophizing about the meaning of life or making love instead of studying. Some of the most educational parts of my college experience, truly. And the music still brings joy, inspiration, and awe to my life—and surely to millions of others—a decade out of college. David Gilmour has made a massive difference to the lives of many people on the planet. The world would be a much poorer place without him and his music. He has lived—I would say—a deeply meaningful life.

Yet, there is something profoundly unsettling about his story as well—and indeed, about the story of just about anyone who has made a great difference in the world.

A year before he became famous, David was roughly the same musician, with roughly the same musical gift, and the same die-hard determination to make an impact on the world of music and live a meaningful life. At that time, however, the world didn't care much about whatever impact he wanted to make on it or what "meaning" he wanted to create within it; in fact, in exchange for his musical gift, the world barely rewarded him enough to keep himself alive. One of the most monumental musicians in the history of rock nearly died as a starving artist, before he and his band got "discovered."

All of us—at least the most idealistic among us—want to make a difference in the world, whether it's in business, the arts, politics, philanthropy, science, or technology. At the very least, we want to make a difference in our communities. This is what feels meaningful to us: making a difference, having an impact, living for a purpose.

Yet, there's a paradoxical aspect to "making a difference" and "having an impact." The world doesn't always *care* whether we want to make a difference or have an impact on *it*. In fact, it can be downright hostile to us when we try. The world doesn't automatically open its arms to us just because we have good intentions. It may laugh at our great sense of "purpose" or, more commonly, simply yawn and turn its head to something else.

At the highest levels of success, there's a capricious aspect to making a difference in the world and living with purpose, which we must come to terms with squarely before we start talking about "secrets to success," "success skills," and so forth. Indeed, I asked David about the secret to his success, and he gave me a frank answer: "I got very lucky. Luck plays a big, big part in the kind of success I've had. They say you have to make your own luck, but I'm not too sure of that sometimes. There are a lot of people I know who had the same determination I had, followed my same path and threw their lot into the music business without going to university, and didn't end up making a successful living playing music. They were thereafter stuck in jobs which were fairly hand-to-mouth. They were not doing what they could have done with their lives if they continued with their studies. It's absolutely not a course I would recommend to anyone, *unless* you were absolutely 110 percent convinced that your passion was something you had to do and you would be willing to forsake a lot of other things for it."

Very few of us, when we dream about the kind of impact we want to make on the world, dream about things we could achieve with little risk. Very few of us dream of staying anonymous middle managers, or paper pushers lost in sprawling bureaucracies for the rest of our lives. That doesn't feel like much of a purpose at all.

No, our dreams and purposes are the stuff of romance, adventure, and excitement. We dream of becoming famous, wealthy, of making a big mark on the world. We dream of becoming rock stars. If not literal rock stars, like David, then some other kind of star: a famous athlete, actor, writer, filmmaker, artist, politician, lauded scientist, CEO, or millionaire or billionaire entrepreneur (such as some of the entrepreneurs I interview in this book). Or we dream of making an impact in a traditional profession, such as law, medicine, or academia, or making a great impact in our community in a position of leadership or charity. Perhaps we dream of being a star teacher and making a difference in hundreds of children's lives.

Yet, such dreams of making a difference always involve risk. The more you want to be a star in your respective field—whether it's being a teacher, a doctor, a lawyer, or an artist, musician, or entrepreneur—the more risk you will have to take in your career choices. Few people become stars in their industry, make a difference to the lives of lots of people, or find a sense of purpose in their career simply by sticking to the script and hewing close to well-trodden paths.

You can take a stadium full of highly talented twenty-one-year-olds with lots of drive and determination, all passionate about making an impact on the world in the ways young people dream about, in fields such as music, art, writing, acting, filmmaking, politics, policy, science, technology, media, philanthropy and charity, or entrepreneurialism. Out of this whole stadium of talent, only one or two of these young people will become superstars in their respective fields, on the level of a David Gilmour.

Many in that stadium will end up flat on their asses, broke. That's a terrifying prospect. In response to such prospects, out of fear, many young people in that stadium will stop sticking their necks out in their careers, clinging to safe scripts in their careers, where there's little risk of failure and equally little risk of achieving anything truly remarkable.

What distinguishes these one or two superstars who reached their dreams and made a huge difference from the rest of the talented, ambitious, idealistic individuals in that stadium?

I've asked many superstars their secret for success. While they all mention talent, persistence, drive, determination, believing in yourself, never giving up—the standard chestnuts of the self-help literature—the most honest and self-aware of the superstars, such as David Gilmour, add an additional factor to the list. They also pay respect to the role of serendipity, synchronicity, and random chance. The stars shone on them. The gods smiled upon them. The right place at the right time. Simple, blind luck.

They don't call it a "lucky break" for nothing.

If there wasn't risk involved, and the fear that accompanies that risk, we wouldn't be dreaming about it, we'd have already done it. (The grocery store is always hiring checkout clerks. If your dream was to become a checkout clerk, you could be living your dream right now. But I'm willing to bet that's not your dream.)

So, how do we reconcile our deepest dreams of making a difference in the world—our dreams of leading a meaningful, impactful life, a life of purpose—with the stark reality that the world doesn't always care what kind of difference we want to make or give us an A for effort?

Navigating these rocky existential waters is one of the most important aptitudes you could develop. Err too far in either direction, and it's very unlikely you'll end up happy in life. Err too far on the side of reaching for lofty dreams within your career, without any attention to existing market risks and constraints, and you may end up, as David did at twenty-one, in a hospital for malnourishment, at least metaphorically speaking. And few people who end up in that place of starving-artist-hood have the fortune to get out, as David eventually did.

Yet, err too far in the other direction, giving in to fear and sticking to the safe path, without even a nod to the larger impact you want to make, the greater purpose you want to achieve, and you may end up feeling like you missed out. You may enjoy some level of predictability or security in your income, but it won't feel very satisfying to you inside. Few people would call this "success."

Therefore, at the outset of any discussion of success, what you need is not another motivational rah-rah lecture on "believing in yourself" or "never giving up" or "working harder," the standard fare of other books. What you need is an honest discussion of how to navigate gracefully among dreams, risk, and ruin in the real-world marketplace.

■ THE CONFLICT OF MAKING AN IMPACT VERSUS LIVING A PREDICTABLE LIFE

I'm going to say something that has probably never been in print before in a business book. It's probably never been in a business book because, at face value, it sounds kind of depressing.

The bigger the impact you want to make on the world or in your chosen field—the bolder your purpose is—the greater the risks you're going to have to take. Which means, the greater the chance that you'll end up making *no impact at all*. Other than the impact of your ass hitting the floor and failing at your purpose.

In a moment, I'll elaborate on why this conflict between safety and making a difference, between predictability and living your purpose, exists. I'll also provide a detailed plan for navigating these rocky waters. But first, consider the following family drama, which plays out in thousands of households across America each year.

Dad and Mom have scrimped and saved for years, maybe even decades, to send their daughter to college, so that she can have a leg up on life. When Daughter gets to college, she decides to major in drama, or art history, or feminist critical theory. A fight ensues:

PARENTS: But how are you going to *earn a living* from being a drama [or art, creative writing, philosophy, literature, poetry, feminist critical theory, underwater basket weaving, etc.] major? Where are the employment ads that say, "Now hiring full-time drama majors"?

DAUGHTER: But Mom and Dad, this is what I'm *passionate* about in life. Do you want me to live life as a faceless office drone, enriching a bunch of corporate fat cats, and let the art inside of me die?

PARENTS: Of course we support your passions in life. We just want you to have a *backup plan* in case the acting thing doesn't work out. You're so smart, you've always been such a good arguer. Why don't you think about becoming a lawyer, like your cousin Sue? Then you can act on the side, on weekends. Acting is a wonderful *hobby*.

DAUGHTER: You just don't understand me! Life isn't just about boring job security! There are bigger things out there, more meaningful things, than how much money is in your bank account. You'll always regret being the ones who didn't allow me to go for my dreams [etc., etc.].

Similar arguments play out when high school students tell their parents they're not planning on going to college, or when college students tell their parents they're dropping out. Cameron Johnson, a wildly successful serial entrepreneur, self-made multimillionaire (and college dropout), recounts two such arguments with his parents.

The first arose during his high school years, when he told them he wasn't going to go to college, as he was too busy building his already-successful businesses.

> "Michael Dell doesn't have a college degree," I told them. "Bill Gates doesn't have a college degree."
>
> They pointed out that I was not Michael Dell or Bill Gates. I was their son, and they wanted me to get a good education![1]

Cameron succumbed in that argument and started as a freshman at Virginia Tech. However, soon after starting college, a similar argument arose, when he informed his parents he was leaving college to build his business.

> They said, "No, you're not."
>
> I said, "Mom, Dad, look at all the basketball stars and football stars who go right from high school to the NBA, or the actors and musicians who don't bother with college because their careers are already in motion. There have to be business stars, too, who don't need to go to a four-year program to learn their field. If I go through four years of college, I'll just be on a level playing field after four years—whereas now I have an *advantage*. Spending four years in school means I'll be four years *out* of the business world. Everything changes like lightning in the Internet world, and they'll have caught up to me."
>
> My dad said, "A college education doesn't hurt anyone."
>
> I said, "I agree, but it'll still be there ten years later if I still want it."
>
> He said, "Cameron, you can lose your house, you can lose your company, you can lose your money, you can lose your wife—but you can't lose your education. It's the one thing you'll always have."
>
> I said, "That's true, I don't disagree, but I *am* getting an education—a real-world education. Even though I'm not in the classroom every day, I'm still learning, and at a faster pace than my friends in college, because they're trying to learn about these things in the classroom, whereas I'm learning these things by actually doing them."[2]

These types of family dramas and arguments, in my opinion, boil down to arguments about our sense of *safety* versus *heroism* in life. Safety and heroism are almost always opposed. Imagine a movie in which the hero exposed himself to no risks or dangers, took no chances, and in fact wrapped himself in bubble wrap to protect himself from everyday slips and bruises. The movie consists of him walking on the sidewalk, on a nice sunny day, in this protective bubble wrap, to go to the store to purchase a few ingredients for dinner. Finito.

Sound like a very exciting movie?

Kids, in their idealism, want to make a big impact on their world. They want to change the world, to feel like their existence makes a difference. They want a big sense of purpose and excitement. They want to be heroes. No kid dreams of being an anonymous paper pusher or a faceless office drone.

Parents want their kids' lives to feel meaningful and satisfying as well, but they see that the kinds of careers that young people tend to dream about (arts and entertainment, literature, blogging, social media, sports, activism, entrepreneurialism, etc.) are also very risky.

And on that point, the parents are absolutely correct: these endeavors *are* more risky. In other words, there's a greater chance you'll end up flat-out broke if you follow them than if you become, say, a dentist or an accountant. So naturally, in their inviolable, nonnegotiable role as parents to protect and look out for their children, they tend to advocate safer, less risky, more predictable, more conformist paths as their children contemplate a career. They tend to talk about "backup plans" and "fallbacks," and to think about their children's creative passions and quests for meaning as "hobbies."

Why does this conflict between safety and heroism, impact and predictability exist? For a very simple reason. Almost by definition, "having an impact" or "making a difference" or "living a purpose" involves going beyond what already exists in any given workplace, organization, field, marketplace, or society. It involves innovating, or exercising leadership. Bryan Franklin, whom we met in the Introduction, defines leadership as "creating a future for others which wouldn't have happened otherwise." If what you're trying to achieve would have happened just the same without you, it's hard to say that you're having that much of an impact or that your purpose is very significant.

Yet, trying to change the course of the status quo—that is, trying to have an impact, living into a great purpose in your career—is also financially riskier than not doing so. This is just as true if you're a traditional professional (doctor, lawyer, or manager) trying to achieve big things within your company or your field as it is for people in artistic/entrepreneurial careers, for two simple reasons:

- People tend to feel safer and more comfortable with the known over the unknown. An "impact" is a change in course, so if you want to make an impact in your field, you're asking people to venture into the unknown. The more of a change of course your innovation or leadership represents, the more you are asking people to abandon safety and comfort, which is not usually something they're willing to do without overcoming a great deal of resistance.
- There may be entrenched interests who are quite happy with the way things are now and who aren't interested at all in your "impact," thank you very much. In fact, they may say you can take your impact and shove it! Try to rock the boat too much, make too much of a change, and these people may try to oust you from the organization, community, or marketplace, or even try to harm your reputation or career prospects. Anyone who has dealt with office politics knows this. Any artist or entrepreneur who has tried to do anything innovative knows this.

If you want to become wealthy or famous, which I presume you do if you're buying and reading a book on success, then you're going to need to make a difference in the lives of *many people.* (By definition, it's impossible to become famous, and it's also very difficult to become wealthy, if you impact the lives of only a few people.)

Yet, when you're trying to have an impact on the lives of large numbers of people, two additional challenges arise, unique to the interactions of people in groups:

- Making an impact on large groups of people involves *leading* them in some way. Yet, seeking to be a leader is akin to seeking what economists call a "positional good." A classic example of a positional good is a penthouse apartment. You can't have a penthouse apartment unless there are apartments below it. Not everyone in society could have a penthouse apartment. Similarly, you can't have leaders unless there are followers. Not everyone in any given situation can be a leader (unless you live in

Lake Wobegon, Garrison Keillor's fictional town, in which "all the children are above average"). In the real world, not the world where everyone gets a ribbon and a gold star, there will always be competition to lead people. The more people you want to lead, the stiffer the competition. And the stiffer the competition, the less you can be sure you'll win.

▥ Those who do end up leading often achieve leadership, amass wealth, fame, or support, or make an impact on the world, largely through the effects of word of mouth. Followers/customers/fans convert other people to followers/customers/fans, who convert more people to followers/customers/fans, until a big group— which business author Seth Godin calls a "tribe"—has amassed around that given leader, company, or artist. This is how most artists, musicians, actors, writers, and entrepreneurs who become famous and wealthy do so—through the viral-effects word of mouth. When word of mouth takes off, its effects are extremely rapid and dramatic (the "tipping point" that Malcolm Gladwell writes about). Yet, word of mouth is one of the least predictable things on the planet. No one really knows what the next word-of-mouth sensation will be. There's a capricious nature to word of mouth, fame, and fandom, which has even a bona fide genius like David Gilmour giving a strong nod to the role luck played in his success as an artist.

In your career, whenever you are faced with two paths, you will almost always be facing a choice between one path that is more predictable (in which you're more or less a cog in a predetermined script) and one that offers the chance to make a bigger impact (e.g., a leadership position) but has more risks associated with it. This is as true for a lawyer or corporate manager as it is for a start-up entrepreneur or a musician.

Another way to see it: at any point in your career, you'll usually be choosing between one path that is safer and one path that has the potential to feel more meaningful to you, between one path that is more certain and one that offers more of a chance for a sense of purpose and heroism. It's hard to be a hero if there's no risk involved.

A good way to think about "living a meaningful life," to a first approximation, is "making a difference in the lives of people you care about." It's no wonder our sense of meaning is so tied up with myths and stories—the heroes of myths and stories take risks in order to make a difference in people's lives. If you're not making a difference in anyone's life, it's unlikely you'll feel that your own life has been meaningful. You may end up, like the title character in "The Secret Life of Walter Mitty," living a mediocre life and merely daydreaming of heroism.

This is, as Thoreau put it, a "li[fe] of quiet desperation." Truly making a difference and living into a meaningful purpose has all kinds of dangers associated with it, including the dangers of failure, rejection, even ruin and going broke.

So, how do we navigate our desire for safety with our desire to make a difference in the world? How do we navigate between our desire for heroism, adventure, and romance and our desire for some level of predictability in our lives? How do we reconcile our idealistic dreams with the harsh realities of the marketplace?

These are the questions I answer in the rest of this chapter, indeed in the rest of this entire book. One thing I'm not going to give you, I promise, is a bunch of unrealistic fluff, yet another cheery pep talk about "never giving up on your dreams." Whenever I hear that kind of motivational guru-speak, I think of someone standing next to me as I contemplate a bet on a roulette wheel, telling me: "Think big! Never give up on your dream that putting your entire life savings on the number six could pay off big. And if you lose, double down—borrow if you have to—and keep going! Don't give up! You'll hit it big one of these days!"

The chance of becoming a true star in any given field, on the level of a David Gilmour, or some of the other self-educated mega-famous or mega-rich people I feature in this book (such as billionaires John Paul DeJoria, Phillip Ruffin, and Dustin Moskovitz), is orders of magnitude tinier than the chance of picking the winning number on a roulette spin. It's more like picking the winning number several spins in a row.

I don't advocate gambling. So I'm not going to tell you to quit college, or quit your comfy corporate job, to pursue your acting career or your singing career or your writing career.

So, am I telling you to give up your dreams, stick with the societal program, get that boring, safe job, and do just as your parents told you? No. The problem is, there are serious (though much less frequently acknowledged) risks to that path as well. If you're not particularly passionate about accounting, corporate management, law, or engineering (the traditional professions), and you go into those fields to please your parents, or to placate your own fears about the risks of following your creative passions, it seems very unlikely to me that you'll end up happy with your career choice. You will always be plagued by a nagging sense of "What if?"

Sure, there are a lot of risks of following your passions—the risk that you'll have to move back into your parents' basement as an adult, for example, or face near death as a "starving artist." But, as Randy Komisar points out in his book *The Monk and the Riddle*, there are also a lot of unacknowledged risks to *not* following your passions, of sticking too close to the beaten path in the name of safety and predictability. These include:

"[T]he risk of working with people you don't respect; the risk of working for a company whose values are inconsistent with your own; the risk of compromising what's important; the risk of doing something that fails to express—or even contradicts—who you are. And then there is the most dangerous risk of all—the risk of spending your life not doing what you want on the bet you can buy yourself the freedom to do it later."[3]

Randy is a partner at the legendary Silicon Valley venture firm Kleiner Perkins Caufield & Byers. A serious meditator and student of Buddhism for many decades (and a fellow graduate of my alma mater, Brown), he's one of the only people in Silicon Valley who could talk with equal authority on structuring multihundred-million-dollar rounds of private equity financing and the finer points of Buddhist philosophy.

I talked with Randy at his office on Sand Hill Road in Silicon Valley. He told me that, a lot of the time, people put off taking any steps toward living a more fulfilling life, with the idea of "keeping their options open." Yet, according to Randy, the idea of "keeping your options open" is an illusion.

Randy pointed out to me that the words "decision" and "decide" stem from the roots "cise" and "cide," to cut off and to kill, also the roots of many other words related to cutting and killing, such as "incise," "concise" (cutting out nonessentials), and "homicide." Thus, a decision is to cut off, or kill, other possibilities.

"People feel like, unless they're affirmatively making a decision, they're not making a decision. They think, 'How can you fail if you're not making any decision, not cutting off any possibilities?' The reality is, you're making a decision all the time. You're making a decision not to follow a path that might lead you to fulfillment.

"Even though the choice to do something you don't love, to 'keep the options open,' may seem like a passive decision and therefore less risky, you can't pretend you're not making decisions. So the real question is 'What risks are you taking by those decisions you're *not* making?' Not making a decision to create a fulfilling life now is in fact a decision—it cuts off certain paths in the future. The biggest risk is what we classically refer to as the middle-aged crisis. You become forty-five years old and realize that you're not the person you wanted to be. You haven't accomplished what you thought you were going to. The reality is that the vast majority of people today, even when they are on their deathbed, find that their regrets largely center around things they didn't do, not things they did do."

Randy calls the safe-and-narrow path, which pretends to incur no risks but which incurs the biggest risk of all (regretting your life at the end of it), "The Deferred Life Plan." In his book, he gives a simple formula for living this infelicitous Deferred Life Plan: "Step one: Do what you have to do. . . Step two: Do what you want to do. . . . The lucky winners may get to step two only to find themselves aimless, directionless. Either they never knew what they 'really' wanted to do or they've spent so much time in the first step and invested so much psychic capital that they're completely lost without it."[4]

So, according to what I've described so far in this chapter, we face a serious dilemma: Either we follow our passions and purpose, and incur a significant risk of ending up as a starving artist, or we follow a safe, predictable, boring path, and incur a significant risk of ending up full of regret in our lives.

Neither option sounds very palatable. Is there a way out of this bind? Is there a way to combine the relative safety and security that our parents advocate with the passion, meaning, creativity, idealism, individualism, and freedom that teenagers and twenty-somethings dream about? Is there a way to get the best of both worlds?

Yes, I believe there is.

I'm about to share with you a very specific plan for living the meaningful life of your dreams, making a difference and escaping the rat-race/herd/cage of the predetermined societal/parental script, while also making it *less* likely that you'll end up poor than if you followed the aforementioned societal script. I call it the "Art of Earning a Living."

To explain this art, let me tell you the story of someone who has navigated these dynamics of dreams and dangers with great elegance in the real world. And no, he's not a gazillionaire, and he's not famous. But he's managed to create an amazing life for himself.

■ ANTHONY SANDBERG AND THE ART OF EARNING A LIVING

For some reason, when many people reach a certain level of material affluence in life, and find that the things they had to do to get there are starting to feel meaningless, many such people begin to develop a keen interest in . . . *sailing*.

And when they do, Anthony Sandberg is right there, ready to take them out onto the water. "That's when they come to sail with me! They realize that maybe they were missing out on something. My world is about opening adventure up to people who have deferred that their entire lives in favor of checking all the right boxes and following the script." Anthony runs one of the largest and most successful sailing schools in the world, the OCSC Sailing School on the Berkeley Marina (http://www.ocscsailing.com). His story is directly relevant to this chapter.

Now sixty-two, Anthony dropped out of Dartmouth his senior year in 1971. Tensions were boiling in the United States around the Vietnam War, and during those final years Anthony was at college, the campus protests against the war were reaching a frenzied height.

Anthony spent most of his time organizing busloads of people to go down to Boston, New York, and Washington, D.C., to participate in the protests. When the invasion of Cambodia started in 1970, "schooling didn't mean anything to me anymore. I wanted to be where what's really happening in America. I took off that last term, and started organizing students full-time in D.C. So I never got a degree. I suppose I could go finish and get one now [chuckling], but I'm not sure it would do me any good."

Sandberg was the first person in his family to attend college. His father was a cook and his mother was a waitress. He grew up in lower-middle-class Hawaii, and then California, in what he describes as a troubled family life.

Wanting to escape, he left home and high school at sixteen, got a job on a ship, and sailed around the world. He returned to high school later that year, though he moved out of his home and was supporting himself fully on his own from that point on.

Dartmouth was impressed with his self-determination and the writings he showed them about his self-funded sailing adventure. They offered him a full scholarship.

While he did well his first two years there, toward the end of his time at Dartmouth—in addition to the little matter of barely attending class due to his organizing—he began to feel a profound cultural alienation from his peers as they readied for life beyond graduation. "At the same time, my senior year, all my friends—who had long hair throughout college—started cutting their hair and buying suits. It was like watching lemmings getting ready to jump. The biological clock kicked in, and they had to please their parents or please whatever they thought the process was. They didn't seem to me to be in touch with what they wanted in life. In fact, there were no rewards for doing what you were passionate about. There were rewards for behaving."

After leaving college, and after the protests died down, Sandberg drew on the same enterprising spirit that got him into college in the first place, and he supported himself from a number of entrepreneurial ventures. He started a sporting goods business, then a leather goods business. He got crew jobs on multimillionaires' yachts in the Mediterranean, Greece, Turkey, Croatia, and Spain. He then joined the Peace Corps in Nepal. "I was spending time with the richest people on earth, and the poorest people on earth."

When he got back from the Peace Corps, he kept on tinkering. "I was curious about a million different things that I wanted to explore." He got passionate about the budding solar energy industry. He apprenticed himself for six months to a top plumber—in those days solar energy involved water as a heating element—and started a solar installation and plumbing company, hiring licensed plumbers beneath him. At this time, he also began teaching sailing part-time at sailing schools.

It was at one of these schools that he got a piece of advice that changed his life forever. "I had a very well-heeled and important client. He said, 'Anthony, without a doubt, you're one of the best sailing instructors I've ever had. But, there is no future for you in being a sailing instructor. You need to capture what you do, identify it, and codify it, so it can be taught to many, many people. First teach it to a team, and then beyond.'"

A lightning bolt hit Anthony through that one piece of advice (read Success Skill #2 on finding the right advisers in life). He became possessed with the vision of starting his own sailing school. At that time, sailing was only for superrich elites. There weren't accessible sailing schools then, like there are today (with Anthony's school being a prime example of one—he started the trend). He wanted to take his passion and love for sailing and make it accessible for as many people as possible.

"I was living in my plumbing van at the time. With a fever, staying up late every night in my van, I wrote out a business plan. Every aspect: how the boats should be cared for, how people should be trained, how visitors should be greeted, what the progression of studies will be.

"I started the school by borrowing boats on the Berkeley Marina. How do you borrow a boat? Well, have you ever seen an empty marina? [Laughing.] They're filled with boats that are owned by people who don't know how to sail them, and who will sell them to somebody else every three years. I walked the Berkeley Marina, saying to people, 'Look, I'll take care of your boat, and I'll teach you how to sail, if you let me use it for my school during the week.' I had my pick of the boats! Honestly, I think a kid could still do that today, it hasn't changed a bit. [Laughing.] As I was doing that, I would get one client, then three, then five. I bootstrapped it entirely. No investment, no debt. A six-dollar business license."

The school grew and grew from there. It now occupies a spectacular six-acre campus facing the Golden Gate Bridge. In his thirty-plus years in business, Anthony's school has taught over twenty-five thousand people to sail, and now employs over eighty staff members, managing a fleet of over fifty boats and yachts. He lives in a gorgeous apartment directly overlooking the bay, part of the school complex. In the course of his work, he has led flotillas of sailing students and adventurers throughout Antarctica, Patagonia, Turkey, Greece, the Galápagos, the Caribbean, Central and South America, Tahiti, Australia, and the South Pacific, and regularly finds time for his own wild sailing adventures as well.

Although he's lived an incredibly rich life so far, and plans to keep the school going strong, Anthony is now in the process of figuring out what the second stage of his life is all about. He knows it has something to do with teaching entrepreneurialism to kids. To that end, he's been mentoring underprivileged children in the Bay Area on how to start businesses. "I don't want to teach them general classes. I want to find the ten kids who want to learn how to be an entrepreneur. I can teach them to start a business out of nothing. Give me two twigs, and we'll start a business out of it."

Anthony wants to teach kids entrepreneurialism for a very specific reason. He believes the future of our planet depends on young people learning these skills.

"We are in a critical state right now. We've got maybe ten years to save our oceans. And there are all kinds of problems of that magnitude. However, I believe the future of our world is not going to come from the nonprofits. I think it's going to come from business— because business is incredibly powerful. I just don't think that holding bake sales and begging for little handouts by nonprofits is going to act quickly or powerfully enough. Business knows how to get things done. But it has to have a conscience, it has to want to make the world a better place and not just make a profit at any cost. It clearly doesn't today."

Anthony Sandberg may not be famous. He may not be a Silicon Valley billionaire. But he is a wealthy man, in every sense of the word. And to achieve this wealth, he never once deferred any meaning, purpose, adventure, or excitement in his life. He has always gone *toward* meaning, purpose, adventure, and excitement. His life is profoundly meaningful to him and to the many people he teaches and leads.

"Our motto at the school is 'Inspire Confidence,'" he says. "It's not 'Learn to Sail Better.' It's about being confident to take that little journey from the shore, and then a little further, and a little further, and all of the sudden, the whole world becomes your playground."

So this is the "Art of Earning a Living." It is the art of creating a career path that *both* provides a high likelihood of financial security *and* allows you to follow your dreams and make a difference in the world.

To understand what it involves, let's go back for a moment to the argument between Parents and Daughter at the beginning of the chapter.

The parents and their child are arguing about the relationship between money, financial security, and safety on the one hand and passion, purpose, meaning, and making a difference on the other.

The parents and the daughter—though they are on opposite sides of the argument—are all operating with the same basic presuppositions: Money and financial security are completely separate from living with a sense of purpose and creating a meaningful life. These spheres bear no relationship to each other. The parents are advocating basically a dull, boring life, in which the daughter pursues a career she cares nothing about (and even finds morally repugnant) in exchange for financial security. The daughter is advocating a life of passion, purpose, and meaning, with no thought or regard for how she's going to pay the bills.

The Art of Earning a Living is the art of finding creative ways of bringing the spheres of money and meaning together and making them overlap significantly.

I call it an art because it's not always apparent how to best achieve financial stability while at the same time making a difference in a way you care about. Remember, we're not talking about "work-life balance" here—the "write plays in your spare time as a hobby while you're a lawyer" philosophy espoused by the parents. We're talking about creating a path where your work *is* your life's purpose *is* your income *is* your meaning *is* the difference you're making on the planet. Significantly more elusive—yet infinitely more rewarding—than the much-hyped "work-life balance."

The Art of Earning a Living requires a great deal of self-inquiry into what, exactly, the difference you want to make is, and also a lot of creative, entrepreneurial problem solving to figure out how you could make decent money while making that difference.

You're going to have to create a solution unique to you and your circumstances. No similar solution will have ever existed before, for a very simple reason: in the whole of human history, no one has yet made the difference you want to make. If they had, the impact you want to make wouldn't be a "difference" anymore, it would be a sameness! Making a difference, not a "sameness," means doing things no one has done before, at least, not for the people whose lives you want to impact.

And doing things that no one has done before—that is, leadership—involves uncertainty, risk, and danger. Which means, as Anthony suggests, losing sight of the shore. The greater the impact you want to make in your field, market, career, industry, or profession, or in the world, the farther you have to travel from shore.

I'm not going to pretend there aren't dangers in trying to make a difference. But in this book, I am going to give you a set of tools and skills that will minimize the dangers and maximize the chance of making a difference. Starting right now.

■ FOUR STEPS TO ALIGNING YOUR MONEY AND YOUR MEANING: PUTTING THE ART OF EARNING A LIVING TO WORK

Since I'd never have you try something I haven't applied extensively in my own life, later I'll be sharing with you the story of how I used these very tools to go from being broke, miserable, and desperate to building my own dream career for myself, which is both meaningful to me and lucrative. But for now, let's dive into the Four Steps to Aligning Your Money and Your Meaning directly.

There are three groups of people I'll be talking to in this section:

A) You'd be happy spending the rest of your life earning what you're now earning, if what you're doing now felt meaningful to you, but it doesn't.

B) You'd be happy spending the rest of your life doing what you're doing because it feels so meaningful to you, but you're not earning enough money doing it.

C) You're not happy with either the money you're earning or the meaning of what you're doing to earn it. In other words, Shit City.

I'm going to address people in groups B and C first; I'll address group A in a moment.

■ STEP 1: Get on Your Feet Financially

If you're in group B or C, there's really only one thing to do next. Get on your feet financially. I was in group B big-time during my "wannabe literary bad boy" phase, for much of my twenties, which I'll describe later in this chapter. I could have happily gone on for the rest of my life writing that stuff (God save the readers!), but the money simply wasn't good enough for me; there was no money.

If you're in group B or C, get on your feet financially, however you can. That's what most of the people in this book did. They got financially stable, from a young age, often their mid-teens. Get a square job, a corporate job, a temp job, a boring nine-to-five. Don't feel anything is "beneath you" so long as it pays. Wait tables if you have to. Give up your "art," "purpose," or "meaning" for a little while and know what it means to be financially stable. Get a kinesthetic feeling in your body of how it feels to have enough money to pay rent, to pay your bills on time, to take your sweetie out to a nice restaurant.

The best way to get financially stable, once you have some kind of job—any job—is to exhibit the entrepreneurial leadership values on the job, described in detail in Success Skill #7, "The Entrepreneurial Mind-set versus the Employee Mind-set." This is how I did it and how all the self-educated entrepreneurs in this book did it.

▌ STEP 2: Create More Room for Experimentation

This step (and all the rest) applies to groups A, B, and C mentioned above. (Presumably those in group A are already financially stable and thus have already completed Step 1.) The next step in Aligning Your Money and Your Meaning, once you're financially on your feet, is to create more room for experimentation.

Finding a comfortable meeting ground for your money and your meaning is going to require a lot of experimentation. Experimentation takes time. It takes money. And it takes room to fall and to fail.

Having the financial stability gained in Step 1 makes it a *lot* easier to start taking some measured risks in your life. Anthony Sandberg, for example, started his sailing school when he already had money coming in from his solar and plumbing business. Elliott Bisnow, whom we'll be meeting in Success Skill #2, started his Summit Series when he already had money coming in from his real estate newsletter business. My wife, Jena, worked a variety of unfulfilling jobs before she developed her health-coaching and yoga-teaching career, which was more fulfilling to her. And again, she waited until she had solid money coming in from her health coaching and yoga before she took the next step and opened a wellness center. Frank Kern, whom we'll meet in Success Skill #3, worked a variety of shit jobs as he was building his Internet marketing business.

It's just *so different*—and better—figuring out how to make a difference in the world and find meaning in your life when your bills are covered and you have a secure roof over your head. It's *way* less stressful than trying to do it when you're broke. And, once the hurdle of supporting yourself is already passed, you'll be much less likely to take a path that leads you to being broke again. Paying your bills on time is a seductive feeling, and once you get in the habit of it, you won't want to go back.

Now, one problem you may encounter once you're financially stable is that the time it takes to create that financial stability in your life is so great, there's nothing left over for anything but following the dictates of your job. This is where Step 2 comes in.

You need to free up time and space for some experiments in leadership, innovation, making a difference, and finding meaning. If you're working freelance gigs (as I was during this period), then there's always a way to find a few spare hours each day for starting a pursuit that might feel meaningful to you. If you're working seventy-hour weeks at a corporate job, however, there will be very little space left over for anything else but that.

In this case, you should begin taking some risks at work. See if you can get buy-in from your boss to focus more on *results* you achieve, rather than focusing on hours logged. There are some great books on how to make this transition, including *Why Work Sucks and How to Fix It: No Schedules, No Meetings, No Joke, the Simple Change That Can Make Your Job Terrific* by Cali Ressler and Jodi Thompson; Chapter 12 of Tim Ferriss's *The Four-Hour Workweek*, titled "Disappearing Act: How to Escape the Office"; and also *The Custom-Fit Workplace: Choose When, Where, and How to Work and Boost Your Bottom Line* by Joan Blades and Nanette Fondas.

Flextime, working at home, telecommuting, working from your laptop and your mobile phone—these just aren't the foreign concepts they were even five years ago. There's really no excuse for not creating some flexibility in your workday now if you want it. The only excuse is your own fear and lack of imagination—and those aren't good enough.

■ STEP 3: With This New Space in Your Workday, Begin Experimenting!

With some increased flexibility in your workday and workweek, or at least some buy-in from your boss about the idea of getting evaluated based on results rather than hours, you can now experiment with taking some risks toward making a difference within your organization, workplace, or industry. Read Success Skill #7, and adopt an entrepreneurial mind-set at your workplace. Solve problems that you weren't "hired" to solve. Contribute in high-leverage ways you weren't hired to contribute. Leading always feels more meaningful, impactful, and creative than following.

Read Seth Godin's *Linchpin: Are You Indispensable?* This is the best book I know on the topic of exercising more leadership within your organization—which Seth calls being a "Linchpin"— no matter what your formal title or job description is. Become a Linchpin in your organization. Most of the people featured in *The Education of Millionaires* worked their way up their early jobs by doing so even if they'd never heard of Seth Godin.

If you're already working in the field you plan to stay in for the rest of your life, and you don't want to become an entrepreneur within that field, then you're right where you need to be in the Art of Earning a Living. Keep seeking out opportunities to exercise more leadership in your workplace (read Success Skill #7 and apply the entrepreneurial mind-set at your workplace). Keep looking for ways to stick your neck out, to take risks, to innovate, to make a difference, in the name of taking your organization to the next level.

With the newly flexible hours in your day and week (from Step 2), you can also begin experimenting more intensively with potential sources of meaning, passion, and purpose outside of work, from artistic endeavors to charity and causes.

Many people are quite content to leave things here: they have a career that pays the bills and in which they're increasingly making a difference and finding meaning, through exercising leadership. And they also have time during their day or week to pursue meaningful passions outside of work.

Seth Godin recommends this path for many people. He told me: "For fifty thousand years, humans did what they were passionate about, and then they did something else to eat. I don't think there's anything written down to say that those days are gone forever. We don't have a poetry shortage. There's plenty of poetry. No one gets paid to write poetry. If you want to write poetry, write poetry."

There's really not much downside to this path. It works. Worst case, you have a day job that pays the bills with increasing artistry, creativity, and leadership, *and* you get to explore your passions (for poetry, singing-songwriting, charity, etc.) on the side.

■ STEP 4: Striking Out on Your Own (for Those Who Want to Change Careers, Become Entrepreneurs, or Become Self-Employed)

If your current field, industry, company, or organization does not reflect your deepest sense of purpose and meaning, however, then you're going to need to go beyond Step 3 in Aligning Your Money and Your Meaning. You don't want your passion and meaning to come either from your current job or organization, or "on the side"— you want to find a new main dish. With the flexible hours in your day and week gained in Steps 2 and 3, begin experimenting with things that might one day become both a source of meaning and a source of serious income for you outside of your current job.

This might mean starting a small business on the side, moonlighting in a second "start-up" career, pursuing self-study to prepare for a different career, or finding ways to earn money from your artistic and creative passions.

Whatever it may be, if you want to make a living from it and leave your current job, you're going to have to do a deep dive into the success skills in this book, particularly marketing, sales, and networking. You're going to have to wrap your own passions, talents, and purpose—the things you care most about and are best at—in the package of these fundamental success skills. If you know how to do *that*, you get paid a lot, *and* you're living your passion and purpose. Keep reading. A major pitfall in this journey is that we are so conditioned to thinking of money and meaning as separate, we overlook creative ways that we can bring them together. If you use your noggin—and the success skills in this book—you can find a zillion ways to interface your creative skills, passions, visions, and dreams with the already-existing worlds of capitalism and commerce. I'm not going to say this will be an easy or risk-free task. However, the stories throughout this book should provide plenty of examples and inspiration on how to do it.

As I was interviewing Seth Godin (who went to Tufts and got an MBA from Stanford), we were sitting in the main dining room of the architecturally stunning Capital Grille on Forty-second Street in Manhattan. Seth told me: "People have this idea that either you're a cog in the machine, just working for the man, or you're out singing onstage, making your living that way. It seems like there's a lot in between—there are a lot of people who may not have what it takes to become the next famous musician, but who are finding ways to make money with what they care about.

"Think about this restaurant right now. It's not really like any restaurant in New York City that I've ever been in. Where did it come from? It's not here because someone made chairs or china, which are available to everyone. It's here because someone's putting on a show. And they're charging many times what they would get if they were selling it from a street cart.

"I'm saying that's 'art.' Someone didn't just copy it. Someone had to take various components and put them together, to create something that was worth experiencing, and sharing, and talking about. On the back of that, you can build a business that makes tons of money selling food.

"The art here, the experience of seeing it, that's free. Anyone can walk in this place, look around, get it, and leave. The souvenir part—the experience part, the owning-the-table-for-two-hours part—that's what they make money from.

"McDonald's fooled us into believing that the purpose of industry was to churn out standardized quantity at low cost. This place reminds us that, no, there's an alternative to racing to the bottom. And that is, racing to the top."

Are you ready to race toward the top and combine money with meaning? Keep reading—the remaining stories and skills in this book show you how.

■ **PORTRAIT OF THE ARTIST AS A YOUNG FUCKUP: HOW I WENT FROM BROKE, MISERABLE WANNABE SUPERSTAR TO FINANCIALLY SECURE, CREATIVELY ENGAGED PROFESSIONAL AUTHOR**

I told you I wouldn't recommend anything to you that I hadn't applied in my own life. So here is my own story of how I applied the

Four Steps to Aligning Your Money and Meaning, in my own life. Through following these steps, I was able to transform myself from being basically a miserable, broke loser, just four years ago, to having my current career, which is both profoundly meaningful to me and financially lucrative.

■ Pre-Step 1: Broke and Miserable Loser

Seven years ago, at age twenty-seven, I became possessed with the idea that I wanted to write and publish my first book, a manuscript of creative nonfiction I was working on, and become a literary superstar.

Laid off from my first postcollege job in corporate America, after the dot-com bubble, I moved back with my parents into the room I lived in as a teenager, with the idea that I would enjoy subsidized rent while I pursued my passion of writing and tried to make it as an author. My parents tolerated this because I also offered to use my writing skills assisting my father on a professional project for which he needed help; this was my day job, which also paid my basic expenses and some rent to my parents.

I ended up writing a wildly sexual, experimental, caffeine-pot-and-wine-charged attempt at autobiographically based comedic nonfiction, almost wholly devoid of any structure, weaving in manic political rants and fragments from my senior honors thesis in international relations at Brown ("Black Masks, White Guilt: Cultural Appropriation, Multicultural Consumerism and the Search for a Meaningful First World Existence"). My literary idols were Henry Miller, Hunter S. Thompson, Michel Houellebecq. I was certain my name would be joining their names at the table of "bad boys" in literature. The manuscript was titled, ironically enough, *Rock Star Envy.*

Here is a selection from one of the twenty-two rejection letters sent to my agent at the time:

"I couldn't tell whether he was trying to write a satire/be humorous when he discussed things like his ecofeminism, or whether he was trying to write a straight memoir. His story picked up speed and kept me interested when he let his too brief anecdotes breathe and become a linear narrative, but the asides, rants, and portions of his college thesis distracted me and stopped the story in its tracks."

Another letter, from a famous literary editor at a major New York publishing house, in its entirety:

"I'm going to pass on this project. Mr. Ellsberg's writing is not strong enough to overcome the simple fact that he is not a very likable person."

At the time, of course, I viewed these letters as pure confirmation of my worst suspicions: the corrupted aesthetics of middle-class consumerist mediocrity and philistinism, the complete venality of corporate publishing pandering to those tastes, the wickedness of the profit-motivated media-entertainment complex—unable to recognize the genius of Art even if they were hit over the head with a two-pound manuscript of experimental nonfiction-in-fragments.

Over time, my views of this episode in my life mellowed and matured. The word "undisciplined" was used by several different editors rejecting my manuscript, and I have come to see that they were right—in fact, all the rejections were right.

I was a cocky kid, convinced that I was creating a new form of writing (doing away, for example, with the oppressive confines of narrative arc, plot, or character development) and that my vision was poised to take over the world, whether the world cared or not.

You could say I was trying to blaze a trail. And perhaps I was doing so.

But there was a problem with this trailblazing. No one really wanted to go wherever the trail I was blazing led. In fact, *I* didn't really know where it led. In reality, it led to some dark, tangled forest bog in my depressed soul, with peat so thick and brush so dense that the trail back out got erased no sooner than it was blazed.

After a second round of submissions of *Rock Star Envy* bombed, in 2006, I finally got the message: I was not going to make a living as a bad-boy literary *enfant terrible* of memoir writing. If I wanted to continue to pay rent and buy groceries, I would need to be more flexible about how I interfaced my main set of skills (writing and editing nonfiction) with market realities.

■ STEP 1: Freelance Copywriter (Getting on My Feet Financially)

And so began my journey in the Art of Earning a Living, in 2007, at age twenty-nine. I began seeking out every gig I could get. Editing gigs. Ghostwriting gigs. Copywriting gigs. I helped people self-publish their books. I wrote book proposals for aspiring authors. Anything that had $$$ attached to it, and somehow involved words, I would do it. (How did I get all these gigs? Mostly through networking. Read Success Skill #2 on how to be a great connector!)

I moved to Buenos Aires, for a while, where I knew I could live very cheaply, worked for mostly Australian clients over the Internet (it's a long story), and pursued my freelance commercial writing and editing writing full-time. I brought in $8,280 of gross income in 2007, which I was able to live on with a combination of living in pesos and drawing down some money I had saved from my last corporate job.

At the end of 2007, I moved into a $350-a-month room in San Francisco. I kept my business humming. The recession hit in 2008, but through mastering the skills of marketing, I expanded my business by 600 percent, to almost $50,000 in gross income per year in both 2008 and 2009, on a totally flexible freelancer's schedule. I also moved out of that tiny room in San Francisco into better digs.

Obviously, things improved from a monetary perspective. I was no longer going deeper and deeper into debt to cover my living expenses while I "went for my dreams" (as the motivational books put it), hoping some editor at a publishing house would bestow upon me a windfall advance.

I was developing a valuable set of skills. Not editing/writing skills, which were already fine. I'm talking about the success skills in this book, particularly sales, marketing, and networking. Out of necessity (and following the steps I'll provide in detail in coming chapters), I became good at connecting with potential clients, selling them on the idea of working with me, and leading them to where they wanted to go in their projects. Money started to flow. I had passed through Step 1 of the Aligning Your Money and Your Meaning.

(Step 2 in the Aligning Your Money and Your Meaning is all about creating flexibility in your workday, which allows for more experimentation in integrating your money and your meaning. Because my income in Step 1 was already derived from freelance work, I fortunately had plenty of flexibility—one of the great benefits of being a self-employed freelancer. So I got to skip directly to Step 3.)

▉ STEP 3: Freelancer Copywriter with a Side Passion of Writing Books

Once money started to flow in 2008 and 2009, and I was on finan-cially firm footing, I very quickly began asking myself: Is this how I want to spend the rest of my life? This is the next step of Aligning Your Money and Your Meaning.

In his book *The Monk and the Riddle*, Randy Komisar advises you to ask a simple question about your current mode of income: Would you be willing to do *this* for the rest of your life?

The point is not that you *will* do it for the rest of your life. But would you be *willing*? If this was all there was—no brighter tomor-row, no magic promotion or raise or investment that vaults you into the shrouded next level.

Just this. Now.

Would you be happy with this the rest of your life?

If the answer is no—if the thought of doing your current gig for the rest of your life makes you totally depressed—then you owe it to yourself (having only one life to live) to figure out what kind of pursuit you *would* be willing to live till the end.

And in so doing, it's important to look at the whole package, both the money and inner rewards. Is the *whole package*, the money and the meaning, of your current life tolerable to you if this was it for the rest of your life? If either one (or both) of these aspects is off, then you've got to start making the appropriate adjustments.

Writing my "subversive" incoherent mess of a memoir might have been metaphysically rewarding to me at that time (Pre-Step 1). But at a certain point, the whole "starving, debt-laden artist" thing was no longer appealing to me.

So at first, I swung totally in the other direction (Step 1) and focused entirely on paying the bills. Which made sense for a while—it was like "financial therapy," weaning me off my artistically un-derearning ways of the past.

But as soon as I was on my feet again financially, and I had some flexibility in my workday to ponder such things (Step 2), Randy's question popped into my mind. And the clear answer to his query was no. I would *not* feel satisfied spending the rest of my life as a book proposal writer, direct-response copywriter, and marketing consultant. Not to say it was a bad situation. A lot of people would have killed for that setup, with such solid money on such a flexible schedule. But I had to add something in order for my life to feel meaningful.

I always knew that my great passion was writing books. Not editing other people's books, not writing book proposals for other people's books or marketing them. But writing my own. That's what I was originally doing in my "starving memoirist" phase.

Well, with Steps 1 and 2 handled, I now had the flexibility to write on the side, exploring this passion, yet without having to do it in a "starving artist" way. I wrote a proposal for what became my first published book, *The Power of Eye Contact*. My income in 2008 and 2009 included $10,000 each of those years in advance money from that book. That certainly wasn't enough to quit my day job, but it at least contributed to my income and allowed me to explore even more this passion on the side.

For these two years on my path of the Art of Earning a Living, I was solidly at Step 3. I had a great freelance income on a flexible schedule, and I was reengaging with my passion for book writing.

■ STEP 4: Toward Full-Time Author

However, in 2010, I got the idea that I wanted my passion—book writing—to be my main income. This is Step 4 in Aligning Your Money and Your Meaning with integrating your money and your meaning fully. I continued to grow my freelancing day job, in a still-shaky market, by 50 percent in 2010, to $75,000. I'm proud of this growth in the freelancing business over the past four years—about 75 percent per year annualized, including two years of a recession. I credit this growth to the sales, marketing, and networking skills I describe later in this book. (It's often easier to get a far greater return with much less risk by investing in your own earning power via sales and marketing skills, than is available on the stock market. See Success Skill #5 on investing in your own earning power.)

But in line with my new resolution, I continued nurturing my side career, in a more serious and devoted manner than before. It paid off big-time for me. I came up with the idea for this book, wrote the proposal for it, networked my way to a fantastic literary agent, and received a six-figure offer from Penguin. Now in 2011, I am massively toning down my freelance business, turning my attention almost exclusively to my career as a book author, and starting to conceive of the next book project.

My own Art of Earning a Living, so far, culminates in this book. It is both the most financially lucrative and the most personally meaningful project I've ever had the privilege to be involved with. Through a lot of trial and error and going through the Four Steps to Aligning Your Money and Your Meaning I describe here, I seem to have found the sweet spot of overlapping money and meaning in my life.

How will you meld together money and meaning in *your* life?

This is one of the most important skills you'll ever develop. By definition, it can only be studied in the real world, outside of class, because the method of instruction is trial and error, with real-world feedback. I hope the stories I provide in the book—and the steps I've given you here—offer inspiration for getting started.

■ WITHOUT FAILURE, THERE IS NO LEARNING (OR, WHY ENTREPRENEURIALISM IS LIKE DATING)

One of the capacities that will be invaluable to you as you begin to work through the Four Steps to Aligning Your Money and Your Meaning is developing a different—and I believe more realistic— relationship to risk. Indeed, if there's one single trait that sets all the self-educated millionaires I interviewed for this book apart from other people, it's their relationship to risk.

Critics of my book will likely say that what sets them apart is they simply took *bigger* risks than others: the people I interviewed were simply the *winners* at the roulette wheel, and I failed to talk about all the people who played at the wheel and got wiped out. (This line of critique would charge me with a fallacy of statistical reasoning known as "survivorship bias": making assertions about some process based on conclusions drawn only via looking at the "winners" of that process, without taking into account the experience of the—usually much larger—sample of losers.[5])

And yet, I don't believe the people I feature in this book simply took a bigger bet than everyone else and happened to get lucky and win. Rather, I've seen that they have systematically and intentionally developed a style of working that allows them to take *lots* of small bets—bet after bet after bet after bet—all the while making sure that they don't get wiped out of the game if one or many of them go south. In other words, I believe that for most of the people featured in this book a trait even more important than luck was *resilience.*

Most people, when they think of the idea of starting a business, see it as an *incredibly risky* proposition, one that entails not just egg-in-the-face, but *total ruin.* They are nearly hysterical about the risks they could incur if they left their safe, boring jobs. Images of would-be entrepreneurs living homeless on the street after their ventures failed keep many people who dream of starting their own businesses stuck in comfortable, boring corporate jobs for the rest of their lives.

I believe this is a distorted view of entrepreneurialism. Most of the self-educated people featured in this book took pains to make sure that their "downside was not so exposed," to use the parlance of investing: they made sure that a failed business would not mean total ruin; it would just mean a few scrapes, a few good lessons learned, and up they are again at a new one. No biggie. They are calm, relaxed, and cool about failure, not hysterical and terrified, because they view failure as necessary for *learning.*

Take the story of Mike Faith, owner of Headsets.com, which does millions in sales each year of headsets for hands-free phoning. Mike was mildly dyslexic, and started falling behind in the United Kingdom's equivalent of high school. He never felt he fit into an academic environment—abstract academic skills were neither his strength nor his passion—so he decided to leave school at age fifteen.

His career after that, for many years, began to look like a ping-pong match of entrepreneurial ventures, one after the other after the other in rapid succession. He started in door-to-door sales at fifteen, selling window insulation, all the while living at home with his parents (living at home with parents is a powerful way to limit one's financial downside, as many twentysomethings are now being forced to discover).

He was so good at sales, he bought his first car at seventeen with money he earned, and bought his first home at twenty-one, enabling him to finally move out. Soon, he got into the business of buying up assets of bankrupt companies and selling them at auction for a tidy profit. He then got involved in the rising UK property market of the late eighties. When that crashed, he lost everything. "By my mid-twenties, I had made my first million, and lost my first million."

For many people skeptical of starting a business, this is the end of the story in their minds: welcome to life as a desperate pauper, they imagine, the penance for taking too much risk.

But for Mike, this was only the beginning. (Indeed, a great many of the people I interviewed for this book have at least one bankruptcy under their belt.) Here's where the differing mindset around risk comes in. Ruin? *Eh,* says Mike. "It's good for you to go through that experience. I think for someone to be successful in business, you've got to have that edge where you're prepared to take chances and fail, and—here's the key—pick yourself back up."

Here's where the *resilience* comes in. For Mike, his failure wasn't condemnation to perpetual ruin. He *started out* with the assumption that life has risk. Rather than see failure as something to be avoided at all costs (as most of us see it), he instead designed his life and mind-set around the *inevitability* of failure and how to cope with it. Instead of viewing his first big failure as ruin, he simply decided to view it as an opportunity for an interesting change in life plans.

Mike and his wife sold all their remaining possessions in 1990. With $1,000 in their pockets, they followed generations of enterprising spirits before them and moved to America.

He took a day job at a software company, but soon he was back at his entrepreneurial ventures on the side. He started a company selling the labor law posters that human resources departments were legally required to display at workplaces. Soon he had a hundred thousand customers. Then he got into selling posters with area code and ZIP Code maps and turned that into a $2 million business within years.

"We were using phone headsets in the poster business. The headsets were pretty crappy. It was hard to get any service on them. And I couldn't buy what I wanted anywhere. I tried and I couldn't get it. To me, that's enough of a data point to say there's a business there. Because if I can't find it I know I'm not the only one. Other people can't find it. There's an unserved niche in the market, something people can't find but they want. It's just a question of how big the niche is. And I thought, 'Everyone uses the phone, this is a big market.' I decided to be in the headset business.

Six weeks later I was in the headset business." The company now does $30 million a year in phone headset sales.

Hearing Mike talk, you could be forgiven if you thought you were listening to a different breed of human. The way he—and nearly all the entrepreneurs I interviewed in this book—relate to risk is *completely different* from the way most of us do. To be sure, they aren't banking their entire life future on one single dream or bust (say, becoming a rock star, à la David Gilmour). But rather than never try their hand at any dream at all, and sticking to a safe-but-boring course instead, they keep trying one dream after the next, maximizing their inner and outer resilience for the in- evitable failures. They fail early and often, and turn courses on a dime, until *something* begins to gain traction.

"I can't help it. It's an addiction. It's a compulsion," Mike told me with a mischievous grin, from his fancy San Francisco offices. Nearly everyone I interviewed for this book has this attitude about starting businesses. What makes it different from, say, a gambling addiction, is that these people are masters of making sure they stay in the game when luck inevitably turns against them. Unlike a gambling addict, they have consciously cultivated a lifestyle of resilience. They are ready to pick themselves up, dust themselves off, adjust course, and try something else when they fail. That is the essence of learning. Without failure, there is no learning. These people are not addicts of gambling; they are addicts of *learn- ing* in the real world. And learning in the real world involves fail- ure. Lots of it.

"People who have been successful are still as likely to get it wrong as right going forward. They just try more things," Mike told me. "That's the difference." Mike's advice for young peo- ple who want to combine their passion with their money? "Start with the passion and the drive. You've got to have that hunger. From that passion and desire, go actually do some stuff. Try some little businesses. Get some failure under your belt. Find out what works and doesn't work, and don't worry about the failures, worry about learning."

By far the most common objection many people raise in dis- cussions about whether it makes sense to try out an entrepreneur- ial side gig in service of pursuing your dreams is the oft-cited statistic that 95 percent of small businesses fail within their first five years. This statistic brings up images of 95 percent of all small-business owners ending up on the streets begging for change to feed their kids after they sell off their house to pay off business debts.

"That statistic is a bunch of crap," Josh Kaufman, author of *The Personal MBA: Master the Art of Business*, told me. He pointed out to me that the statistic is based on the number of people who file Schedule C forms (profit or loss from business activities) and other forms related to business ownership, then stop filing such forms at some point. Yet, as he says, "It's calculated on the number of businesses that cease to exist within five years, not that go bankrupt or whose owners' lives are ruined forever and ever. Sometimes companies are making money, but they're not making enough to make it worth it, so they go do something else. Sometimes the business got acquired. That's a really *good* thing. 'My business ceased to exist because I got paid a lot of money to sell it to some other company and it got absorbed.' *All* of the many ways that a business could cease to exist are wrapped up in that one number, which gets interpreted as a doomsday 'Oh my gosh, so many people are failing in business and ending up in the soup lines!' kind of statistic."

One of the best ways to avoid this kind of horror-story scenario when reaching for your dreams, even if your business doesn't end up working out, is to start a service business. Usually, overhead and start-up costs are low, you don't need to borrow a lot (or any) to get started, and you can begin generating revenue immediately. Even if the business doesn't work out, the consequences of failure are usually minimal, and if you do end up being one of those 95 percent who fail to file a Schedule C within five years, you're not going to end up on the street begging for change. It's just not that big of a deal. You can close up shop on that business, go back to your day job, and try something different another time, no big deal.

"The very best things you can do when starting a new business," Josh told me, "are, number one, keep your overhead as low as possible, and number two, make sure you're getting recurring revenue as quickly as possible. If your revenue is semi-predictable, you can just grow and grow based on the cash that the business is throwing off, instead of having to get investments, loans, and so forth."

In his book, which he presents as a business education in a book without the need for $100,000 of debt (http://www.person almba.com), Josh talks about a concept called "iteration velocity."

He quotes Google CEO Eric Schmidt: "Our goal is to have more at bats per unit of time and money than anyone else." Josh (who has an undergraduate degree from the University of Cincinnati, but who educated himself in his real-world business savvy without an MBA) writes that "When creating a new offering, your primary goal should be to work through each iteration cycle as quickly as possible. Iteration is a structured form of learning that helps you make your offering better; the faster you learn, the more quickly you'll be able to improve." Basically, it means, try something new but small and low-risk, see how it works, keep it if it works well, and don't be afraid to turn on a dime (or "pivot," as many entrepreneurs say) if it doesn't work. It involves *intentionally* exposing yourself to lots of small, survivable failures, so that you can get feedback from the real world, adjusting course as quickly as possible to avoid investing too many resources down a dead-end path.

I'm amazed at how many people won't go for their dreams because they're scared of that 95-percent failure statistic or some version of it.

Let's consider an analogy.

While I have absolutely no scientific data to back this up, it seems to me a reasonable guess that 95 percent of all dates are failures.

Now, imagine what would happen to our species if all people, when they heard of the low success rates of individual dates leading past the first date, freaked out and said, "OH MY GOD! I'M NEVER GOING TO GO ON A DATE AGAIN! I MIGHT GET REJECTED!" This generation would be the last.

Fortunately, when it comes to dating, humans see that there is a big difference between the high likelihood that *any single date* will fail and the very low likelihood that *all of your dates for the rest of your life will fail.*

Doing something entrepreneurial is, much like dating, a numbers game. If you can keep your financial and emotional losses low each iteration, and not jump off a building if the business (or date) fails, well then, you can keep trying and trying. Eventually, most everyone can find a creative blending of passion and money that works for them, just as eventually most everyone can find a great date that leads to something more.

Beyond the pure numbers game aspect of these two different human endeavors, here's another parallel between creative entrepreneurship and dating: if you don't allow yourself to get completely devastated and wiped out from a failure, you can actually *learn* from your failures, and thus improve your odds with each iteration.

I could insert a lot of jokes here about the countless dating blunders and bloopers in my twenties; they could fill a book. But suffice it to say, when I finally went on my first date with my wife, Jena, I had learned enough from all those blunders to avoid the clod-head mistakes of my past and to woo her properly that one spring night in 2008. And *that* was the date that really mattered. You only need one, in a whole lifetime.

■ DUSTIN MOSKOVITZ'S STORY

In early 2004, Dustin Moskovitz was working a twenty-hour-per-week job as a computer system administrator, on top of forty or so hours a week of classes and homework as a sophomore at Harvard.

And then there was this little side project he and some of his dorm buddies were working on, called TheFacebook.com.

It's hard to believe, but there was a time when Facebook was not a sure thing as one of the most significant phenomena in the history of human communication and social life. There was a time when it was a few kids sitting in a dorm room, and it had sixty or seventy thousand users—far fewer users than many now-folded companies have boasted before.

"The big risk was, there were these big incumbents. We thought, if they could just clean their act up, they would surely beat us. Friendster, MySpace, even LiveJournal at the time was millions of users bigger than us," Dustin told me.

"A guy called Adam Goldberg started CU Community at Columbia the semester before we started Facebook. He's a friend of mine now. He had a really well-designed social network. As soon as he saw us go our multi-college strategy, he started to do it too, aggressively. At the time, it did not look like a foregone conclusion. It looked like a good business opportunity, but there were plenty of other players, and it seemed plenty likely that they could beat us. And we were also thinking, Google could just jump in at any moment. They easily could have won in 2004. Now, of course, it's a different story."

Dustin and his college buddies, roommates and fellow co-founders Mark Zuckerberg and Chris Hughes, famously decided to move out to Palo Alto that summer, 2004, with the intention of going back to Harvard in the fall. "But by the time the end of June rolled around, it was more like a hundred and fifty thousand users, and we thought, 'OK, this is actually pretty difficult to do, even without having sixty or eighty hours a week of classes, homework and paid work. We started asking ourselves, 'Is it really feasible to go back next semester, and build this company, and do school?' Very quickly, we came to the conclusion, 'No, we'll probably fail at both if we try that.' So Mark and I decided not to go back to Harvard."

At this point in his story, I asked Dustin: "For so many people in the world, getting into Harvard is pretty much the pinnacle of achievement—the thought is, once you've graduated from Harvard, you're pretty much set for life. So here you are, you've achieved that pinnacle, and you have this site which is getting incredible traction within six months, but without knowing for sure back then that you weren't going to get beaten down. How did you decide to take the risk?"

"First of all," he said, "Harvard allows you to stop out for an indefinite period of time. So I could go back anytime. My friends might not be there anymore, I might have to start over socially. That was a risk. But it was a pretty small risk compared to the opportunity at the time.

"I called my parents and said, 'We'll stop out for a semester and see how it goes.' And my dad was like, 'Great! I can't afford the tuition next semester anyway!' [Laughing.]

"By the summer, it was a big deal. In terms of consumer Internet sites, it was growing really quickly. We had advertising on the site. It was clear we could make some money off of it. We thought there was a real business there. We also knew, however, that it wasn't a done deal by any means—there were many other entrants for this winner-take-all prize, which definitely could have beaten us in those years.

"But here's the thing. We knew we were developing skills. These were plenty marketable skills. People knew who Facebook was. And we could go back to Harvard whenever. It just didn't feel that risky."

As we've seen in this chapter, people often have a sense that if you leave some stable situation, such as school or a comfortable job, in order to try a more meaningful but less certain pursuit, you'll end up completely forlorn and destitute if the pursuit doesn't work out.

That's almost always an exaggeration. The odds of starting one of the most significant social and business phenomena in history and creating a company with a multibillion-dollar valuation are exceedingly minute. There's no question in my mind that Dustin, Mark, and the rest of the early Facebook team are geniuses, and incredibly hardworking. But I'm confident that they would concede that there was also a great deal of serendipity in just how massively it paid off for them.

Does that mean your only options are either a tiny chance of striking it massively rich or a big chance of going bust? Not at all. As we've been discussing this entire chapter, there's so much in between. In a blog post entitled "One in a Million," Seth Godin writes, "The ardent or insane pursuit of a particular [risky] goal is a good idea if the steps you take along the way also prep you for other outcomes, each almost as good (or better). If . . . bending the market to your will and shipping on time and doing important and scary work are all things you need to develop along the way, then it doesn't really matter so much if you don't make the goal you set out to reach."[6]

The point is, if you're learning valuable business skills while you also pursue your dreams, you win either way. You win (obviously) if the venture works out, but less obviously, you also win if it fails—few things provide better real-world education in business skills than a good hard failure.

But this win-win only applies if you're actually immersing yourself in the business side of what you're doing as you go for your dreams. Seth continues, "Does spending your teenage years (and your twenties) in a room practicing the violin teach you anything about being a violin teacher or a concert promoter or some other job associated with music? If your happiness depends on your draft pick or a single audition, that's giving way too much power to someone else." Learn the business side of your craft, and you'll come away with applicable, marketable skills no matter what.

For Dustin, of course, going for his dreams paid off. For several years, Mark Zuckerberg was the world's youngest-ever self-made billionaire. But Dustin is eight days younger than Zuckerberg. When Facebook's valuation soared in 2010, Dustin's chunk surged to over two billion, and he took Zuckerberg's place as the world's youngest. Dustin has already started his next venture, Asana (http://asana.com), which aims to revolutionize workplace collaboration as thoroughly as Facebook has revolutionized the way we socialize.

I don't normally outdress billionaires, but in this case I did. I was wearing a black Hugo Boss suit (no tie) to my interview with Dustin at a Mission-neighborhood café near Asana's offices in San Francisco—and he was wearing jeans and plaid. "I don't really tend to buy expensive things and haven't changed my lifestyle a great deal since starting Facebook. As such, I don't have much interest in making my net worth accrue any further. I believe in the ability of capital markets to create positive impact on the world, but I'm also going to give quite a bit of it away."

Dustin and Zuckerberg have since signed Bill Gates and Warren Buffett's Giving Pledge—in which they have all vowed to give away at least half of their wealth. In a letter announcing his pledge, Dustin writes, "As a result of Facebook's success, I've earned financial capital beyond my wildest expectations. Today, I view that reward not as personal wealth, but as a tool with which I hope to bring even more benefit to the world. . . . Over the next few years, [my partner Cari and I] will begin to identify the causes to which we can make the most leveraged contributions. We will donate and invest with both urgency and mindfulness, aiming to foster a safer, healthier and more economically empowered global community."[7]

HOW TO FIND GREAT MENTORS AND TEACHERS, CONNECT WITH POWERFUL AND INFLUENTIAL PEOPLE, AND BUILD A WORLD-CLASS NETWORK

People thought twenty-year-old Elliot Bisnow was either crazy or stupid when he started calling up complete strangers, inviting them to join him on an all-expenses-paid ski trip to Utah, and then *charging the cost of their flights, hotels, skiing, and meals on his personal credit card.*

But Elliott Bisnow is neither crazy nor stupid.

In 2005, Elliott was entering his junior year at the University of Wisconsin–Madison when he spotted a great way to make a difference for someone he cared about. His father had started a real estate investment newsletter, Bisnow.com, which had amassed a loyal following, but which had no revenue yet. Elliott saw an opportunity to help the family business. He came up with the idea of selling advertising in the newsletter and—to use a technical term—started selling the shit out of that advertising space.

"I'd wake up at five A.M. in my dorm, every day, sometimes four thirty. I would do follow-up e-mails on the business from five to six. I had a tennis scholarship to college, so I would go to tennis practice from six to seven. It's late fall in Madison, and I'm mopeding through the rain and sleet to be back in my dorm room. From seven thirty to ten I was making sponsorship calls and closing big sponsorship deals. Junior year I didn't go to class the whole semester. Here I am in my dorm room, closing ten-thousand- or fifty-thousand-dollar deals. I had multiple computer screens, multiple cell phones, I'm just cranking, cold-calling, making sales."

One day, during his freshman year, Elliott saw a bunch of smoke coming out from under the door of the resident adviser's room. Curious, he opened the door and found Anthony Adams silk-screening T-shirts. It turned out he was doing about $1,000 per month selling funny shirts. That paid for his college tuition, and the room was free for being an RA.

Elliott asked him, "How do you have your own business?"

Anthony said, "Well, I have an LLC, I have a bank account, and I just sell the T-shirts."

Elliott was puzzled. "I don't understand—don't you have to work for somebody to do that? Who hires you?" Anthony explained to him what an entrepreneur was.

"Wait, you mean I could actually make money without having to work for another person?" Elliott asked Anthony. Anthony nodded.

"Well, what job will you do after college?" Elliott asked. That question was met with a stare that had "You dumbass" written all over it.

Elliott's young mind was thoroughly blown by this new concept—that you didn't need to work for a boss to earn money. He figured he could start a T-shirt company too. He spent the rest of the year trying, yet failed miserably. Sophomore year, he started a consulting business, trying to get all the stores in Madison to hire him to bring in college students to brainstorm marketing solutions for them. That one bombed too. (One particularly embarrassing fuckup: he intended to e-mail a prospect a pitch, but instead e-mailed him the Excel spreadsheet containing logs of all his sales calls for the same pitch, including detailed notes on his calls with that specific prospect.)

But, Elliott says, "You learn by doing, and failing. By the second business, I understood how to put together the business. My pitch was getting better and better. By the third one—the real estate newsletters—I had two years of pitching and trying to sell under my belt. Those two years were incredible—the learning curve. Now with the newsletters, I had a better product to sell, and I actually got the gist."

Through Elliott's sales leadership and his tireless hard work (and skipping all of his classes), he built the real estate newsletter into a seven-figure business. He decided—since he wasn't going to class anyway—it was time to take a leave of absence from college and focus on growing the business.

At a certain point, Elliott desperately needed help—he was managing way too much on his own. He decided he needed to hire some more people in the company. But he had no idea how to proceed. How do you hire someone? What do you look for? Where do you look?

He figured there must be some other young entrepreneurs in the country who had faced these questions, so he began doing some research. He found that, indeed, there were others out there. He came across lists like *BusinessWeek*'s top 25 entrepreneurs under 25, and the "Top 30 Under 30" from *Inc.* "These kids became my new idols," Elliott told me.

Using the sales skills he had developed in launching three businesses (two of them failed and one was now successful), he began cold-calling young CEOs off the lists. If the key to great sales is to have a great product to sell, then Elliott had dreamed up perhaps the greatest pitch in all history: "Come on an all-expenses-paid ski trip to Utah with me and a bunch of other top young CEOs, I'll fly you out there first class, we'll all meet each other, and we can share information and knowledge." As Elliott says, "It's not that hard to convince someone to go on an all-expenses-paid ski trip." Beyond the skiing, most of the young CEOs had never met each other and were thrilled with the chance to meet other top young leaders.

Twenty CEOs joined together on that first trip, which occurred in April 2008. They included Josh Abramson and Ricky Van Veen, cofounders of CollegeHumor, Vimeo, and BustedTees; fellow college dropout Blake Mycoskie, founder of TOMS Shoes; and Ben Lerer, cofounder of Thrillist. The average age of the participants was twenty-six.

Five weeks before the trip, Elliott was in the hole forty grand on his personal credit cards to cover the trip. Ever the enterprising mind, he used his self-taught sales skills once again to call up new corporate sponsors to see if they'd pay for the trip; he got the entire trip covered by sponsors.

The trip was a massive success. "They had never met a ton of other young entrepreneurs. For three days, they were stopping their lives and meeting amazing other people, doing business together, learning from each other. We made these great friendships," Elliott said. The trip went so well, in fact, that Elliott decided to do another trip six months later, for sixty young business leaders. Naturally, he found sponsors to pay for that as well. Dustin Moskovitz attended the second gathering, as did Tony Hsieh from Zappos.

The trips took on a life of their own, grew and grew. Elliott brought on some friends to help him, Jeremy Schwartz (a Berklee College of Music dropout), Brett Leve, and Jeff Rosenthal, and the gatherings morphed into what is now Summit Series (http://www .summitseries.com), an annual invitation-only gathering of young entrepreneurs, innovators, and thought leaders, which has been called by *Forbes* "the Davos for Generation Y." The *New York Times* says, "There is no blueprint for what Mr. Bisnow and his associates are doing. Perhaps the closest analogy is Davos, if the yearly forum held in Switzerland for billionaires and heads of state were somehow crossed with MTV's 'The Real World.'"[1]

The tipping point for Summit Series occurred in 2009, when the White House Office of Public Engagement wanted to put on a roundtable with young entrepreneurs. Someone from the office had heard that Summit was the hottest business networking conference for the Facebook generation. So they contacted Elliott and asked him and the Summit Team to put together the event for the White House, which they did. Bisnow and his team of merry twentysomethings had arrived at the central halls of global power.

Now, Elliott rolls with Bill Clinton, Mark Cuban, and fellow non-college-graduates Ted Turner, Sean Parker, Russell Simmons, and Twitter cofounder Evan Williams, all of whom have participated at Summit Series gatherings. Aside from Facebook cofounder (and college dropout) Mark Zuckerberg, Elliott is now quite possibly one of the most well-connected twentysomethings on the planet. As a *Forbes* profile of Summit asks, "Do you know of a more influential networking event for a new generation of geniuses? If so, let me know."[2]

Elliott has left the family newsletter business in good hands and is focusing entirely on Summit. It's his second multimillion-dollar business, and he has also raised over $2 million for charity from participants at the events. (By the way, Elliott never returned to Madison after his "leave of absence.")

I met with Elliott and the other cofounders and executives— all in their twenties—in Miami, where they were renting a group home together. The eight of them collectively choose new cities to live in every few months, all over the world, where they meet people to invite to their conferences and work remotely via laptop and cell phone.

I asked Elliott how he accounts for his success in life at such a young age. He told me point-blank, "I attribute my success so far, 100 percent, to the people I've met and learned from. It's not even a question. [Motivational author, and college dropout] Jim Rohn says, 'You are the average of the five people you spend the most time with.' And on a bigger picture, you are a reflection of the twenty or thirty people who give you the best advice. Everything is about people. It all starts with you surrounding yourself with great people who you can learn from.

"The problem is, most people view college as their learning experience, then they graduate into the 'real world'; as soon as they're done with college and out into the 'real world,' they're done learning. I view *life* as learning. It's all learning for me, all the time. I'm literally nonstop learning. Most people are like, 'As soon as college is done, I'm done with books.' I read books every day. I talk to people every day. I'm always out looking for new people I can learn from."

There it is. From one of the world's most successful twenty-something leaders: if you want to be successful, and make a huge impact in your life, *find exceptional people to learn from, and surround yourself with them.*

So how do you find these powerful guides and teachers in real life, outside of the classroom? "Great networking is not about quid pro quo. It's not a back-and-forth. It's about give-give-give as much as you can, and if I see you succeed, I'm really happy. And, if I'm your friend, you're going to pull me up with you. If you have everyone in your network asking each other, 'How can I help you? How can I help you? How can I help you?' you're going to go far in your life. If you're genuine, and you want to help people—give, give, give—it comes back around."

I can hear the more cynical of my readers saying, "Well, that's easy for Bisnow to say. He was running a seven-figure business and had a forty-thousand-dollar credit line when he called to invite those CEOs skiing to get advice from them. He could afford to take risks. I don't have a seven-figure business, and I certainly can't risk forty grand in credit card bills to pull off a stunt like that. How does this 'giving' stuff apply to *me* in *my* situation?"

Great question. I'm glad you asked!

■ HOW I FOUND TWO OF THE MOST AMAZING MENTORS IN THE WORLD

When you're just starting out on your path to success, and you want to find mentors farther along the path than you, what do you possibly have to *give* someone who is much more powerful, connected, and successful than yourself?

Let me tell you a story of two of my most powerful mentors and teachers in life, Bryan (whom we met in the Introduction) and college dropout Eben Pagan, one of the world's most renowned and respected teachers of marketing skills for entrepreneurs—and how I connected to them.

If we were to predict Eben Pagan's level of future success from his high school and college career (as most parents, teachers, and school officials do), our estimates would have been quite low.

He thought school was a "waste of time" as he grew up in Oregon in the '70s and '80s, in what he describes as semirural poverty. He got middling grades at best with a spotty attendance record. He spent most of his teen years playing in a Christian rock band. He dropped out of community college after one semester to tour full-time with his band.

"I was doing the music thing for roughly five years, with different bands. I went on tour with one band, then recorded an album with another band. Fairly soon, however, I came to realize that it was very difficult to 'make it.' Everyone's got a dream as an artist, and it's very difficult to make that dream come true. I wanted to have success in my life. I wanted to be able to live the lifestyle I wanted. Growing up in my town in Oregon, I didn't know anyone who was successful or wealthy, and I didn't know anyone who *knew anyone* who was successful or wealthy.

"Just intuitively, though, it seemed like rich people and real estate tended to intersect. So I decided to go learn about real estate and get my real estate license. But I was a miserable failure in real estate. I recall I sold one-and-a-third homes my first year. And these were cheap little homes. Total, I earned a couple of thousand dollars. I was still working part-time in a manual labor job."

Not an auspicious career start. However, if we were to use his

high school, college, and early career record as a predictor of Eb-
en's future success, we'd be way, way off.

As a result of getting into real estate, Eben discovered something that would later prove to be central to his life: he learned
how to educate himself in sales and marketing. He got started
when he attended a workshop by a real estate sales and marketing
trainer named Joe Stumpf, in Eugene, Oregon. "I immediately recognized I had to somehow work for this guy and soak up his
knowledge. But I didn't know how I was going to do that—here he
was, leading big group workshops all over the country, and I was
barely scraping by.

"So I started calling up his outbound telemarketers. These
guys are trying to sell you on something, so they'll talk to anyone!
I told them about my experience at the workshop and became
friendly with them. Once, I found this set of Tony Robbins tapes at
Goodwill for ten bucks, and I knew one of the guys I was talking
to there would like it, so I packed the tapes up and sent them to
him. Things like that.

"One day, they sent me some audiotapes of Joe. I called them
up and said, 'The audio on this program is not good—I think it
could be a lot better.' I had a background in sound from my band
days. Turned out, coincidentally, their audio guy wasn't working
out, and they let him go. So I talked to the general manager of the
company, and I went to work for them. I worked there for three
years, doing audiovisual seminars. I had never done audiovisual
seminars, but I took my knowledge of gear and made it happen.

"This turned out to be the most significant decision in my
business career—to find someone who is massively successful and
go to work for him. Through that, I got into the world of marketing
and sales. I discovered a lot of the past marketing and sales geniuses, like Claude Hopkins and Eugene Schwartz and John Ca-
ples and David Ogilvy, and read all of their books. I read Robert
Cialdini's book *Influence: The Psychology of Persuasion*, which
was very impactful on me.

"I started applying all I was learning about marketing and
sales to consult with real estate businesses how to market and sell
themselves. And my clients were having such success with it, I
was able to work about a week a month and live quite comfortably
on that."

On the side of this successful consulting career, Eben began
building up a business selling products and services (mainly

e-books, membership communities, Web-based trainings, and in-person weekend workshops) focused on helping men and women be more empowered in relating to the opposite sex.[3] He built this into a $20 million business (in later chapters I'll go into more detail about some of the secrets by which he did this).

So many people started asking him how he built his business so rapidly, he opened a second division of his business, which teaches info-marketing skills to entrepreneurs (http://gurublue printblog.com). In the world of Internet marketing, he's a living legend, widely considered one of the most advanced practitioners of these skills in the world.

His company, Hot Topic Media, now brings in around $30 million a year in revenue and employs about seventy people around the globe. He founded it himself, and grew it over a decade with no investors. He is now a self-made multimillionaire, and would never have to work another day in his life if he didn't want to. But he's not about to retire to an island in the Bahamas—he loves leading and growing his business and often works twelve-hour days by choice. He runs this business off his MacBook, and he spends his time either working from his home office, which has a majestic view of the Empire State Building, or on the go, attending and speaking at conferences around the globe.

I first heard about Eben when a friend of mine joined Eben's home study program. My friend let me listen to one of the recordings, on how to write a direct-response sales letter. I had been earning my living for several years writing book proposals on a freelance basis. Within a short period after listening to that one recording, I was earning more from writing sales letters for clients than I had ever earned writing book proposals; I'd often earn $1,000 for a few hours' work, and my clients would come back for more, because the sales copy—which I'd learned how to write through Eben—was earning them so much money.

I knew Eben was someone I needed to learn from and connect with. When my friend told me he had signed up for a live course with Eben, and that I could come on a bring-a-friend ticket, I leapt at the opportunity. Of course, it's hard to connect with a teacher personally when he's on stage in front of two hundred people, most of whom have paid thousands of dollars to be there, and all of whom want his attention, advice, and help.

That weekend blew me away. One comment in specific stuck with me from that weekend. A person in the crowd asked, "How can I connect personally with powerful mentors who will guide me in my life and business?"

Eben said, "Leadership is like a fountain. Imagine the leaders are the water near the top, ready to burst out of the fountain. The water about to burst out is being pushed up by water below it. If you want to succeed, *find leaders who are doing amazing things in the world, and push them up.* Find powerful people and help them reach their goals. If you're of service to them, they will be of service back."

Almost a year later, I was at the Burning Man festival in Nevada with Jena. I heard through the grapevine that Eben was at the festival and that he'd be giving a talk. Jena and I have a friend named Annie Lalla, who is an amazing relationship coach, but who was struggling in her business because she was resisting learning sales and marketing skills. I *forced* Annie to join me at the lecture, dragging her there kicking and screaming, so that she might learn something about marketing from Eben.

Little did I know that I had just brought to Eben his future fiancée. (Now *that's* quite a way to "push the water up"!) Of course, at the time, all it involved was us standing around him after the talk, shaking his hand and asking him questions about his talk. But later it turned into much more than that, for Eben and Annie . . .

When we got back from Burning Man, I saw a post late one night on Eben's blog, saying he was organizing a small, private gathering in Ojai, California, with relationship teacher David Deida, one of the experts I'd learned most from about how to have a great relationship with Jena. I *leapt* out of my desk chair, ran to our bedroom, woke Jena up, and yelled, "Eben is hosting a private gathering with David Deida later this month! It costs twenty-five hundred dollars a person to attend and it's in California. We're *going*!" Jena mumbled something semi-coherent about talking about it in the morning, and went back to sleep. I called Annie and told her about the opportunity; she said she fell madly in love with Eben the second he opened his mouth at the talk at Burning Man (he is a rather dashing fellow), but she hadn't gotten further than hand-shaking after Eben's talk. She signed up instantly.

Jena questioned me about the wisdom of spending that much for a weekend. But I told her: "One connection with a powerful teacher can change your life forever. Is that worth it?" She surrendered to my enthusiasm and agreed to join me. All three of us traipsed out to Ojai together from New York. I knew that I wouldn't be able to connect personally with Eben when he was on a stage in front of two hundred people. But at a gathering with only thirty people, in an intensive personal growth weekend workshop where he was going to be one of the fellow participants, I had a shot.

At the workshop, Eben saw how powerful and solid my relationship with Jena was, and he started asking *me* questions about my relationship with Jena! This was a dream come true. I knew, now, that I had found my way to help Eben and push the water of his leadership up the fountain. Stunned that he was asking *me* for guidance, I gulped and gave him everything I had. He later invited Jena, Annie, and me to hang out with him twice personally to pick our brains about our relationships.

He is now not only a wonderful friend to Jena and me, but also a great teacher and mentor to us in our careers; I've learned more from him about making my way in the world than I learned in sixteen years of formal education.

And the rest, between Eben and Annie, was history. Eben moved from LA to New York to live with Annie, and they are now engaged.

If that story of how I met an amazing mentor—who has taught me way more free of charge than any college professor ever did for tens of thousands of dollars—sounds like a long and twisty road, that's because such stories in real life almost always are. There's no quick-shot formula for connecting with powerful mentors. Elliott did it through inviting leaders to ski trips. I did it via Burning Man and a relationship workshop. These may be extreme lengths, but one good mentor can literally change the direction of your entire life. It's worth the effort.

Here's a story about how I met a second great mentor in my life, Bryan Franklin, whom I introduced you to in the Introduction.

I had kept hearing about this guy Bryan (http://www.bryan franklin.com) through friends of friends. He was supposed to be one of the most successful executive coaches in the country. He was only thirty-eight, but he had been earning $1 million a year for the past *ten years* coaching executives at some of Silicon Valley's hottest firms, including Google, Apple, LinkedIn, and Cisco, on sales and leadership. He ran a yearlong sales, marketing, and leadership training program that cost $18,000; a client of Jena's had taken the program, and Jena said she was amazed by the business results she saw this client getting from the program.

It all seemed kind of preposterous to me when I first heard about this. I mean, c'mon. A thirty-eight-year-old earning a *million bucks a year* coaching fifty-year-old executives at multibillion-dollar companies on sales and leadership, and doing so since his twenties? What the hell did he have to teach them on sales and leadership that they didn't know for themselves? And eighteen grand for a *single year* of training with him?

Nonetheless, I was intrigued. Who *was* this dude?

Jena had met him once, and when Bryan found out she lived in New York, he mentioned he was interested in starting one of his yearlong programs there. I didn't know much about him beyond what I had heard above, but I wanted to know more. I got in touch with him and said, "I know a lot of people in New York, and I could probably get you in front of a roomful of people who might be interested in hearing about you." He said he'd be in New York in a few months, and he'd take me up on my offer.

Jena and I put the word out through our community. The pitch was basically, "We don't know much about this guy, but what we've been hearing is amazing, so come join us in a free lecture he's giving, which we're organizing, and we'll all learn from him together." Enough people trusted our judgment, and then invited their friends, that the room was packed with over seventy-five people, for a lecture called "How to Take Your Business to the Next Level."

The lecture was worth it (you'll be hearing a lot of the content, and more from Bryan, later in the book) and I knew I wanted to be a student of this man. Jena and I eventually packed three more rooms over several months. From this, he put together his first New York yearlong sales, marketing, and leadership training program, in which Jena and I participated.

Jena and I hosted him and his fiancée Jennifer every time they came to town. We promoted him in every way we knew how, introducing him to business partners and even clients. (I introduced him to Eben, and they've since become good friends and Bryan has even spoken at one of Eben's live events.) Jena and I always asked ourselves, How can we give more to him? How can we contribute more? How can we be of service more? How can we help him get what he wants more?

(We even started coaching him on his nutrition and eating

habits! He would always come to our house eating junk food, and had a gut to show for it. We pestered him about this, saying, "You talk so much about personal growth—well, this is one area you haven't mastered yourself. It's time to shape up!" He finally started listening to us.) We figured, if all this help could win us the opportunity to even just be around his business mind for just ten minutes here and there and soak up his knowledge, it was worth it. He has become one of the most significant teachers and mentors in our lives and businesses, and also a close friend. I am profoundly grateful for the influence these two college dropouts, Bryan and Eben, have had on my life, an influence that touches this book on every page.

■ INVESTING IN YOUR CONNECTION CAPITAL

So, if you want to recruit powerful mentors and teachers to your team, the secret is giving. Giving. Giving. Support them. Figure out how you can help them, and do it. Be the water beneath them, pushing them up the fountain. Be enterprising about it—figure out ways to give and to support them that will blow their mind.

And, while you may *hope* to get something in return, you must always do it with absolutely zero *expectation* of getting anything in return. The vibe has to be one of giving, not taking. Simply be grateful for the opportunity to help someone who's doing amazing things in the world. Very likely, it will come back to you (it always does, in my experience). But you can't focus your attention on that, or it doesn't work. Focus your attention on how you can be of service.

In my stories about connecting with Eben and Bryan as teachers, I highlighted examples of two different kinds of things I was able to give them. These two things, which I'll explain in detail in a moment, are both examples of what I call "connection capital."

Capital is something used to create value, which itself is not depleted significantly in the creation of that value. (A hammer is used to create a house, but is not significantly "used up"—the way nails and wood are—in the creation of that house.) In a capitalist society, she who owns the most capital is the wealthiest and has the greatest means to become wealthier still.

Some people spend their time amassing financial capital—

cash, stock, bonds—and real capital such as buildings. In turn, I've noticed that many people I interviewed for this book spend an inordinate amount of time, effort, and money investing in the growth and maintenance of what I've called "connection capital."

Connection capital is anything that can help you expand your network of connections (your "tribe," as Seth Godin calls it), and is not significantly used up in expanding this network. The two biggest forms of connection capital are (a) your already-existing connections and (b) your ability to give good advice.

Your Already-Existing Connections. I connected Eben to Annie, who turned out to be one of the most important people in his whole life. I couldn't have done this if Annie wasn't already in my network. As a result of this connection, Eben became a tighter part of my network. I connected Bryan to Eben. I couldn't have done this if Eben wasn't already in my network. As a result, Bryan became a tighter part of my network.

It's one of those rich-get-richer, need-money-to-make-money kinds of situations. There's no denying it: the bigger your network is, the bigger it becomes. The more connections you have, the more you make still. For a simple reason: the more people you have in your network, the more they connect you to other people, and the more people who want to join it. Lots and lots of people want to be connected to Elliott Bisnow because he knows lots and lots of people.

This is the snowball effect in action; once you get a good network going, the growth can be fast and dramatic. In fact, no other asset I know of can grow so quickly. Because it's comprised of people and of caring. And people, unlike dollars or bonds or stock shares or globs of gold or factory machines or plots of land, talk to each other and connect each other over the things they care about.

Elliott Bisnow held his first, small ski trip in 2008, just two and a half years before I am writing this. Now he's at the helm of one of the greatest business networks on the planet. "Bisnow's ascent to the mobile tech elite happened so fast even he is surprised," a *Washington Post* profile about him said in early 2010, just a year and a half after that first fated ski trip. "Nobody thought I was cool until a year ago," the article quotes Elliott. "I wasn't popular in high school. . . . I didn't fit into cliques or sit at the cool table at lunchtime. Same thing in college."[4]

Being able to connect people to each other is a *massive* asset, which in turn helps grow the amount of people you know, which in turn grows your ability to connect people. Get the snowball rolling, and it may surprise you how fast it grows.

The question is: How do you get the snowball rolling when you don't even have a pebble of snow? How do you use your network to grow your network when you don't *have* a network yet? This is a crucial question, which we'll address later in the chapter. But first, let's talk about the second major component of connection capital.

■ A SWISS ARMY KNIFE OF ADVICE

The second major component of connection capital is your ability to give relevant and valuable advice.

Give advice? To someone who is more successful and powerful than you? Huh?

Absolutely. Here's how.

Eben says that the three areas of life the majority of people spend most of their time worrying about are money, relationships, and health. In my experience, very few people have all three of these areas buttoned up in their life, at least not as much as they like. If you're talking to someone whom society deems more successful than you, it's probably the case that they are more successful in only *one* area (business, marketing, sales, fame, etc.).

In my experience, almost every person I've met who is, by societal standards, much more successful than I, is also struggling with at least *one* area or issue about which I know quite a bit more than they do. They're human, just like you and me, and humans have problems.

I'm going to teach you two questions that, if you put them into use at parties, events, and conferences, will change your life forever and will grow your network faster than you ever thought possible:

1. What's most exciting for you right now in your life/business?
2. What's challenging for you in your life/business right now?

If it's a personal context (cocktail party, dinner party, etc.), ask about their life; if it's a business context (conference, networking event, etc.), ask about their business. Note: These shouldn't be the first words out of your mouth when you initially meet someone. Of course not. You've got to have some trust and rapport going in the conversation first. But if you start peppering these questions in your conversations with new people you meet, and then honestly try to help them with whatever goals, aspirations, or challenges they mention in response, you'll be amazed at the networking magic that occurs.

I often find that when I ask these questions of people whom I'd like to mentor or guide me, I have insights, resources, or connections that could help them in the area of whatever they answer. Whatever the answers to these questions are, I listen attentively and compassionately, and if I know of someone or something useful to these causes or issues, I recommend it. I am *constantly* seeking out ways I can be of service to the people I talk with, in ways that are meaningful and impactful to them.

Maybe it's a health concern that they mention, or a relationship issue, maybe even some specific aspect of their business with which I have experience and they don't. I refer them to books, courses, and websites that have been useful to me in dealing with whatever issues they mention, and could help them as well. I often make a note and *send them* the book I've referred them to. And of course, I refer them to other people I know who can help them with that specific issue, goal, or problem. (See the section on the value of "Your Already-Existing Connections" in this chapter.)

Sometimes, just an ear to listen, an empathetic understanding, or a dose of commonsense guidance is a *massive* gift you can give. You think rich, powerful, and well-connected people don't struggle with anything in their lives?

In the case of Eben, through asking these questions I was able to give him relationship advice and also to connect him to Bryan, who became a great friend. When there was some question as to whether Eben and Annie would become an item, Bryan ended up "laying it down," bro-to-bro style, about why Annie was a perfect match for him and why he'd be crazy to let her go. (I also introduced Bryan and Annie—see a pattern here, about how this stuff works?)

In a like manner, even though Bryan is by societal standards far more successful than I am, I still give him advice—about health and nutrition, which is one area I know a lot more about than he does, from my life experience and self-education.

Furthermore, I didn't just wait for him to ask me for this advice. Once we had become close enough, I *called him on it*. I basically *told* him he needed to pay more attention to his health and his eating habits, an area of his life I felt he was neglecting.

That is one of the most powerful things you can give someone, ever: a wake-up call. To my surprise, rather than rejecting, ignoring, or dismissing my suggestions, Bryan actually listened and incorporated what I suggested. As a result I went from being someone he liked to someone he truly valued in his life.

You have to do all of this advice giving with clean intentions, with humility, and in a total spirit of service. Usually, you can't do it right away. You must already have built up some rapport and trust together. And you must do it extremely tactfully, with a great deal of social intelligence. (If you feel you need to brush up on your own social intelligence—including your sense of tact—a great place to start is the book *Social Intelligence: The New Science of Human Relationships* by Daniel Goleman. I highly recommend this book: social intelligence is something we learn almost nothing about in our formal education.)

With all these caveats in place, if you can give someone a loving wake-up call in an area of their life where they've got a major blind spot, or just some well-placed advice that helps them overcome a problem or get one step closer to an important goal, they will be forever grateful.

I even gave Bryan quite a bit of marketing advice. How did I, who earns a fraction of what Bryan earns, and who was looking to him for business guidance, give *him* marketing advice?

Simple. While he's an absolute master of sales, and of word-of-mouth marketing (the methods he'd used to fill his coaching practice and his other coaching programs), I saw from my own study of copywriting that he didn't know a lot about direct-response copywriting. I started coaching him on copywriting, and even writing some of his copy for him.

Here are several areas where you can often give valuable advice to—and therefore greatly serve—people who are more powerful and successful than you are. You'd be amazed at how open potential mentors are to receiving help. And if you help them, they will help you. These areas below include, but expand upon, Eben's triumvirate of health, money, and relationships.

MARKETING AND SALES. I have found that most people who have built their businesses around marketing don't know jack about sales. And most people who have built their businesses around sales don't know jack about marketing. If you learn about both, as you should if you want to be successful in life (see Success Skills #3 and #4), you can often provide business advice to a surprising variety of people, as I was able to do with Bryan.

In particular, you should learn about direct-response marketing and copywriting, the type that Eben teaches. Direct-response is all about generating sales and revenue *now* (as opposed to "brand" or "image" marketing, which consumes large amounts of money to generate revenue in some vague, distant future, if at all). If you can help people generate sales and revenue *now*, you'll never be a wallflower; you will always find people wanting to talk with you and wanting your advice.

A few months' worth of studying direct-response from Eben and others whom we'll meet in Success Skill #3, and a year's worth of applying it in the real world, has taken me quite far; I've done consulting for several multimillion-dollar companies and now know more about direct-response than probably 99 percent of people in business. I don't say that to brag; I say it to highlight how low the bar is—it's a real blind spot for most businesses, indoctrinated as they are with the gospel of brand marketing. If you study the resources I list in Success Skill #3, you will know more about direct response than 99 percent of businesspeople too.

I've been astonished at the caliber of people I've been able to connect with, simply from this little bit of marketing knowledge. It's like a cool party trick. In fact, I was at a party, where I had the opportunity to meet the famous novelist Erica Jong. I asked her what she was excited about, and she told me about an anthology she was putting out the next year. As she told me about it, I could see right away that the marketing efforts planned by her big corporate publisher would be helped by some direct-response efforts on the Net. I began giving her unsolicited marketing advice for her book launch. A few minutes into this, she grabbed a pen, scribbled down her contact info on a paper, and said, "I *have* to talk with you more." Erica is now a friend, and not only have I had the honor of helping her quite a bit on her book marketing, but she has also been extremely generous with advice, guidance, and help in my writing career.

I probably would not have been able to bring her into my life as a friend without having built up the connection capital of valuable advice, which I was able to give her at that party, on a topic important to her.

The fun continued. Erica invited me to a party she was throwing, where she introduced me to her PR agent, Sandi Mendelson. Same thing. I started giving Sandi some marketing ideas around social media, which I had been studying a great deal. Sandi invited me to her office to continue the discussions, and we've since done business together. Sandi was also responsible for my meeting my literary agent Esther Newberg, who played a huge part in this book coming into being, as Esther connected me to Portfolio. It all started with some unsolicited marketing advice to a novelist, at a party.

It's almost a cliché and an inside joke among my friends now. Whenever I meet new people, I compulsively start finding out what they're up to, and then giving them unsolicited marketing advice on it. Maybe it's cheesy. But I'll be damned, it works. In almost all cases, I find it's greatly appreciated. If you find yourself saying, "Yeah, but I don't know as much about marketing as you do," remember, I only studied Eben's stuff for a few *months* before I started applying it in the real world. If you really are going to tell me you can't be bothered to study something for a few months in order to get all the benefits I've described here, please, now, return this book for a full refund, plunk yourself down on your couch, and flip on the tube. Seriously!

FOOD, WEIGHT, AND NUTRITION. Most people who are successful in the worlds of business and money are highly driven. And many people who are highly driven ignore their health; their success so far has come at the expense of their health. If in the course of your life and self-education you have learned to overcome your own chronic health challenges, or have achieved your ideal weight or learned a lot about nutrition, fitness, and healthy lifestyles, you'll often know a lot more about these topics than many successful businesspeople do—particularly if you read up on these topics and experiment with what's best for you in your own life. As with all advice, you need to be extremely tactful in bringing these topics up. But if the conversation steers in that direction, in response to your "challenges" question discussed above, you'll often find that people are desperate for advice in these realms. You can often be of tremendous service, much more than you realize. I was able to do this for Bryan around his formerly abysmal, now fantastic eating habits. As a result, I served him powerfully, and in so doing brought him closer into my tribe.

SPIRITUALITY, PURPOSE, AND MEANING. If you've thought a great deal about the more existential, philosophical aspects of life, and have come to some personal wisdom or understanding in these areas through your own life journey, providing support in these realms is often a *great* way to serve people who are more powerful and successful than you are. (See Success Skill #1 on connecting with your sense of purpose and meaning.) Stories of people who "make it" in the world of material success, money, and fame, and then feel "empty inside," are a dime a dozen. In fact, they are the *rule*, not the exception, when it comes to material wealth.

Our society is largely organized around pursuing material wealth. And obviously, I have nothing against material wealth, honestly gained; in fact, I'm actively working to bring more of it into my own life. But most people don't realize, until they have it (if then), that beyond bare minimums, increasing your material wealth doesn't bring remotely commensurate increases in well-being. It just doesn't.

Thus, I've found that, almost without exception, wealthy, successful, famous, and powerful people I've met struggle with spiritual and existential questions of meaning, purpose, and inner fulfillment in their lives. They are often *thrilled* to have someone talk about these issues with them, and to lend an ear. In fact, I've found that powerful mentors are often *more* likely to struggle with these questions on a day-to-day basis than less materially successful people. For a simple reason. Many less wealthy people either (a) are so desperate to *get* wealthier that they bulldoze over these more philosophical questions entirely in their mad race up the ladder, or (b) have already come to peace with the existential questions of their lives, in which case they're not struggling with these questions—they're just out in the world, serving their purpose, or enjoying their lives with gratitude, or both.

If they're not totally caught up in amassing more wealth and power, however, it's the wealthy ones who often *struggle* with these questions. They've reached the top of the ladder, and they realize that the whole mad race to the top was in many ways a farce to begin with—it simply doesn't deliver the lasting fulfillment it was supposed to. So they begin pondering these bigger questions of the meaning of their lives.

Of course, there are many wealthy, connected, or powerful people who are totally switched on spiritually and existentially, and are using their power and influence for a greater purpose, to change the world. (These are the best people in the world to know because they are creating our future. Get under their fountain and push them up as much as possible.)

But many others in this position are deeply confused, lost, unhappy, even despairing in their lives. If you have reached some peace, reflection, or wisdom about the spiritual or existential questions of your life, you can often offer a great service by sharing this peace and reflection with those whom you wish to become your teachers in the realms of business and money. Often, just having a real, honest, human-to-human conversation about life's biggest questions can gain you a new friend for life.

HOBBIES, PASSIONS, AND CAUSES. You can often connect with influential people through shared hobbies and passions. Of course, this knowledge has been keeping golf courses running for centuries. I happen to have no interest in golf whatsoever, so I'm not going to write to you about golf. But I've found that cultivating a wide range of cool, hip, discussion-worthy hobbies maximizes your chance of being able to *share with* and *give to* amazing people you meet.

I'm passionate about Cuban music and salsa dance, for example. I met my wife when I was teaching a Cuban salsa dance class at Burning Man. That was without question the single most significant instance of "networking" I'll ever experience in my life. And it all happened because I had cultivated a passion for salsa dance.

I have a friend, Hitch McDermid, who, through many years of study, became a top teacher of AcroYoga, a form in which one person (a "base") lies on the ground on his back and balances a partner (the "flyer") through a series of beautiful and challenging poses, on the base's upright feet and arms. If you meet Hitch at a party, you may very well find yourself "flying" upside down, balancing on his outstretched arms and legs—definitely an interesting way to meet and connect with someone! In fact, through some people he met at a party, Hitch got connected to the mega-famous electronica group Thievery Corporation, and began providing AcroYoga to them backstage before their shows.

If you know a lot about vintage wine, or gourmet cooking, or fine tequila, or tango dance, or travel in Latin America or Southeast Asia, or Buddhist meditation and philosophy, or massage, or kite boarding, or social media marketing, or contemporary art, or some other interesting, cool, hip, unusual, sexy hobby or interest, it's very likely you'll be able to share your gift among people you want to connect with. (Of course, more "straight" hobbies like sailing, football, and baseball can work too. Though there's a bit of a "join the club" effect with these, which makes it harder to stand out and truly broaden someone's horizon. Are you really going to tell someone something they don't already know about baseball or football?)

RELATIONSHIPS. In most cases I've seen, there's not much of a correlation between success in business and money, and happiness in relationships. If anything, I've seen a *negative* correlation. A friend of mine involved with a long-running, high-level business networking group said that at the twentieth reunion of the original founders, nearly all of the members—mostly men—had been married at the start of the group and were now divorced.

The reason is obvious. Many people who achieve great success in the worlds of business and money do so at the expense of their relationships, by focusing on their business entirely and ignoring their relationships. And many business luminaries I've met, both men and women, are such control freaks that they're terrified of the surrender, loss of control, and vulnerability involved in opening their heart. (It's called "falling" in love, and not "stepping safely down the stairs of love," for a reason.) Simply put, many financially and materially successful people are terrified of opening their hearts and don't know how to even if they wanted to.

If, through your own experiences and self-education in life, you have learned to open your heart and surrender to love, or just to manage the ups and downs of dating and relationships smoothly, you may be able to serve your desired mentors by guiding them gently into deepening their relationships, opening to emotional intimacy in their lives, and finding or creating more love in their lives. If you do give this gift, this service of the heart, you will have given one of the greatest gifts possible.

Really, it's all about becoming a "trusted adviser" to people you want to connect with. Being a trusted adviser to a successful person is, simply put, one of the most powerful ways to become successful yourself. You should definitely read *The Trusted Adviser* by David Maister, Charles Green, and Robert Galford, and *Networking with the Affluent* by Thomas J. Stanley, two of the best books on high-integrity, no-sleaze connecting I've read.

Stanley's book lists many different ways you can serve powerful, influential people you'd like to connect with. (Remember, as with everything in this chapter, the giving has to be done in the spirit of pure service, or it feels icky!) These methods include "The Talent Scout," "The Revenue Enhancer," "The Advocate," "The Mentor," and "The Publicist." Read the book for more details, but these are all fantastic ways to be of service to people you want to learn from.

Another great resource, which adapts some of these strategies for the digital and social media age, comes from David Siteman Garland (http://www.therisetothetop.com). In his article "From Tim Ferriss to Seth Godin: How to Interview and Build Relationships with the Most 'Influential' People in the World," he emphasizes the same point everyone else is making in this chapter—when you find creative ways to serve people you'd like to connect with, "ask for nothing [in return]. . . . By doing [that], you will separate yourself from 98% of the pack." He then outlines a specific, detailed process for finding creative ways to be of service to influencers on the Web. This is required reading for anyone interested in the topic of this chapter.[5]

Here is one single, very wise blog post that will probably go further in helping you achieve your purpose in life—if you put it into practice—than entire courses in college. And it's available for free on the Web, along with an infinite number of equally powerful free resources, some of which I'll be pointing you toward in this book. (See why more and more people are beginning to scratch their heads about the value of $100K college tuition bills and decades-long loan payments?)

Your self-study and learning in one of these areas of advice giving is highly liquid; it can often be traded for learning in another area. Because few people are truly well-rounded, if *you* become well-rounded in these areas of marketing and sales, health and nutrition, spirituality and personal philosophy, and interesting hobbies and passions, you will almost always have something to help people with. It's like a Swiss army knife of service, ready in your back pocket for any occasion.

And, as you *give* more, and *serve* more, you'll eventually attract the right teachers in all these areas, who will help you *learn* more . . . which will allow you to give more and serve more . . . and on and on. Forget all that quantum X-ray stuff in the movie *The Secret*. This is how the law of attraction works in the real world. "The happier you are in giving," self-made multi-entrepreneur

Russell Simmons told me, "the more people are excited to be around you. You become 'sticky.'"

■ HOW TO BECOME A WORLD-CLASS CAPITALIST OF GIVING

Often, when a young person is starting out in the real world beyond school, wanting to connect with a powerful mentor, teacher, or contact, she recognizes this fundamental point of connecting via giving. But she doesn't have a lot to give, so she volunteers to give the only two things she has on ready tap at this stage in her development, her time and her elbow grease, in hopes that these will buy her some access to the influencer.

This is fine, for a time. History is replete with stories of young up-and-comers who gave themselves over to a more powerful mentor in time-intensive service, and worked around the clock in apprenticeship, in exchange for valuable teachings and connections, later becoming successful themselves because of it. Benjamin Franklin, an elementary school dropout, started out his illustrious publishing and writing career (author, among other things, of one of the most widely read autobiographies in history) as a legally indentured servant in his brother's printing shop at age twelve. (Though they don't often involve legal indenture anymore, in modern times this is called an internship.)

However, if you start out making this trade of time and elbow grease in the hope of gaining teachings, make sure you're able to convert those teachings quickly into connection capital (i.e., into a network of connections and the experience that allows you to give valuable, high-impact advice, thereby providing more value to your network, drawing in more connections).

For a simple reason. Relying on time and elbow grease and service as your main form of giving—potentially valuable as these gifts may be—severely limits your scope of giving. There are only so many hours in the day, and so many hours of elbow grease you can give before you conk out. In twenty-first-century business parlance, this form of giving is "not scalable," or "not highly leverageable." They reach their upper limit of scope quickly.

In turn, connection capital is a highly scalable, highly leverageable form of giving. (I know I sound like a dot-com business-plan writer here! But hey, I like applying this business-speak to concepts that are fundamentally poetic and metaphysical. Humor me!)

When I was hanging out with Elliott, he dashed off three introductions to potential interviewees for my book, including one to self-educated fashion designer Marc Ecko. Within twenty-four hours, I already had an appointment set up to interview Marc, one of the most influential people in the world of fashion; there's not a chance I would have gotten that interview so quickly (if at all) without the amazing introduction from Elliott.

This introduction took Elliott minutes to compose, and yet it helped me and my project immensely. Those few minutes he spent earned him a lifelong fan in me.

Would there be any chance he'd be able to win a similar amount of appreciation, goodwill, fandom, and desire to serve him back on my part by spending hours and hours of his day, say, fetching me coffee, scheduling my appointments, and making photocopies for me? The image of Elliott Bisnow, one of the world's most connected twenty-five-year-olds, spending time fetching coffee or writing reports for anyone is absurdly laughable.

Yet, that is precisely how many twentysomethings, including many twentysomething college graduates, spend their days, in their entry-level corporate shit jobs. The difference between the lowly impact most twentysomethings experience day in and day out in their shit jobs (with all the attendant existential angst, feelings of resentment, and bitterness) and the massive impact Elliott Bisnow can have on someone's day with just *two minutes* of his time shows the power of connection capital.

By developing connection capital—that is, your "emotional bank account" of trust and goodwill among your already-existing contacts, and your bank of experience and knowledge from which you can give valuable advice—you can decouple the impact you make on others' lives from the *time* you spend making it. You still need to spend some time to have an impact—Elliott still needed to spend a few minutes composing those e-mails. But those few minutes were so profoundly helpful to me, as opposed to, say, two minutes of coffee fetching from a similarly aged college grad in a corporate shit job, because those two minutes were mixed with a very powerful form of capital—specifically, Elliott's network of trust and goodwill.

It's just like anything else in business. You mix labor with more capital (technology, skills, support services, etc.) and you get more productivity out of each minute of labor. Now, economists tell us that education is one of the most important forms of capital investment—it's human capital. And I agree with them entirely on that point.

Where I disagree, obviously, is what *form* your investments in education should take. Economists, when they talk about human capital investment, are almost always talking about formal education. As I've been arguing, and I'll continue to argue throughout this book: unless you want to go into a profession for which formal credentials are strictly required—such as medicine, law, academia, and so forth, or in which they are strongly preferred, such as rising up through the ranks of a corporate or government bureaucracy along with the rest of the herd—then in my opinion, formal schooling past the basics is an extremely weak form of investment in your own human capital.

What kind of human capital do you truly develop in today's formal higher education? The ability to write mediocre, turgid academic papers. The ability to cram all night for tests on things you will forget the next week and never use again in your life. The ability to study Monday, Tuesday, and Wednesday nights, and party Thursday, Friday, Saturday, and Sunday nights. The ability to navigate a social landscape full of binge drinking and Adderall popping. The ability to follow orders and do as you're told. The ability to manage long-term loan payments on $20,000 to $100,000 of debt.

These, and a starter business wardrobe, will buy you a mediocre entry-level job and a lot of job insecurity. You get these meager returns on your investment in formal education for the simple reason that—when all is said and done, when all the lofty rhetoric from teachers and pundits and politicians about the value of higher education evaporates under the harsh sun of a recession—these skills don't add much of value to anything or anyone in the marketplace. So, only modest rewards flow to those who have invested their time and effort in developing them. That means shit entry-level corporate job, shit entry-level corporate pay—if you're one of the lucky ones to even get a job.

Compare these forms of modestly valuable collegiate human capital with the kinds of things you can (and have to) learn on your own, educating yourself out in the real world: How to network and connect with powerful teachers and mentors (the subject of this chapter). How to start and manage a business. How to market and sell effectively (Success Skills #3 and #4). How to lead others. How to discover your sense of purpose and meaning (Success Skill #1). These forms of human capital produce mountains of value and are handsomely rewarded, either by the marketplace or by your own life satisfaction and well-being.

It is possible to learn these things in college, but they are usually learned through extracurricular activities such as student government; leadership in cultural, charitable, political, or Greek organizations; sports teams; peer support groups; and so forth. Yet extracurriculars are essentially a form of free (or low-cost) self-education. The more you focus on these, the less you'll be focusing on the formal curriculum you're paying (and going into debt) to study in college.

Elliott Bisnow is vastly more successful than most twenty-five-year-olds (by wild orders of magnitude) because he focused entirely on investing in developing this kind of real-world human capital, the kind that actually produces real-world results and is valued in the real world, rather than bullshit academic-based human capital, which is only valued in the sheltered context of academia, or by out-of-touch, large bureaucratic employers seeking fresh drones for their entry-level jobs.

Elliott wasn't born with this valuable human capital; he didn't inherit it. He bootstrapped investments of time and elbow grease to develop it, putting in the effort of learning how to sell, during those first two years (while skipping class) in his Madison, Wisconsin, dorm room. Those investments paid off in the form of the ability to sell, which is hands down one of the most economically valuable forms of human capital in existence (see Success Skill #4). He parlayed these sales skills into financial capital in the form of his seven-figure business, which gave him access to credit, which allowed him to buy those ski trips. He parlayed those ski trips into honest-to-goodness human relationships (i.e., connection capital) with people who are themselves tremendously connected.

In other words, he invested his other forms of capital (sales skills, financial capital) into connection capital—the ability to help people massively in the space of two minutes just by making introductions within his network. Multiply two-minute periods like that, day in and day out as Elliott gives, gives, gives to all the people around him (and they give, give, give back to him) in this highly leveraged way (small amount of time, big impact), and you begin to see the genius of what Elliott has created for himself. You

begin to see what separates him from nearly all other twentysomethings, indeed, from nearly everyone else in the working world:
Elliott has decoupled his *labor* from his *capital*, and focused on
building some pretty amazing capital for himself: a world-class
tribe of people he helps and who help him. He has become a
capitalist—a capitalist of giving and service to others.

The second form of connection capital—that is, the second
form of giving that can expand your network of teachers, mentors,
and guides in life—is as we've seen, advice giving.

There's a paradoxical aspect to this—after all, you're *seeking*
advice, so how is *giving* advice going to get you advice?

Well, how do you get more love? By going out and asking for
lots of love? By begging for it? Pleading for it? That may work, tem-
porarily, on a very insecure person, for a low grade of needy, desperate love.

But the way to get really high-quality, pure-grade love in your
life is to *give* high-quality, pure-grade love. By high-grade, I mean
clean—free of neediness or the expectation of return, not with the
intention of getting some back. If you do it with that intention, it
deteriorates into neediness and desperation. Give widely and generously, to all those around you (particularly focusing on your
own tribe), and somehow it comes back to you. It's just the way it
works. I don't know why, but it works. It's the same for all things
of value. To get value, give value.

So, what are the kinds of value you can give? We've already
talked about time and elbow grease. This is what most twentysomethings give, for low pay and low appreciation, in their
bureaucratized corporate jobs in which they're just following orders, supplying labor for someone else's brilliant plan. That's a
dead end.

Then, there's giving connections. Once you've got a great network in place, *that's* a highly time-leveraged form of giving. Meaning, once you've built up a great network, it doesn't take much
time—just a phone call or an e-mail—to connect two people within
your network, or to connect someone you just met with someone
you already know. These connections can be life-changing for people. And, assuming the connections are always well thought-out,
and they provide value for both people being introduced, it's pretty
much an infinite, inexhaustible form of giving.

And finally, there's giving great advice. Granted, it may take you years or decades to build up the appropriate knowledge base, but once it's there, giving advice from it can take just minutes, and it can be incredibly powerful and life-changing. If someone is having trouble with their business, or their relationship, or their health, and you give them a juicy suggestion that sets them on the right course and changes their life for years to come, you've just provided *massive* value in the space of a brief suggestion.

You've probably marveled at doctors or lawyers who earn $500 or $1,000 an hour dispensing their advice. It seems almost incomprehensible—someone earning over *one hundred times more* than a BA pouring coffee earns for the same marginal hour of effort? It also seems like a prima facie argument for more and better graduate education, if you want to get ahead in life.

Well, how would you like to earn *$6,000* per hour for your advice, with no college degree?

I shit you not.

Welcome to a mini-lesson in the power of learning how to give really good advice.

■ HOW TO EARN $6,000 PER HOUR WITH NO COLLEGE DEGREE

A few years ago I was doing some marketing consulting for a client on a retainer of $5,000 per month. On an hour-for-hour basis, it was probably working out to about $250 per hour. Not a bad gig. I was earning more per hour than many lawyers, and certainly more than most PhD psychologists in private therapy practice—all with skills I had learned purely through self-study. I felt satisfied with the value I was providing the client, as they were earning multiples of my retainer each month in higher revenue and profit.

At a certain point, though, it became clear that the company would benefit from a little heavier marketing firepower than I was able to provide; it was a large company, and they had the cash flow to invest in even more advanced marketing ideas than I knew how to give them.

So I suggested they bring in Eben—one of the world's foremost experts in Internet marketing—for some consulting. The CEO looked at some of Eben's videos online, and he was intrigued. He gave me the green light to talk to Eben and inquire about his consulting services.

It turns out, Eben doesn't often do consulting. He's so busy working on his Internet business, which brings in $30 million a year in revenue (close to $100K per day), that it just doesn't pay for him to take hours away from his workday to focus on paid hourly labor. If he spends several hours on someone else's business for pay, he gets the pay, but he never gets the products of his labor back. If he spends a few hours creating an Internet video that he sells, he can keep selling that video for the rest of his life. The gift that keeps on giving. Leverage. Scalability.

Nonetheless, from time to time, Eben informed me, he did do consulting work, particularly if it came in through a friend. He wouldn't keep the money; he'd give it to a charity, the Safe Conflict Project (http://www.safeconflict.org), run by his best friends, Amber Lupton (who did not complete college) and Nathan Otto. It would be his form of volunteerism.

His fee?

Fifty thousand dollars per day.

That is, around $6,000 per hour.

It sounds preposterous on its face. Earning more in one *day* than many recent college graduates will earn in an entire *year* of labor (if they're lucky enough to have a job), and more than many people around the globe will earn in their entire lifetime.

Before we take up arms and call for the socialist revolution to redistribute Eben's wealth to the poor twentysomething college-grad cubicle farmers in corporatelandia, however, let's pause and reflect for a moment.

Why is an hour of his help so highly valued on the marketplace, when an hour of a recent college grad's help is typically valued at 1 percent or less of his rate?

It's because Eben has focused his education on accumulating real-world skill sets and knowledge—human capital—which have allowed him to give *very, very good* advice. Specifically, this advice allows him to have a massive impact on individuals' and organizations bottom lines in a short period of time, such that those individuals and organizations are willing to pay top dollar for an hour of his attention and advice.

What does this have to do with our focus here on connecting with powerful people? Giving good advice—as we can see in the case of Eben—is one of the most highly valuable gifts you can give someone, and one of the most highly leveraged ways to connect with people. This means that an hour of attention from someone who has really good advice to give is valued in the marketplace a lot more than an hour of someone who has elbow grease and "hard work" to give.

Imagine if your advice was valued at $6,000 per hour and you could just dole out these $6,000 hours to anyone you pleased. Think you'd have more people wanting to connect with you? This is an incredible asset to be able to draw on for giving, giving, and giving more. As we've been discussing, it's a phenomenal form of connection capital.

In turn, most of us have focused our education, in the classroom and beyond, on much lower-leverage knowledge: How to follow orders and be obedient little schoolboys or cubicle jockeys. How to do as we're told. How to follow workplace manuals, protocols, procedures, classroom assignments.

We get paid less and are valued less by other businesspeople with whom we might want to connect because these skill sets have a lower impact on business results. We've basically just trained ourselves to be cogs in a machine. Now, with highly educated Chinese and Indians happy to do this kind of by-the-book work for us, many of us are finding that these skills we've been training sixteen years to develop have no impact in the workplace at all; we're out of work. Software programs might even take our job.

Eben, Elliott, and the other people I interview in this book get paid more than you and I do, and have more people wanting to connect with them in their business network, because they have a higher impact on the world and on other people's businesses than you or I do. Specifically, they *learned* how to have a higher impact, through the skill sets and knowledge we'll be talking about in this chapter, and in this book.

This sounds slightly offensive. Higher impact? Don't all human beings have an impact? Don't we all matter?

Of course we all matter. And of course we all have a massive impact—in certain lives at least. Our impact on the people we love, and on the people who love us, is much greater than the impact anyone else will have, no matter how much or how little money we all earn.

But we're talking about money in this particular discussion. And in a capitalist economy, in general (and with some significant exceptions) money flows to the people who make the most impact on the most people who have the most money. That's just the way the game works. You can rail against it, you can call for a socialist revolution. But as long as you're still opting to play the game, you might as well learn the rules of the game.

Brian Tracy, one of the most successful motivational authors, speakers, and sales and leadership trainers of all time, and a high school dropout (before later enrolling directly into an MBA program with no high school or college), writes: "The amount of money you earn is the measure of the value that others place on your contribution. . . . To increase the value of the money you are getting out, you must increase the value of the work that you are putting in. To earn more money, you must add more value."[6]

Personal development author and blogger (and graduate of Cal State, Northridge) Steve Pavlina expresses a similar theme in his book *Personal Development for Smart People: The Conscious Pursuit of Personal Growth.* He talks about the "contributor" mind-set versus the "moocher" mind-set, which is the essence of what we've been discussing in this entire chapter—the giver mentality versus the taker mentality. He writes: "Under the contributor mind-set, you receive money as payment for your social service. The money you earn is society's way of saying: 'In exchange for your valued contribution, you are hereby granted the right to extract equivalent value from society at a time of your choosing.' . . . The only real limit on your income is how much societal value you can create. If you want to earn more money, develop your skills and talents to facilitate the creation of lots of social value. Focus on giving, and the getting will largely take care of itself."[7]

From a certain perspective, these viewpoints are quite problematic. Can these authors really say that the Wall Street executives who received multimillion-dollar bonuses, while evaporating trillions of dollars of shareholder value and nearly causing a worldwide financial meltdown, were providing "social value" worth millions of dollars? Is the guy who gets rich building yachts for multibillionaires really providing that much social value in the grand scheme of things?

These perspectives ignore vast failures in market efficiency, which stem from conglomerations of power and concentrations of wealth, which lobby for favorable policies and distort market forces, making a mockery of the neat charts of the "efficient markets" from Economics 101. The world rewards people a lot more financially for polluting rivers than it does for planting trees, even though society benefits more from fresh air than from polluted rivers.[8]

On a day-to-day level, however, within your normal career in an industrialized economy, there is much to what Tracy and Pavlina are saying. Both authors rail against adopting the idea that you will earn the money you want to earn in life simply by showing up for work and doing what you do, without regard for how much tangible value you are actually creating in real people's lives.

Zig Ziglar, another legendary motivational speaker, author, sales trainer, and self-made multimillionaire (who dropped out of the University of South Carolina to pursue a career in sales), has said, "You can have anything you want in life, if you will just help other people get what they want."

The problem is, the concept and skills of "helping other people get what they want"—which is the main method by which we can connect with powerful mentors and teachers in life, as well as by which we will earn the money we want to earn in life and achieve what we want to achieve—is nowhere to be found in our formal educational curriculum, from elementary school through college. We learn how to study abstract things, rattle off facts, take tests, write academic papers, and basically follow instructions.

In turn, Eben, Elliott, and the other people featured in this book focused their self-education on gaining skills that allow them to contribute to other people, in higher-leverage and higher-impact ways. Specifically, they've focused on the ability to provide valuable, high-impact, high-leverage advice and leadership in the main areas of concern we've identified earlier: money and business, sales and marketing, spirituality and purpose (which often are expressed in the business world by the word "leadership"), and health and relationships.

These are the areas people tend to "want things" in. If you learn how to help them get what they want in these areas—as the self-educated entrepreneurs we're learning about in this book have done—you can connect with anyone you want to. And you can earn a lot of money as well. Because these are areas near and dear to people's deepest desires, fears, worries, and dreams—and they'll want to be around you and connect with you, if you can help them with these areas.

I can't explain exactly what the relationship is between giving widely within your network, with no expectation of anything in return, and giving in a professional relationship in which you're getting paid, but I know that there is one.

For some reason, the more you adopt the giving mind-set in your personal relationships and your network, with no quid pro quo, the more people want to be around you and connect to your network. (That much is obvious.) But also, the more they want to hire you as well. I don't know exactly why that is, but that's been my experience and the experience of others I've seen.

It may be because people trust givers, and therefore want to hire givers. They know they'll be taken care of. They know they'll get great value. They know that if anything goes wrong, it will be cleaned up and fixed. They know that you're not just doing it for the money; you're doing it because you care.

The reverse also holds true. The more you get your money and material needs met, the easier it is to take your mind off these material needs and focus on helping others. Of course, there's not a direct, linear relationship between wealth and the giver mentality. Obviously not. Many wealthy people are stingy, misers, greedy, takers, hoarders, selfish. And many financially poor people are incredibly giving of the heart, and even of their modest financial resources.

But, in general, it's easier to give when your cup runneth over. Joseph Simmons dropped out of a mortuary science program at LaGuardia Community College when his hip-hop career took off, as "Run" of Run-D.M.C.—a pioneering group in the early eighties that undeniably changed the face of popular music around the globe. Now a practicing Pentecostal minister, Reverend Run encourages his followers to get their financial house in order and cultivate prosperity, for the purpose of being more available to serve others. He tells them, "It's hard to help poor people when you're one of them."[9]

In *Linchpin: Are You Indispensable?*, which is the best book ever written on the central importance of giving within a business context, Seth Godin writes: "It's difficult to be generous when you're hungry. Yet being generous keeps you from going hungry."[10]

There's no question, this attitude we're exploring here is a paradox. Give to get; get to give. Gifts that you get paid for and are part of your career, gifts that you don't get paid for and aren't part of your career. None of it can really be analyzed rationally. At some point, you just wrap your head around the paradox and "get it." In this view, the wealthiest people are not the ones who are hoarding the most value—they're the ones who have the most value flowing in and out of their lives.

Multi-hundred-millionaire Russell Simmons, cofounder of the Def Jam record label and the Phat Fashions line, who dropped out of City College of New York to become a concert promoter and artist manager, writes in his book *Do You!*: "Piling up zeroes in your bank account, or cars in your driveway, won't in and of itself make you successful. Rather, true success is based on a constant flow of giving and receiving. In fact, if you look up *affluence* in the dictionary, you'll see its root is a Latin phrase meaning 'to flow with abundance.' So in order to be truly affluent, you must always let what you've received flow back into the world."[11]

You may scoff at this sentiment coming from a wealthy person and think, "Well, why don't you give all your hundreds of millions away?" Sorry to sound harsh, but—to whomever is asking that in a begrudging manner: Russell Simmons is giving away more than you, *and* he's keeping more than you for himself. He gives more and he gets more. He's simply making a bigger impact than most of us do on the planet. He's doing more in the world. And he's doing that because he's developed more *affluence* than you and I have developed, in the precise way he defines it: he's got more value flowing in and out of his life.

Accountants talk about stocks and flows. The money in a bank account, for example, is a stock, while the deposits and withdrawals are a flow. When we talk about wealth and affluence, we usually have in mind the amount in the stock. What Simmons and Seth Godin and Run are suggesting is that affluence is perhaps better indicated by the amount of the *flow*. The more value that flows in and out of our lives, the more we and others benefit, and the more affluence is generated.

Simmons uses his stocks and flows tirelessly to spawn all kinds of different charities and initiatives, focusing largely on youth empowerment and voter registration. He wouldn't be able to have this effect if he were poor. (In fact, most charities, nonprofits, and advocacy groups in general would not exist if rich people weren't funding them.) Maybe it's time to stop begrudging self-made affluence and instead see how we can create it for ourselves, so *we too* can give as generously and widely as Simmons is giving.

You can begrudge Eben Pagan and his $50,000 day rate. But let me ask you something. If *you* had the power to earn $50,000 in a day—because your skill set was that highly valued on the marketplace—and give that money to your favorite cause or charity, *wouldn't you do it?* Eben does this all the time.

You can begrudge Elliott Bisnow and the Summit team for living in nice houses and traveling together to exotic locations all over the world. But they've also raised over $2 million for charity among their tribe. Wouldn't you like to raise $2 million for your favorite charity?

In my experience, these people are just giving, giving, giving, all the time. They give when they get paid—far and above and beyond the minimum amount necessary to do an OK job. And, they give of their time and resources outside of work. Give, give, give.

No wonder so many people like to be around them, and their networks are so huge. We like to be around givers. All the world loves a lover, and all the world loves a giver.

Furthermore (and even more attractive): these people give generously without denying themselves. One thing I see in common among all the successful self-educated people I've met—which is different from the way most other people think—is that they tend not to see a contradiction between living a comfortable life for themselves and helping others.

Most of us tend to hold these two as separate. We tend to focus either on improving our own material circumstances without much attention to improving the world, or giving ourselves over completely to some cause (impoverished martyrdom). These two spheres correspond roughly to the two main types of jobs recent college grads go for: entry-level corporate jobs and entry-level nonprofit jobs.

I never understood my fellow Brown graduates, who said they wanted to "make a difference in the world," and then went into $36,000 jobs licking envelopes at some nonprofit organization while eating ramen noodles at night. Whatever difference spending one's time licking envelopes for $36,000 a year makes in the world, it's a fairly low-leverage difference. Furthermore, whoever ends up licking those envelopes didn't need to study for four years in college to do so, and my fellow Brown grads who took these kinds of jobs could have spent their years between the ages of eighteen and twenty-two learning the skills and mind-sets of having a real impact on the lives of other people, the way the people in this book learned. Instead, they take these kinds of jobs because they assume that if there's money, profit, or commerce involved, it's not making a difference, it's greed.

The entrepreneurs in this book, in turn, understand that true giving generates wealth, and true wealth helps you give more.

They understand flow. They understand affluence.

Much of the rest of this book is given over to self-education in the different tools in the Swiss army knife of advice giving, specifically: sales, marketing, connecting with influential people, how to invest in and increase your earning power, how to build a personal brand, how to take responsibility for your own success, and getting in touch with your purpose and meaning on the planet.

Diving deeply into your self-education in these real-world skills for success and leadership pays a double benefit. Not only will learning as much as you can about these areas improve your own life and business. They are also the main business areas in which other people seek advice. Developing experience, skills, and knowledge in these areas is a direct investment in your connection capital because it allows you to give a highly leveraged gift (valuable advice and guidance) to many people around you, increasing your circle of connections and contribution and also drawing the right teachers, mentors, and guides into your life. This connection capital, once in place, can pay "interest and dividends" for decades to come, as you use it to provide value, both personally and professionally, to the people around you.

Do you see how this all works by now? It's all really, really simple.

Give give give. Give give give. Give give give. Give generously within your network, and to people you hope will be in your network one day. Always inquire within yourself, and within your deepest creativity, how you can be of greater service. Without keeping track and without concern for a specific quid pro quo.[12]

Once you get a true network of co-support and mutuality going on, the giving and service and help start going around in this amazing community circle in ways more powerful than you can imagine.

■ HOW TO GIVE WHEN YOU'RE JUST STARTING OUT AND YOU'VE GOT NOTHING TO GIVE

There are still cynics among my readers who are starting to grumble. I know, I know. I had the money to fly out to Eben's talk in LA, and to go to Burning Man, and to an expensive weekend in Ojai to connect with him. I had a connection to Bryan in my social circle, and the network to be able to introduce him to a lot of future customers. I had already learned enough about marketing to give Bryan—a successful businessman—credible marketing advice. And I happened to be close friends with the amazing Annie Lalla, marriage material through and through, whom I was able to introduce to Eben.

In other words, my networking cup already ranneth over. I had a lot of "capital" to work with in my giving. But that's precisely the point. I had developed this capital—the ability to earn good money, knowing lots of people in New York, gaining access to great marketing teachings, and counting among my friends amazing people like Annie—largely because of *past* connecting, giving, and networking. It's a cycle that grows and grows over time, once you get hip to this dynamic. The more you give, the more you get, and the more you get, the more you have to give.

But you ask, "What if I have *nothing* to give. What if I'm *broke* and can't jaunt around the country to Ojai, or to wild bacchanalian parties in the Nevada desert, to hobnob with powerful mentors? What if I know *no one* and have *no network* to connect anyone else to? What if I have *no advice to give whatsoever*? What if I'm just starting out and basically have nothing on this planet? How do I give to amazing teachers and mentors *then, hhhmph?*"

OK, OK, you're really persistent on this point! Well, worry not. There is a great answer. The answer is: if you're just starting out on your path, and you've got nothing else to give, then give your enthusiasm and your willingness to implement other people's advice. This is worth a lot more than you think.

Keith Ferrazzi (http://www.keithferrazzi.com) is the author of the *New York Times* bestsellers *Never Eat Alone and Other Secrets to Success: One Relationship at a Time* and *Who's Got Your Back: The Breakthrough Program to Build Deep, Trusting Relationships That Create Success—and Won't Let You Fail.* These two books are absolutely required reading if you're interested in anything in this chapter—two of the best books on networking and connecting ever written. Keith, who graduated from Yale and holds an MBA from Harvard, is widely considered one of the world's top experts on success through relationship building and other so-called soft skills.

I asked Keith about how to give when you feel you've got nothing to give. He told me: "People always ask this question, when they're starting out, what do I have to give? But it's just the opposite—you have a lot to give when you're just starting out. The greatest gift you can give another person is the feeling of making a difference, a legacy, an importance.

"I get too many requests from kids who will reach out to me and say, 'Mr. Ferrazzi, I saw your speech, or I heard you on something or other. Can I have dinner with you, or coffee with you, and pick your brain on things?' And this is totally the wrong way to go about it. I want to say to them, 'Read my books, then talk to me.' The rudeness of wanting me to regurgitate what I've already written down and spent years telling people is ridiculous.

"The *right* way to go about it is to be generous with the person you want to connect with. And in this case, the generosity is: *you tell a story*. Tell a story about how you drew inspiration from their teachings and their example, how it impacted your life, and all the ways you're passing that gift on to others now. If you move me enough with what you've accomplished with my teachings and how you're serving others, then *yes, of course* I want to help you. I've helped all *kinds* of young people who have reached out to me with their stories of the amazing things they've done applying the concepts in my books. When I invest my time and effort in helping a young person, the dividend I receive in return is their gratitude, and their success."

Keith told me a story of how he put this concept into action when *he* was the young person seeking advice from a powerful mentor. "When I was kid, I built a relationship with the chairman of Baxter International at the time, Vernon Loucks. At least once a quarter, I would ping him, send him a simple update e-mail, and let him know how his advice was beneficial to me—how I applied it, how it's been helpful, then thank him effusively, praise how much I respect him, and then follow up right after that with another question. A quarter later, I'd tell him how I applied *that* advice, and what happened then. It was a lovely cycle. I stayed in touch with him for years and years and years, and it was a wonderful relationship."

Elliott Bisnow told me: "Everybody loves to give advice. If you ask someone in a genuine way to sit down with you, talk to you, give you advice, most people are happy to do it. It's shocking how few people go and ask for advice. If you call someone and say, 'Hey, I love what you're doing, I think it's incredible. I'd love your advice on something,' most people will sit down and give you advice and talk with you and mentor you. But most people just never do that.

"There's so many things that people just never do, which are available to them. It's all about *not* going through the motions. Going to high school, going to college, playing sports. This is just doin' what you're supposed to do, in an archaic system that doesn't really teach you. The notion that college is learning, and if you don't go to college you're not learning, is very silly. It's all about learning, all the time. And I felt in order to maximize my learning, I needed to learn different things than science and math and ancient history. In college, I realized, I was a people person. Just as, if you want to be a lawyer, you need a law degree—I realized I was a people person, and I needed to get educated in the game of life."

Welcome to your education in the game of life.

WHAT EVERY SUCCESSFUL PERSON NEEDS
TO KNOW ABOUT MARKETING, AND
HOW TO TEACH YOURSELF

Twentysomething college dropout Frank Kern was taking orders at a fast-food Greek restaurant in Macon, Georgia, when a college buddy of his he hadn't seen since dropping out walked in to order some fries.

The old college friends were excited to see each other, but also a bit surprised to find themselves on opposing sides of a fries transaction. Frank exclaimed, "Dude! Great to see you, man! I heard you were in med school. How's it going, man?"

And the friend replied, "Oh, it's going great, man! Hey, what are *you* up to these days?"

"Um, well . . . I'm here, um . . . working at this fast-food restaurant."

Around the same time, Frank suffered another disheartening experience. It was Christmastime, and he wanted to drive to see his parents for the holiday. "I realized I didn't have enough gas in the tank to go see them and then make it home. And it was like ten miles away. And I didn't have the cash to buy the gas."

Working for minimum wage in a fast-food restaurant. Not enough money to buy gas for a twenty-mile round-trip. These are the typical scenarios we imagine when we think of someone dropping out of school. When Frank dropped out, his parents kicked him out of the house, saying, "Enjoy life as a fry cook." So far, he was not proving them wrong.

But what these cultural expectations for dropouts miss is that people can turn around. Whether you're a fast-food server or a cubicle jockey in a mindless corporate shit job fresh out of college, you're not going to create anything better for yourself unless you make a fundamental shift: from viewing yourself as a passive follower of paths other people set for you, to actively taking responsibility for creating your own path toward success, however you define it. Thus, how much education you have doesn't really matter; what matters is whether you make this fundamental shift in mentality.

For Frank, the shift happened after these two humiliating experiences. He realized he wanted something better for himself. He decided he didn't want to live broke and powerless any longer.

Frank's grandfather was a self-made multimillionaire who had dropped out of school after eighth grade. He started out his working life as a young boy in sales, worked his way up through the car-dealing profession, and eventually came to own a chain of car dealerships in Macon. He had then parlayed those earnings into very successful real estate development. (Except for one flop: he partnered with a fellow Macon resident, who had a sixth-grade education, named James Brown—yes, the one whose music you dance to at parties to this day. Unfortunately, the restaurant, James Brown's Gold Platter, didn't sizzle like the music did.)

Frank was aware of his grandfather's success, but hadn't paid a lot of attention to it. Now he began to think, "If he could achieve all that without a degree, maybe I could be that successful too."

In his youth, Frank hadn't taken himself, or his future, very seriously. He remembers feeling profoundly alienated from school. "From third grade forward it all went to shit. I started losing interest in school when I was getting bad grades for 'penmanship'—and my mother would hassle me for getting bad grades for my handwriting. I remember thinking, 'Who gives a shit? This is stupid.'"

Frank's idols in high school, in the late eighties, were Duane Allman, Jimi Hendrix, Jim Morrison. (Note: What do all of these musicians have in common?) "I partied really, really hard. I didn't think I would live very long. To me, living very fast and dying very young was what you were supposed to do. So I never thought very far forward in terms of career planning. I was in a band; we were terrible. We played typical drunken eight-hour-guitar-solo Southern rock."

Frank worked as a desk clerk at a hotel during high school. It was an eight-hour job, from three in the afternoon until eleven at night. "I was like, 'If this is what the real world is like, I don't want to live in this world. I'd rather just die. I'd rather just blow it out—wreck a motorcycle or something, or get shot, or OD. I just didn't care."

In college, at the University of Georgia, Frank lasted the minimum amount of time you can last, prior to academic dismissal. Three academic quarters. Partying too hard, living the wannabe rock star life, kind of like my wannabe literary star phase in my twenties, though apparently with a lot more alcohol. I asked him if he thought of himself as some kind of romantic rebel at this time. "No, that would glamorize it. I was really just a kid who was lost, who didn't have any hope. I'm going to party as hard as I can, and maybe I'll end up some old biker dude or something. I did not want to live, if I had to live in what I called 'the cage,' which was a nine-to-five bullshit job."

After dropping out and moving out, he got a job as a Pizza Hut delivery guy, then various food prep and dishwashing jobs, then a job installing electric underground dog fences, all the while playing in his band. (It's interesting how people who opt out of "bullshit" corporate jobs usually instead end up in even *more* "bullshit" service jobs, if they don't possess the type of entrepreneurial skills and mind-sets we're learning in this book. They see nine-to-five corporate office jobs and low-pay service jobs as the only two options for making one's way in the world.)

Over the next several years, he bounced in and out of college. Whenever he'd get tired of whatever minimum-wage job he was working, he'd reenroll in college, with the idea that he'd get his degree and get a better job. Yet, his natural skepticism toward formal schooling continued. "I was studying in the School of Business at Macon College, and looking at the guys who taught there, and realizing none of them were rich. We all parked in the same parking lot, and the professors were driving old used Honda Accords. And I was like, 'Wait a minute!'"

Sometime during this ping-pong back and forth between enrolling for college and dropping out for minimum-wage jobs, he hit rock bottom. And vowed he was going to create something better for himself, outside of both corporate office jobs and minimum-wage service jobs. Which is when he began hanging out with his grandfather intensively, studying his life, and soaking up every bit of knowledge he had.

"In the end, I learned more from him than in all of my schooling. He was a salesman, to the bone. He taught me the importance of sales. What I learned from my grandfather was, the key to making money was to cause something to get sold. Whether you sell it yourself, or you employ someone to sell it and you get some of the money. He would always say, 'The only way to make money is to buy something at one cost and sell it at a higher cost. If you do that, and you hustle, you make as much money as you want.'

"I asked him to take me under his wing, and he taught me not so much a skill set, but a mind-set. The mind-set that was: 'You can do anything you want. The people who are professing to be experts, telling you what you can and can't do in life and how to do it, are just a bunch of fucking jackasses. The model that society teaches you to become successful is highly flawed.' And he used his personal story as the example of that, because he had no education past eighth grade.

"When I was still taking some college classes, I would come visit him in the evening, and he would say, 'Well, how much did you get paid for going to class today?' He had very strong opinions about all kinds of stuff. He was of the opinion that if you had a job, you were a pussy."

His grandfather's message of self-employment hadn't fully sunk in during high school (he had been too busy partying and trying to be a rock star), but now he was ready for the message. All of this study and mentee-ship with his self-made grandfather started making its mark. "I finally saw that there was another way. I saw that there were men and women out there who did not have jobs— they were businesspeople, making a lot of money and doing a lot of good in the world, without working for a boss. When I got to meet a lot of his connections, very few of them had ever followed the traditional path of getting a college degree and then getting a job. That's when I became a true believer in my current belief, which is that the way to go is to own your own business. Period. Once I had that belief instilled, I knew there was no other way for me."

Frank began rooting around for different businesses he could start. Eventually, he found his way to the writings of Dan Kennedy. And something happened to Frank, which also happened to me, and pretty much everyone else who finds their way there: everything changes after you first encounter Dan Kennedy.

———————

Dan Kennedy graduated from Revere High School in the early seventies, and then took a job in sales, while he began to teach himself direct-response copywriting. He is now one of the world's highest-paid copywriters, routinely earning $100,000 or more for a sales letter, plus royalties on sales. He is widely considered one of the greatest living geniuses in direct-response marketing, both as a practitioner and as a teacher, and pretty much everyone in the field looks up to him and has learned from him. He writes: "I am a 100% self-educated direct marketing expert. No college, no apprenticeship. Just a study of everything I could get my hands on and diligent application."[1]

At some point, if you're interested in money, and the making of it, you should immerse yourself in the work of Kennedy (http://www.dankennedy.com). He will piss you off, infuriate you, make you shake your fist, make you slam down his book at some point, but still, you need to read him.

What you will get from Kennedy, if you open yourself to his message, is the Gospel of Marketing. At some point while reading him, it will click for you—as it did for me, and for Frank—and you will just "get it." In particular you will get that, if you're serious about financial results in your life—whatever business you're in, however large or small, and whether you're an employee or an entrepreneur—you need to become a lifelong student of marketing. Period.

In Kennedy's words: "The breakthrough realization for you is that *you are in the marketing business.* You are *not* in the dry cleaning or restaurant or widget manufacturing or wedding planning or industrial chemicals business. You are in the business of *marketing* dry cleaning services or restaurants or widgets or wedding planning or chemicals. When you embrace this, it makes perfect sense to set your sights on marketing mastery. If you are going to make something your life's work and chief activity and responsibility, why not do it exceptionally well?"[2]

So what is marketing, anyway? Self-educated millionaire Cameron Johnson, another avid student of marketing in general and of Dan Kennedy in particular (among other teachers I mention here), offers a clear perspective.

Whenever Cameron Johnson has started one of his dozen-plus profitable businesses, many of which he's sold for nice payoffs, he asks a few simple questions: "What do people in this industry need? What's bothering them, hassling them, costing them money, keeping them from getting what they want? . . . *[C]ustomers with needs come along every single day.* There are *always* people and niches with unfulfilled needs. With this approach to business, you don't need to rely on luck, timing, or the fickleness of fads and crazes—just on your own ability to observe and create. Choose a niche, find a need, and then see what could help those people do their job better."[3]

This is the essence of quality marketing. The reason most of us hate the word "marketing" is that most of the marketing we experience did not follow this basic idea. Rather, the marketers happen to have something on hand they want (or were hired) to sell, and they try to push it on us, as if by force.

In turn, if the product or service is designed to solve a *specific unsolved problem* or meet a *specific unmet need*, and if the message is targeted well, so that you happen to be someone with that unsolved problem or unmet need, you will be *happy* to hear about the product or service. Think about the last time some product came along that solved a pesky, annoying, painful problem that had been bothering you for years—perhaps some health problem, or technology problem, or home repair problem, or even a psychological or existential problem. Think of how excited you were when you heard that there was finally an effective solution to that problem— *that* is how good marketing is supposed to feel.

There's another advantage to starting off by solving an already-existing unsolved problem. Not only does it feel better to the customer, it also feels better to *you*, the entrepreneur or executive. Sean Parker, who was the founding president of Facebook and did not attend college, was adamant about this point when I spoke with him.

"The people who are most successful, they had a problem that was gnawing at them, and they couldn't be comfortable unless they did something to solve that problem. It was so clear to them that they needed to do this thing, that every minute they weren't doing it, they were unhappy. It was about an outcome in the world, more than some romantic notion of making it big as an entrepreneur. It was about solving a problem."

What problem did Sean want to solve, when he first spotted TheFacebook, before it was Facebook? It wasn't the problem of how

to check out your friends' friends' hot roommates and coworkers—
though I admit that, when I was single, I did appreciate their solution to that problem.

Sean spoke to me with utter clarity, purpose, and passion about
the problem he set out to solve. "There was no global, persistent,
legitimate concept of identity that traveled with you from site to
site. There was no single sign-in or authentication system. There
was no verifiable notion of identity."

That was the big unsolved problem Sean wanted to solve. "Microsoft tried it with Microsoft Passport. No one trusts Microsoft
enough to do that. AOL tried it with Magic Carpet. Sun tried it
with Liberty Alliance. They were these big top-down efforts, and I
felt like the only way this was going to happen was through a
bottom-up movement. But the bottom-up movement was going to
have to come through some other application.

"I took one hack at it with [online address book] Plaxo. It was
the wrong answer, though. When I saw TheFacebook, it seemed
like the right starting point, a piece of clay that could be molded
over time to solve the right problem. The founder, Mark Zuckerberg, was the most ambitious and smartest person I'd ever met who
had built a social network. He was also the most receptive to my
feedback in terms of where I thought we needed to go. If you look
at Mark's actions even after I left the company, in terms of creating
Facebook Connect and the authentication network, and getting
other websites to use Facebook's data and trying to take your friend
network elsewhere, he's executing that vision flawlessly. And now
that the platform's built, he's answering the question 'How do we
integrate it into the fabric of the Internet?'"

Being that thoroughly consumed with solving a problem will
carry you through a lot of business ups and downs. When Sean
was starting Plaxo, which ultimately failed, he was flat-out broke.
But he kept going, fueled by his vision of solving a major problem.
He told me: "I lived out of a suitcase, homeless, for the first year I
was trying to start Plaxo, pitching venture capitalists. It got to the
point where my last sweater had a hole in it. When I was in one of
the partner pitches with Mike Moritz of Sequoia Capital, who became my investor, I had to be conscious of the fact that I had a hole
in my sweater, so I couldn't lift my arm up beyond a certain point,
where he'd see I had this hole in my sweater. I literally had no
money to buy clothes. Unless you're driven by a desire to solve a

problem, you're not going to be able to stick that out. If you're driven only by a desire for the status that is associated with being an entrepreneur, you're not going to be willing to deal with the humiliation of sleeping on people's couches."

Sean famously connected with Mark Zuckerberg when The-Facebook was an infant, and played a crucial role in making Facebook what it is today, adding central innovations like photo sharing and friend-tagging, and introducing Zuckerberg to Peter Thiel (whom we'll meet later in the book), Facebook's first investor. Facebook is now well on its way to becoming the single point of login and user authentication for a large swath of the Internet. Sean, with a 7 percent stake in Facebook, is now worth billions.

So the first part of marketing has nothing to do with communications or ads or messages. It has to do with the concept of the product or service itself, and how well it is designed to meet needs/solve the problems of a specific target market. Good marketing, Seth Godin writes in *Purple Cow: Transform Your Business by Being Remarkable*, "start[s] with a problem you can solve for a customer (who realizes he has a problem!)."[4] Good marketing, in other words, is not something you do *after* you create the product; the fact that most marketing is done this way is why we hate the word "marketing" so much. If you *start* with marketing—that is, with thinking about, anticipating, and meeting the needs of a market in an original, effective, compelling way—then that market will be *glad* to hear about what you're offering.

Once you've designed a product that actually solves someone's real problem (rather than just solving your own problem of needing more cash!), you'll still need to let those people know about it. The specific type of communication Dan Kennedy teaches, and which I recommend for most small businesses, is called direct-response marketing. This may have a bad ring to you, because there's a lot of very bad (and sleazy and cheesy) direct-response marketing out there: junk mail, late-night infomercials, "But Wait, There's More!, Free Ginsu Knives with Your Order—Only if You Act Now!," and so on.

But, there are also some very high integrity (and non-cheesy) ways to practice direct-response, as we'll be learning later in this chapter. And when you get into it, it's shockingly cost-effective in getting the word out about your company, product, service, cause, mission, or whatever other gift you're giving to the world. It's the preferred marketing method for bootstrappers, people who don't have massive venture investments to burn through in the course of achieving their goals.

What all forms of direct-response have in common is that they're aimed at *causing a specific response to occur*—whether it's joining your newsletter, purchasing your product, making a donation to a cause, or calling a politician to advocate for impending legislation. Whatever you're up to in the world, direct-response will help.

Most marketing you see out in the world (including the marketing you'll learn in undergraduate and MBA courses) is what's called "brand" or "image" marketing. It's loosey-goosey. It's not aimed at any response in particular. It gobbles up massive budgets, with the aim of painting a pretty "picture" in your mind of the product or service, or giving you a warm, fuzzy feeling when you think about it—in the hopes that that pretty picture or warm, fuzzy feeling might cause you to buy it, maybe, one day, down the line when you're in a store and you happen to see the product.

If you're in business for yourself, you don't have time or money for that. You need results *now*. And if you work for a large corporation, you should become their resident expert in direct-response and wow them with the results *you're* able to get for them. (Not in your job description? Wah, wah, wah. Read the section in Success Skill #7 on why you should rip up your job description and flush the shreds down the toilet—if you want to make an honest mark in the organization and rise up through the ranks.)

In his wonderful book *No B.S. Direct Marketing: The Ultimate, No Holds Barred, Kick Butt, Take No Prisoners Direct Marketing for Non-Direct Marketing Businesses*, which is in my view the single best introduction to direct-response available, Kennedy lists "Big Company's Agenda for Advertising and Marketing," which includes:

1. Please/appease its board of directors (most of whom know zip about advertising and marketing but have lots of opinions)
2. Please/appease its stockholders
3. Look good, look appropriate to Wall Street

4. Look good, appropriate to the media
5. Build brand identity
6. Win awards for advertising
7. Sell something

He then lists "Your Agenda" for advertising and marketing, which includes, in its entirety:

1. Sell something. Now.[5]

If you're an entrepreneur, or self-employed, marketing is one of your most important jobs, period.

However, if you work for a large corporation (or aspire to), and you're not in the marketing department, you might wonder: What relevance does all this talk about learning marketing possibly have for me?

There are several important reasons you should learn marketing, even if you work for a large corporation and aren't planning a career in marketing.

1. Marketing is a mentality. It's a worldview that puts customers' emotional reality first, and inquires deeply about their needs, wants, and desires. Do you think adopting that mentality might be good for other parts of the business, besides the marketing department?

2. There's no better way to rise up the ranks of your organization than bringing in new business, or coming up with ideas that bring in new business. Not in your job description? If you're seriously that attached to your job description, one day someone is going to come along in your department who's willing to go the extra mile and go *way beyond* your job description. Whom is the boss going to think of first when it's time for considering promotions? And, if you're using your job description as an excuse for avoiding proactive leadership and initiative, whom do you think your boss is going to think of first when it's time to hand out pink slips? Few employees are more popular with the higher-ups than those who come up with workable ideas about how to bring in more revenue.

3. If you've noticed, your job may not seem so secure these days as it used to. Now is a good time to start thinking about what skills you're bringing to the table if you find yourself looking for work in the future. Not only will these marketing and copywriting skills help you promote *yourself* to future employers when you need to (see Success Skill #6 on personal branding, for Marian Schembari's story), but there is no skill, and I mean no skill at all, more highly prized by potential employers than a demonstrated ability to bring in new business. Employers love rainmakers. They hire rainmakers first, and will never, ever fire them, so long as they continue making rain. Learn to be a rainmaker.

There may even come a time when you are finding it difficult to find employment. Instead of sitting around moaning and watching an empty screen in response to the hundreds of resumes you're sending out, you could try getting some freelance consulting gigs in your field while you look for work. It's a great way to meet prospective employers (vastly more effective than job hunting), and you'll also have some money coming in to smooth over the transition to your next job. The marketing skills you can learn through this chapter will be invaluable in helping you get these freelance gigs. Who knows, the self-employment bug might even bite you, and as you enjoy these freelance gigs, you might just "neglect" to find a new boss to replace the old one!

Frank Kern (http://frankkern.com) "got the message" of the direct-response gospel, as preached by Kennedy and others, and is now himself one of the highest-paid marketing consultants in the world. He engineered a product launch over the Internet that did over $18 million in revenue in the twenty-four hours in which the shopping cart was open.

His retainer for his consulting services starts at $170,000 per year per client. And, following his teacher Kennedy, his sales letter starts at $100,000 per year plus 15 percent royalty (the royalty on sales often ends up bringing in much more than the upfront fee).

He now works a few hours a day, from a beach house over the water in San Diego. A long way from serving fries in Macon and not having money to buy a tank of gas.

I asked Frank for his main message and words of wisdom for readers of this book.

"Understand that no matter what you're doing, even if you

want to be a ballplayer, a rapper, a movie star—nothing happens until something gets sold. Ever. The reason actors make so much money is because their face sells the fucking movie tickets. It's not about their ability to act. The reason the musician gets rich is because he sells a lot of seats and records. Or his song gets used in a movie—it's a license, a sale. The key to making money, and therefore living a life of less stress, is to cause someone to joyfully give you money in exchange for something that they perceive to be of greater value than the money they gave you. The key there is 'joyfully.' Most sales and marketing you study, you learn how to trick people into parting with their money, or badger them into doing it, or make them so miserable that they think you're their only salvation. None of those situations involve the word 'joyfully.'

"We're in the information age, for the love of God! We don't need to teach kids trigonometry. That's why they make computers. It's not like we're going to get stranded on a desert island, without a computer, and need to somehow formulate an algebraic equation. I think it would be very intelligent to teach our kids the language of the world, which is the language of money, the language of sales, and the language of influence. Because they're either going to be an influencer, or they're going to be influenced. They're either going to be a leader, or be led by someone else. There's always going to be two sides to that coin. Which side would you rather have your kid be?"

■ HOW I BECAME A HIGHLY PAID MARKETING CONSULTANT (AND SAVED MY MARRIAGE!) WITH TWO MONTHS OF MARKETING STUDY

If you're not already sold on the importance of learning marketing, seriously, put this book down and go and join the International Socialist Organization—I hear they're recruiting.

For the rest of you, I presume you're pretty excited about what's possible for yourself, for your dreams, for your goals in life, for your material comfort, and for your ability to give your gift and get your message out into the world, through learning marketing.

In this chapter, I'm going to give you a world-class education on *how to teach yourself marketing*. Read those words carefully. I'm not actually going to *teach* you (much) marketing here. That's just not the scope of the book. You know the adage about "teach a man to fish"? I'm not going to teach you how to fish. I'm going to do something better. I'm going to *teach you how to teach yourself* how to fish.

In many ways, that's the intention of the whole book, with every life skill we talk about in this book. We'll be discussing skills such as networking and connecting, marketing, sales, writing powerful business prose, clarifying your purpose in life, learning social media, taking charge of personal finance, building amazing relationships. Such a wide range of amazing topics—there's no *way* I could do justice to all of these in a single book.

So, what I aim for in each course in this book is to give you a guide (and the inspiration) to *get started* educating yourself in these areas. I aim to point you in the right direction. That's all a good teacher can really do anyway. The rest you'll be learning on your own. That's why it's called *self*-education!

I'm going to share with you my guide for self-education in marketing in a moment. But before I do, I want to share a personal story about how learning these skills has impacted my life in a major way. I hope this story will show you that learning marketing is not all just about money.

I fell in love with Jena on our second date, and told her so. She said she was falling in love with me too that very date. I moved from California to New York, to be where she lived, a month later, in June 2008.

Three months after that, in September 2008, the bottom fell out of the U.S. economy.

Overnight, Jena's weight-loss coaching practice, her life's dream and work, became empty of clients, as people slashed their personal expenses. Her sales went down drastically, while expenses stayed the same. The books were completely in the red.

Our relationship was young, and I had previously never given any attention to her business, wanting to keep that separate from our love. And besides, she had a team of very impressive advisers, including an MBA and many seasoned corporate veterans, guiding her. What good could I do when she's getting advice from them? I thought.

Nonetheless, Jena was coming home crying every night. She was staying in the office until 11:00 P.M. trying to save the baby of her business, then she'd come home and we'd often stay up until 1:00 A.M. as I comforted her from the stresses of her day and tried to reassure her. But the situation was not looking good. She faced the unsavory choice—which so many other small business owners faced during that time—of pouring savings into a business that had just collapsed, during a nasty recession when there were few assurances that the money would ever come back again, or getting out and moving on from this life dream of owning her own business.

I was also under a lot of stress financially, as I'm sure you were too during those months. The combination of my financial stress and hers was putting an enormous amount of pressure on our fledgling relationship. As I've told Jena, the *only* time I ever questioned to myself whether our relationship would last was during those fall months of intense stress and pressure on both of us.

But I wasn't going to give up so easily. "Money and love are *already* mixing in this relationship," I told myself. "Money is all we talk about these days!" So I overcame my self-imposed ban on mixing business and love. I vowed to find a way to help turn Jena's business around. I knew it was one of the only ways we could save our relationship because there was just too much pressure on it otherwise and all our dreams seemed to be falling apart.

By a coincidence, I had just been introduced to the work of Eben Pagan and Dan Kennedy, via my friend Brent Smith. Brent is a dating coach (and non-college-graduate) who was earning $10,000+ a *weekend* taking millionaires to Monaco and training them in dating skills (http://www.absolutepowerdating.com). He was a voracious student of every word Eben and Kennedy wrote, and he told me to check out their work.

I listened to some of Eben's recordings and started reading some of Kennedy's books, and instantly I could see that Jena's business would be benefited by their direct-response marketing approach. Jena didn't know what direct-response was (I barely did either at that point), and her advisers were not recommending it either. I saw an opportunity to make a difference and decided to go for it. What the hell, it's not like either of us had much to lose at this point—everything was pretty much crashing in on us. It was a Hail Mary pass of marketing.

The crucial turning point for me was listening to a recording that was part of Eben's "Guru Mastermind" home study marketing course. The recording was called "How to Write a Killer Sales Letter" and featured Eben's main copywriter, Craig Clemens, who has generated over $50 million in sales through his copy.

The key revelation from that recording, for me, was that when you're communicating with a marketing message, you need to *get inside the heads* of your prospects, figure out what matters most to them in their lives, and talk to them about *that*, not about what you want to sell them. They don't care about what you want to sell them. "If you aren't talking to your prospect about their strongest and deepest wants, needs, and desires, you are doing them a disservice," Craig said on the recording.

This one piece of advice upends the vast majority of marketing you'll see out there and marketing training you'll learn in undergraduate and MBA marketing courses. Most marketing focuses on what the marketer wants to sell. That's why we find most marketing so invasive and annoying. Because we don't *care* about what the marketer wants to sell.

Good marketing, in turn, speaks to the prospect about their deepest emotional realities, their innermost desires, and about helping them achieve what they want in those realms. Thus, the best marketing is all about human connection, on a genuine level. If you can truly help your prospect achieve their deepest wants and desires in the area your product or service addresses (and if you can't, you shouldn't be marketing it in the first place), then you are actually doing your prospects a great service by communicating with them about their problems or issues, because few people *ever* meet us on that level, even in our personal lives. It feels fantastic to be heard, met, and understood. If you can do that with your prospects, then they will most certainly want to do business with you (provided what you're selling is an appropriate match for them).

The recording gave a specific process for getting inside of the heads of the people you're communicating with, so you can talk with them about what is *most* important to them. If you talk with them about what's *most* important to them (instead of talking about your pitch, which I guarantee is low in the list of what's important to them), they will listen, and they will trust what you have to say. The process Craig offered was simple: make a list of your prospects' biggest fears, frustrations, desires, dreams, and nightmares around the issue your product or service helps them with. List twenty-five answers for *each* of these categories.

I gave Jena the homework to make these lists, answering from the viewpoint of her prospective weight-loss clients. This was the first time I'd ever given her "homework" around her business, so she looked at me funny—but she was in no position to protest, given how dire the situation was.

She created a beautiful portrait of the inner emotional reality of her prospective clients, via the answers to this exercise. And with that portrait, I began constructing an e-mail to send to her list, which spoke directly to her prospects' most urgent needs:

Are you absolutely, positively sick of constantly feeling self-conscious of your body?

Are you tired of looking into your closet and seeing all the clothes you wish you could fit into again?

Do you feel that your weight is holding you back from doing what you want to do in life?

Do your cravings feel "out of control"?

Do you feel bogged down by lethargy as a result of carrying around extra weight?

Do you fear that you'll never manage to lose the weight?

Does the fear of diabetes or heart disease lurk in the back of your mind?

Are you afraid that you will be relegated to a "small life" because you don't have energy to be out and about creating something large?

Do you feel your body is not trustworthy, that it will screw up the plans made by your mind?

Do your cravings expand to become all-consuming, sabotaging "the weight-loss plan"?

Are you concerned you'll never find the time to implement healthier eating?

Are you sick of feeling like a failure because you fail to lose weight?

I then wrote, in Jena's voice, a story she had told me many times, about how she had struggled with *every one* of these painful bits of self-doubt and self-hatred, before she finally figured out how to get her health, eating, weight, and body image in order. At the end of the e-mail, I provided a specific way for potential clients to get in touch with her if they had been struggling with the same issues and would like to have the same results as Jena.

Jena had never sent anything like this to her list. It totally flew in the face of the "brand" marketing that her board of advisers was recommending to her. She had mostly been sending nice, corporate, boring "Here are the services we offer"–type e-mails to her list. These e-mails, of course, never resulted in any sales, but at least they were safe and comfortable and didn't risk rocking the boat.

Jena was scared about this new e-mail—it was so much more vulnerable and human, so much more emotionally raw, than the normal corporate communications. But she realized this was the time to try something new. This e-mail focused on her *prospects'* needs, not on *her* need to sell them stuff. (Did you see how many times it contained the word "you"?) She gulped, and pressed Send.

The e-mail created howls of protest from some members of her board of advisers. "You're going to ruin the brand we've spent years creating with this!"

But, it also brought in *$8,000* of new coaching business in the space of a single week.

Jena had never seen results like that in the entire history of her business, despite many highly educated advisers giving her marketing advice. (That e-mail, which she has sent to new subscribers to her list many times over the last two years, has generated over $150,000 in new coaching business.)

She became an instant convert to direct-response marketing. She signed up for a live event with Eben, listened to his recordings, and read every book she could get her hands on by Dan Kennedy. Through her efforts, she completely turned her business around, rejuvenating it. Within months it was in the black again—and growing rapidly in the middle of a recession.

As we both expanded our self-education in marketing after this experience, the financial pressure on our relationship disappeared, to be replaced by ease and abundance. We weren't even engaged yet, but I do believe that Eben and Dan Kennedy saved our marriage, because our new relationship might not have survived the financial stress of the early recession had Jena and I not discovered their teachings and implemented them in our lives and businesses. We have a completely new relationship together because of it.

A note on integrity: an objection you might have to all this direct-marketing stuff, and a reason you might dismiss it, is that you think it's manipulative. For example, it might seem manipulative to talk with prospects about their fears of health concerns, or their fears of never losing the weight they want to lose.

These are important concerns. When you talk with anyone about their deepest fears, desires, and dreams, there is a potential for manipulation. That's why you must always check in with yourself and approach these encounters with the highest integrity and the most giving, generous intentions. You must truly believe that what you are offering will benefit the prospect enormously. If, in the course of talking with them, you come to see that what you're offering isn't actually a good match for their needs, then you must actively discourage them from buying it and, if possible, refer them to a better solution.

However, if you have a product or service that you truly believe will benefit someone, then—as my friend the marketing coach Marie Forleo says—you're actually *depriving* them of these benefits if you don't communicate effectively and discuss together with your prospect whether your offering might be a good fit for their needs. You're being stingy and selfish with your gifts, she says, if you don't take the time to learn how to get your gifts out into the world, into the hands of the people who can benefit from them. Good marketing—honest marketing, high-integrity marketing—is the art of getting your solutions out into the world, into the hands of the people who need them and will use them and derive real benefits from them. It's the art of spreading your gifts as widely as possible in the world.

A final coda to the story: I parlayed this experience helping Jena into a sub-career doing copywriting and marketing consulting. Within half a year I was bringing revenue in the high five figures, consulting for individuals and businesses in my network; in fact the copywriting and marketing consulting subsumed my book proposal writing business, which had been my bread and butter for the previous several years.

I don't think what I achieved would be that difficult for anyone else to achieve. It's available to anyone who wants to put some time into learning good direct-response copywriting.

Like Eben and Dan Kennedy and Frank Kern, I didn't have any formal "credentials" to do this consulting. I didn't have an MBA in marketing, or even a BA in business. What I had, instead, is something infinitely more valuable: a growing portfolio of real-world results. If you can help people get the results they want, and you can show them proof that you've helped other people get great results, people just don't give a damn about your credentials. They care about results.

While you can't go out and practice law or medicine or psychotherapy or engineering without academic credentials, for most other fields, boosting up your formal credentials is absolutely the wrong thing to be focused on. Focus instead on learning how to get results, real-world results that people actually care about, and which speak to deep desires, wants, and needs. Your competitors can wipe their asses with their formal credentials.

■ A QUICK-AND-EASY GUIDE TO TEACHING YOURSELF MARKETING IN TWO MONTHS

OK, so you're sold. You're ready to learn high-quality, high-integrity marketing. Well, how do you begin? This guide will show you how to start. You'll be amazed at how many free or low-cost resources there are out there for you, and how quickly you can begin putting your learning into action and get real-world results.

Step 1. Create an e-mail address that is not your main e-mail address and does not go to your main inbox. I'm going to be asking you to sign up for a lot of different free e-mail newsletters, and they will flood your e-mail account, so make sure it's not your main account or inbox!

Step 2. Go to the following websites. Not only should you read everything you can get your hands on in the archives of these sites, but you should also sign up for the free e-mail newsletter available on each site, with the e-mail address you created in Step 1.

You should sign up for these newsletters because *all* of the people I'm going to recommend are master copywriters. You can get an entire education in marketing and copywriting just by comparing and contrasting the different styles of these marketers. Once you begin diving into some of the resources I mention above, you'll see that there is no "one" way to market, no "one" tone you need to adopt. There are so many different tones and styles here, from Dan Kennedy's over-the-top hard sell, to the wickedly funny copy of Marie Forleo and exercise guru Matt Furey, to Jonathan Fields's super-sweet soft sell, and everything in between. If you are offended by a particular style, or it's just not for you, then find a marketer you vibe with more and learn from him or her instead. (All of these newsletters include links at the bottom, which allow you to remove yourself from them if you no longer wish to receive them.)

Once you've exposed yourself to lots of different styles (to see the range of what's out there), you'll probably find one or two teachers or sites whose values and sensibilities match your own. Start focusing your energy on learning from them—while never fully losing awareness of what others are doing out there as well, for diverse ideas and perspectives.

(If you know how to do such things in your e-mail program, set up filters or rules so that each marketer's e-mails go to a different mailbox or folder—it's just easier to manage that way.)

Note: Many of the people I recommend here, including Eben, Marie Forleo, and Jonathan Fields, are personal friends. In no case am I receiving any commission, payment, or other benefit for recommending you to anyone here. Be aware, most of the people on these lists will eventually send you to landing pages, where they sell their products and services. Learn as much as you can from these landing pages, as they're often masterful examples of marketing. But obviously, do your own due diligence before deciding to buy anything.

By the way, all of the people I mention below graduated from college, unless I mention otherwise. But hey, we won't hold that against them.

Copyblogger.com

This site (http://www.copyblogger.com), run by Brian Clark, is an absolute treasure trove of free information on high-integrity marketing. Brian has pioneered a style of marketing he calls "third tribe," which attempts to combine the best from the two camps—direct-response marketing and social media marketing—yet leave behind the worst aspects of each. Specifically, direct-response marketers are great at selling stuff and making gobs of money but, as we've discussed, have in the past had a reputation for being pushy, cheesy, and sleazy. Social media people (bloggers, etc.) have in the past focused on giving away tons of free content, serving their communities, and building great trust for their brand, but in the past they have had a lot of difficulty making money from their efforts. (The image of the "broke blogger" has almost replaced the image of the "starving artist" for the digital era's preferred cliché of high-minded impoverishment.)

Copyblogger.com attempts to bridge and synthesize these two worlds, teaching you a style of marketing that combines the integrity, trust, honesty, and vulnerability of the social media tribe with the money-earning genius of the direct-response tribe, while leaving behind the sleaze, cheese of the latter, and the vows of poverty of the former.

I'm astonished at the amount of free education available on this site. A month of diving intensively into its archives could have more real-world benefit for you than entire years of higher education.

One of my favorite picks on the site is a series on "How to Write Magnetic Headlines." You'll notice the influence of this series on my chapter titles and subheadings.[6]

MarieForleo.com

Marie is a pioneer in the field of entrepreneurialism and marketing for women. However, I think everyone, men and women, should study her stuff because there's something very important in her "feminine" touch to marketing (visit http://marieforleo.com). In the past, direct-response was an all-boys club, and there was a lot of dick swinging going on, with very aggressive, testosterone-laden hard-sell pitches and an emphasis on "Sell! Sell! Sell! More! Faster!" without much concern for how those on the receiving end felt about it.

Marie's great insight was, women don't want to read this kind of marketing, and most women business owners don't want to create it. All else equal, Marie contends, women tend to prefer to do business with people and companies with whom they have an ongoing business relationship, not a one-off transaction. They don't want a bunch of aggressive pressure and don't respond well to it; they tend to respond more to a gentler approach, based on trust, sharing, community, and connection.

Marie was ahead of the curve on this because the whole trend of marketing now—with the emphasis from social media on openness, transparency, honesty, and community—is heading in that direction.

Beyond all this feel-good stuff, she's also wickedly funny, which is reason alone to read her. She's entertaining, and nothing sells like humor.

MattFurey.com

Matt is one of the most respected copywriters and practitioners of marketing through e-mail on the planet. He's known for kick-ass storytelling in his copywriting. Funny, irreverent, highly conversational. A world-class legendary copywriter and marketer. Get on his e-mail list (visit http://mattfurey.com)—you can learn a ton from him emulating his style.

JonathanFields.com

You can't find a more soft-spoken, authentic, sweet, genuine marketing expert out there than Jonathan Fields (visit http://www.jonathanfields.com). You can get an entire business and marketing education reading his blog and going through his archives. Mostly, he just wants to help you—and very rarely, he'll try to sell you something too. A master of high-integrity, high-trust, low-hype, soft-sell marketing.

Seth Godin (http://sethgodin.typepad.com)

I never, ever cease to be blown away by the brilliance and cutting-edge insight on display on this blog. Seth's blog isn't really about marketing, at least not as the word is usually used. It's about changing the world. And to change the world, you've gotta market the change you want to create. Otherwise, no one's buyin' it! That's the general vibe of Seth's work, and you will do well to study everything he writes. The archives on his blog are an entire business education for free. I read it religiously.

Other Great Marketers

You can access a free archive of masterful sales letters by the late Gary Halbert, one of the greatest copywriters of all time (visit http://www.thegaryhalbertletter.com). And you can get a very content-rich free course in copywriting from Gary Bencivenga, another legend of marketing and copywriting (visit http://www.marketingbullets.com).

I also recommend you get on the e-mail lists of the people

we've been talking about in this chapter already (and, to add to their credibility, not one of them has a college degree): Dan Kennedy (http://www.dankennedy.com), Eben Pagan (http://www .gurumastermind.com), and Frank Kern (http://www.frankkern .com). Finally, gotta say it, get on my wife Jena's list (visit http:// www.pleasurableweightloss.com). Many of these other people I've mentioned are die-hard marketing trainers; with Jena, you'll see the results of someone with a real-world off-line business, who taught herself marketing from the ground up in a short amount of time. She writes her own copy, and it rocks.

Step 3. When my father once asked the legendary Norman Mailer for writing advice, Mailer said the main secret was: "Apply Ass to Chair." Meaning, in this case, sit down at your desk, in front of your computer, and start putting this stuff into action. Don't wait for the time to be right. (It never will be.) Don't wait for everything to be perfect. (It won't be.) Don't wait until you "learn just a little more." (There's *always* more to learn!)

Most of the marketing experts I've mentioned here offer free articles, online videos, teleseminars and webinars, and other free resources, which comprise a collective treasure trove for educating yourself in real-world marketing.

No matter what you're up to, whether you're trying to sell your own freelance services or trying to end world hunger, whether you work in a company of one or one hundred thousand, these skills will help you get your product or service or message, or your company's product or service or message, in the hands of the people whose lives will benefit from it. (If no one's life will benefit from it, then why are you marketing it? Time to find a different line of work!)

However, none of these teachings do you any good until you put them into action. You're not going to get it perfect the first time you try. There will be bumps, bruises, slips, trips, and falls along the way. But your failures will themselves be a crucial part of your learning process.

The world needs your gift now. It can't wait for you to keep it to yourself. The way for you to get your gift out into the world is to learn marketing, that is, learn the art of talking with people about their deepest needs and desires, and about why what you're offering might help them meet those needs and desires.

The time to get started is now.

■ MARKETING SECRETS FROM THE POM QUEEN

My family friend Lynda Resnick wanted to go into advertising when she graduated high school, but the advertising agencies weren't having any of it. "No one would hire me. I went in for junior art director jobs. They kept telling me I had promise, but I should go back to school. But that wasn't an option. I had to work. Although my father had the money to send me to the college of my choice, he decided not to. He said I never stuck anything out. Well, at seventeen, that was something I would spend the rest of my life proving wrong," she told me.

Lynda went to a city college for a few months, but was so bored, she left to start working full-time. Like many people without a college degree, Lynda took a job in retail, at a dress shop. But here's where the similarities end between the career trajectory of Lynda and that of most other people with only a high school diploma. "The shop owners complained constantly about the lack of business," Lynda writes.[7]

Most people in such jobs tend to think, "That's not my problem—they're not paying me enough to worry about that. It's their responsibility to generate the business, I just do what they say and collect my paycheck." They toil ten, twenty, thirty, or forty years with such a mentality and wonder why they never raised their station in life.

Lynda, however, exercised some initiative and leadership. (See Success Skill #7 on the entrepreneurial mind-set). She writes:

"To help them out, I drew enchanting little female characters that embodied the mode of the times. Then I worked up headlines and text to accompany my illustrations. The owners placed these homespun ads in the local papers.

"It worked. Customers came in talking about the charming advertising. . . . The owners were only too happy to . . . keep me in the back room creating advertising instead of selling on the floor. . . . I was no longer a salesgirl; I was in the early stages of becoming a marketer."[8]

Lynda had essentially worked herself—through the back door—into the position of marketing director. She left the dress shop and took another job, this time at the in-house advertising department of a larger company. She also started freelancing on the side. (See the section in Success Skill #1, Four Steps to Aligning Your Money and Your Meaning.) She told me, "I did a direct-mail campaign for a charming little store in the [San Fernando] Valley. It made them successful overnight, and it made me successful overnight. After that point, it was easier to find clients.

"I didn't think of it as 'starting a business.' I just did advertising jobs. It started growing, and I had to hire more people to do them. I didn't start out like they do today, with some grand business plan and a bunch of venture money. It just . . . *evolved*." Lynda left the larger company and started her own advertising agency at age nineteen, Lynda Limited, which was highly profitable from the start. This was only a few years after the advertising agencies she had applied to upon her high school graduation told her she'd need a college degree for any entry-level job with them. (See Success Skill #5 on bootstrapping your career and success—Lynda is a textbook example.) She later interviewed for a position as senior art director at her own firm, one of the very people who had turned her down years earlier!

Lynda (http://blog.lyndaresnick.com) has proven herself to be one of the great marketing minds in history. Ever drink one of those double-globed bottles of dark, tangy POM Wonderful Juice? That's her brainchild. Hardly anyone had ever heard of pomegranates, let alone pomegranate *juice*, before Lynda came around. Now it's available in practically every supermarket in America. She's had a string of hits like that throughout her career.

In her book, *Rubies in the Orchard: The POM Queen's Secrets to Marketing Just About Anything*, Lynda continues the theme we've been developing in this chapter. Good marketing is not about pushing your stuff onto an unwilling audience. It's about listening to your audience. Really, really well. At its best, it is not a sleazy endeavor, but a deeply empathic one:

> Since my college career had been measured in months . . . I never took a marketing course. Everything I know about marketing I learned on the job. My lack of [formal] education would have stalled a career in nuclear physics, but it never hindered my career in marketing. You can't learn how to be a good marketer from a textbook. . . .
>
> The most important lesson of all is self-taught. Ultimately, marketing is all about listening. If you don't listen and you don't care, you'll never be a good marketer. You want to be the equivalent of a good friend—someone who cares, someone who listens

carefully, someone who tries to anticipate another's needs. The rest—marketing research, statistical analysis, economics, and finance—are really important tools, but in the end, you have to use all that information to inform your own human instincts. That is where your own sound judgment and the empathy quotient come in.[9]

WHAT EVERY SUCCESSFUL PERSON NEEDS TO KNOW ABOUT SALES, AND HOW TO TEACH YOURSELF

Some years ago, Robert Kiyosaki, author of the internationally bestselling personal finance book *Rich Dad, Poor Dad: What the Rich Teach Their Kids About Money—That The Poor and Middle Class Do Not!*, was in Singapore and granted an interview with a local newspaper journalist.

As they were chatting before the interview, the journalist mentioned that she had written several novels, but they had not been successful in the marketplace. She confessed to Robert, "Someday, I'd like to be a bestselling author like you."

Robert had seen her articles and saw she had writing talent. He asked her why she thought she hadn't been successful. Robert narrates what happened next:

> "My work does not seem to go anywhere," [the journalist] said quietly. "Everyone says that my novels are excellent, but nothing happens. So I keep my job with the paper. At least it pays the bills. Do you have any suggestions?"
>
> "Yes, I do," I said brightly. "A friend of mine here in Singapore runs a school that trains people to sell. He runs sales-training courses for many of the top corporations here in Singapore, and I think attending one of his courses would greatly enhance your career."
>
> She stiffened. "Are you saying I should go to school to learn to sell?"

I nodded.

"You aren't serious, are you?"

Again I nodded. "What is wrong with that?"

"I have a master's degree in English literature. Why should I go to school to learn to be a salesperson? I am a professional. I went to school to be trained in a profession so I would not have to be a salesperson. I hate salespeople. All they want is money. So tell me why I should study sales?" She was now packing her briefcase forcibly. The interview was over.

On the coffee table sat a copy of my first book, *If You Want to Be Rich and Happy, Don't Go to School: Ensuring Lifetime Security for Yourself and Your Children.* I picked it up, as well as the notes she had jotted down on her legal pad. "Do you see this?" I said pointing to her notes.

She looked down at her notes. "What," she said, confused.

On her pad, she had written "Robert Kiyosaki, best-selling author."

"It says 'best-selling author,' not best 'writing' author. . . . I am a terrible writer. You are a great writer. I went to sales school. You have a master's degree. Put them together and you get a 'best-selling author' and a 'best-writing author.'"

Anger flared from her eyes. "I'll never stoop so low as to learn how to sell. People like you have no business writing. I am a professionally trained writer and you are a salesman. It's not fair."[1]

The journalist exhibits the precise mentality that I hope my own book will sledgehammer out of you, if there's even a molecule of that mentality still lurking within you.

I call it the "I'm Above Learning How to Sell" mentality, and it's pretty much the bread and butter of our nation's higher-education system. What *they* sell *you* is the idea that, if you get enough of their credentials, enough letters after your name, then financial security, a great career, and real-world success will just fall in your lap without your having to do anything.

To the extent you haven't achieved the material results you want in the real world, it's because you've bought into this "I'm Above Learning to Sell" mentality. Expunge it from your system. Now. Every last drop of it.

I'm not just talking about selling products and services for money. (If you work in a large corporation and you're not in the sales department, for example, you may not be in a position to sell your company's products or services to clients.) No matter *what* you're up to in life, you have to sell something, whether it's selling an employer on why he should hire you, selling your boss on why she should promote you, selling the members of a corporate meeting on your brilliant idea, selling your employees or direct-reports on why they should put in more effort, selling a donor on why she should donate to your cause, or selling supporters on why they should join your movement to save the whatever or overthrow the what-have-you. Sales is simply persuasive face-to-face communication. It's relevant anytime you are talking with someone and you want a specific outcome to arise from the conversation.

No single skill you could possibly learn correlates more directly with your real-world success than learning sales. And yet—surprise, surprise—it's nowhere to be found on the curriculum of formal education, from elementary school through graduate school. No wonder there are so many broke and unemployed people with undergraduate and graduate degrees.

(And don't tell me that there are *more* broke people without the degrees. True, but beside the point. If they learned to sell, like nearly all the dropouts I feature in this book did, they wouldn't be broke for long.)

Robert Kiyosaki (http://www.richdad.com) is famous for having two dads, his biological father, whom he describes in his books as "poor dad," and a mentor who took him under his wing early, whom he describes as "rich dad." His poor dad had a PhD, worked at high levels within the state education bureaucracy of Hawaii, and—Kiyosaki says in his books—never accumulated much money. His rich dad mentor, Kiyosaki says, had an eighth-grade education, was a successful entrepreneur, and made millions by the time of the mentor's death.

Robert, who listened to his poor dad's advice and graduated college, but listened to his rich dad's advice on almost all other matters related to money, told me: "I learned nothing about sales in school. I love education—but education that makes me rich. In my first job after leaving the Marines, I went to work for Xerox. I was formally trained by Xerox to sell. Every day, five or six hours a day, I'm being trained to sell. How to overcome the fear of rejection. The biggest lesson I had to learn was how to fail *faster*. That was the biggest one because every day, I'd take three sales calls, take three rejections. So all my rich dad said to me was, 'You've got to increase your rejections. The faster you fail, the more you are going to learn.' That's why when I left Xerox at five o'clock, I would go up the street to this nonprofit charity, helping homeless kids, and I would dial for donations at night. I had a goal every night of getting rejected thirty times. The more I increased my failure rate, the more success I had at Xerox."

You can't truly learn anything about sales until the "I'm Above Learning How to Sell" mentality is fully expunged from your system. So, just in case your nose is still turned up even one or two degrees at the idea that you should learn to sell, I'm sharing with you a little talk I transcribed, by Bryan, who mastered the skill of selling in his twenties (it's part of why he's so successful) and who has taught me a great deal of what I know about sales. I think the relevance of this talk to what we've been discussing so far in this book will be screamingly obvious.

■ THE MYTH OF HIGHER EDUCATION
BY BRYAN FRANKLIN

There is a myth in our system about careers and money that most of us have totally bought into. And the reason the myth is in our system is because it was put there by the marketing machine of higher education.

The myth is that if you get better at your craft, if you get better at what you do, you will be more likely to be successful. So, if you're a doctor and you become a *better* doctor than others (by going to the right schools, studying harder, etc.), then you'll be a more successful doctor. If you're a mechanic and you become a *better* mechanic, you'll be a more successful mechanic. If you're a software engineer, and you become a *better* software engineer, you'll be a more successful software engineer.

This is the myth. Why does the higher education machine want us to believe this myth? Well, what are they selling in all of their graduate and professional programs? They're selling, "Be better at your craft. Just take our master's program!"

Yet, if you take the pool of the *world's best* at a particular craft—medicine, law, writing, music, corporate management, acting, *anything*—their success is all over the map. Some of them are wildly successful, some of them don't have two nickels to rub together. You take the world's best actors, from a craft point of view, and some of them are superstars. Some of them are asking you if you'd like to see a dessert menu.

Furthermore, if you take any craft and you look at the most successful people in that craft as a group, their skill level is all over the map. Some are fantastic, and some are laughably bad—in fact, for some of them, you can't understand how they got to where they are, given how bad they are. This isn't true only in acting, it's true in every field.

That's because *success is its own skill*. There's the skill of the craft. Then there's the skill of success. It's an independent education. My experience is, it takes about the same amount of effort to learn the skill of success as it does to learn the skill of the craft itself. So, it might take years to really learn what you need to learn to become a great engineer, or an attorney, or a musician, or a manager.

Well, guess what? It's going to take years to fully own the skill of being *successful* at your craft as well. Fortunately, you can learn this skill of success while you also learn your craft. But don't get fooled into thinking you *only* need to get good at your craft and you'll be set financially. That's the lie of higher education.

Of course, I'm not suggesting that you should be *bad* at your craft or neglect it. While it is true that you don't actually need to be very good at what you do to be successful at it (because success is its own skill), it's just not very classy, or fun, to be successful at your craft when you're not that good at the craft itself. I recommend that you become *awesome* at the skill of your craft, but also become awesome at the skill of success. And don't ever get caught up in the delusion that they're the same thing, because they just aren't.

So, the skill of success. What is it?

In my experience, the skill of success breaks down into three things. The skill of marketing. The skill of sales. And the skill of leadership.

First, marketing. Throw away everything you think marketing is because most of the marketing you've been exposed to, which makes you sick to your stomach, is crappy marketing that doesn't work anyway. Fortunately, you don't have to learn that.

You just have to learn effective marketing, and effective marketing is really simple. It's the ability to get people who don't know about you to know about you. That's it. If you can get people who don't know about you, or your service or your company, to become aware of you, then you're successful in marketing. They didn't know about you, something happened, and now they know about you—that's successful marketing. [Michael's note to reader: direct-response marketing, which I talked about in the last chapter, combines marketing as Bryan has defined it here, plus sales as he defines it below, in one fell swoop.]

The second skill of success is sales. For some people sales is worse than marketing, and for others marketing is worse than sales. Either way, we have this belief in our culture that these two things are icky. That sense of ickiness is one of the things that perpetuates the lie that if you just get better at your craft, you'll be fine—you can just do what you do, without focusing on marketing or selling what you do, because marketing and sales are icky and low-integrity.

It's just not true. You *have* to be good at these things in order to be successful. If you think sales is sleazy, manipulative, or disgusting, it's because what you've been exposed to is bad salesmanship. Any time we're exposed to people who are totally incompetent at their job, it feels like crap. If you're being "sold at," and they're not connecting with you at all, and they have no idea what you want or need, and they're just "blah blah blahing" on about their product or service, they actually don't know the first thing about sales, and their incompetence is what feels like crap to you.

When sales is done well, it's a really simple discovery conversation. The conversation basically follows the following contours: "Hey, what do you really want? What matters to you? Well, this is my ability to provide that. Does that seem like a match to you?" It's just that simple. Sales is the ability to take someone who knows about you, but who has never given you money, and turn them into someone who knows about you and who is also giving you money, if what you're offering is a good match for them. That's it.

In the Fortune 1000, what position is the most highly paid? You think it's the CEO?

Nope.

It's the #1 sales rep.

Second most highly paid?

The #2 sales rep.

Third most highly paid?

VP of sales.

Fourth?

CEO.

The person making the most money in the company is often two or three levels down from the CEO. Why? Because without that star sales rep, 20, 30, 40, 50, or 60 percent of the business of that company would not exist. Why is that individual able to make such an impact on the business? Because that sales rep understands the skill of selling.

The third skill of success is leadership. Leadership boils down to the ability to change the hearts and minds of people. *Not* controlling people; it's a myth that the leader has control. Your leadership consists precisely in your ability to define a future you don't have control over. The leader doesn't have control over what the employees do; she has to *influence* the employees to do what she thinks is best. The more you understand that you have no control at all, and you're dealing with a bunch of people with free will who are going to do what they want anyway, the more you realize that the skill of leadership really boils down to the skill of influence. If you're taking on a role of leading others, people don't do what you say just because you say it; they only do what you say if they're inspired. Which means, you have to study "What influences people?"

[Michael's note to reader: Seth Godin, in *Tribes: We Need You to Lead Us*—which you absolutely must read if you care about the themes in this chapter and the last—spreads the message that "Leadership is the new marketing." I would also add that leadership is the new sales. And good sales is really a form of leadership. And good marketing is also really a form of leadership. When done with integrity, they all blend into each other; they are really all aspects of the same phenomenon. What is that phenomenon? Bryan calls it "guiding others into a future that would not have happened otherwise."]

If you can get people who don't know about you to know about you (marketing), and you can convert them into customers (sales), and once they're customers, you can lead them from point A to point B, you can accomplish anything on the planet.

When you wrap these skills of success around your craft, you can become wildly successful at whatever it is you do. Creating stained glass. Being a lawyer. Running a company. Being a real estate investor. Because being successful at all of these disciplines—indeed at *any* discipline—requires these three fundamental skills of success.

If you want to take your success to the next level, it's really simple. Just press Pause on learning about your craft. Admit that you're good enough for now. (You can always get better later.) And press Play/Record on your learning about marketing, sales, and leadership. If you invest in being better at marketing, sales, and leadership, then the sky's the limit to your success.

There is knowledge in the world about how to do these three things well. They may be a mystery to you, or they may not be, but they're not a mystery at large. There are actually simple things that every one of us can do to be quite good at these things. In fact, the bar is so low, for marketers, salespeople, and leaders—the bar is so laughably low—that you have to get like a D in these things to be extraordinary. It's the easiest class you'll ever take.

■ HOW I LEARNED SALES BY READING JUST ONE BOOK

I am going to now *teach you* how to *teach yourself* the skill of high-integrity, zero-sleaze selling. I'm going to teach you this by telling you the story of how *I* learned to sell.

For most of my life, from my adolescence throughout my twenties, I held the attitude of the journalist in Kiyosaki's story. "I'm Above Learning How to Sell." Around age fifteen, I became a convert to radical environmentalism, and I began piling up various worldviews and ideologies that separated me more and more stridently from mainstream capitalist society. First it was vegetarianism, then veganism, then Buddhism, then ecofeminism, then deep ecology, then primitivism. Then vegan-Buddhist-ecofeminist-deep-ecologist-primitivism. I won't even try to explain what all those terms are, but suffice it to say that throughout my teens and twenties, I didn't really believe in the value of learning sales.

Over this period, I did slowly begin shedding some of the more rigid aspects of these belief systems. But for me, the crisis and tipping point occurred in my late twenties, when I was almost totally broke as an aspiring writer (which I wrote about in Success Skill #1), and I realized I needed to stop pretending as if money was irrelevant to my life, and start learning about the way money actually worked.

Fast-forward to age thirty-one. By that age, I had definitely started to get some financial mojo going in my life and was supporting myself decently as a freelance book proposal writer. But I still hadn't really learned sales. I still basically subscribed to the view, which Bryan dissected for us: If I'm good at what I do, shouldn't that be good enough to make people want to pay me for it? I'm not going to *force* people to buy something they don't already want. That would be uncouth, wouldn't it?

What I still didn't realize—and what most people who are resistant to learning sales don't realize—is that there's a lot of room between just hanging out your shingle and hoping people show up, on the one hand, and *forcing* and *manipulating* people to buy things they don't want, on the other hand. Most people, for reasons of integrity, don't want to do the latter. (And thank goodness.) But they think the only other option is to do the former, so that's what they do to sell themselves: diddly-squat. This is where the mistake lies. There's a lot of room between these two poles, between pressuring people and doing diddly-squat. Between those two poles lie options that both close the sale *and* exhibit high class and integrity.

What first woke me up to this distinction was a half-day coaching session Jena and I paid for with Victor Cheng (http://www.victorcheng.com), a business growth expert who is often quoted by reporters from Fox News, MSNBC, *Inc. Magazine, Entrepreneur, Forbes, Time,* and the *Wall Street Journal.*

After our epiphany with the sales letter for Jena's business at the beginning of 2009 (described in Success Skill #3), we both were forever "sold" on the value of making serious investments in improving our marketing skills. (See Success Skill #5 on investing for success.) So we flew out to California and jointly hired Victor for a $4,000 half-day of coaching for Jena on her business; I got to be a fly on the wall and soak up the teachings as Victor coached her.

In this session, Victor taught Jena an approach to sales inspired by the book *SPIN Selling* by Neil Rackham. It turns out that a team of over one hundred researchers with a budget of $1 million, led by Rackham, analyzed thirty-five thousand real-world, in-person sales sessions made by ten thousand salespeople in twenty-three countries over twelve years. All to figure out the answer to one simple question: "What the hell works in sales?" (My phrasing, not theirs.)

The basic answer is quite simple and refreshing. Everything

you *thought* sales was about, including the scripts, pressure, pitching, gimmicky "closing" techniques, sleazy guilt tripping, truth stretching—in other words, all the stuff that makes you want to *run the other way* when you hear the word "sales"—doesn't actually work very well. Particularly not on "major sales" in which the buyer perceives the price point as significant, the sale happens over many conversations, and the buyer is likely going to have an ongoing business relationship with you or your firm after the sale.

What works then? It's simple. While we normally think of salespeople as fast-talking slicksters, it turns out that the more the *prospect* talks—about their problems, their fears, their frustrations related to the needs your product or service addresses—the more likely they will want to do business with you. Which means, effective sales isn't about spewing off a slick pitch. It's about asking a lot of questions. The *right questions.* And then listening.

What are the right questions? Any question that gets the prospect deeply connected with their frustrations, fears, and desires around the problem that your product or service addresses.

Victor demonstrated his approach on Jena. I was astonished. He knew very little about Jena's business, weight loss, yet simply by asking the right questions, he was able to sell *her* very effectively on her own services! In this improv dialogue, Victor spontaneously played the salesperson, and Jena played a hypothetical "prospect" in her business:

VICTOR: So how much weight do you want to lose?

PROSPECT: About twenty pounds.

VICTOR: And why do you want to lose that weight?

PROSPECT: I want to feel good and attractive.

VICTOR: And why is feeling good and attractive important to you?

PROSPECT: I'd like to be in a relationship, and I just don't feel confident around men. I walk into a room and I feel like I'm invisible, or like my body's disgusting. I feel so out of control around food.

VICTOR: And if you did have more confidence in your life—walking into the room and not feeling self-conscious—how would that impact your life?

PROSPECT: Well, hopefully I'd get into a relationship and have more friends and be less lonely. And hopefully it would benefit my career too.

VICTOR: Let's talk about the first one. Talk about being lonely. How does that feel right now? What is it like?

PROSPECT: It's terrible. I go home and just eat cookies for company. It's a vicious cycle because all I can think of is the cookies. After I eat the packet of cookies I feel sick and I don't want to go out, even if my friends are calling me to go out.

VICTOR: What would happen if this problem didn't get resolved?

PROSPECT: I'd be alone, I'd be miserable, I'd have no kids.

VICTOR: And how would you feel about that?

PROSPECT: Terrible. I want to be a mother. I want to have a family. I want to fulfill that role.

VICTOR: And what you're telling me is, the weight today is quite possibly getting in the way of your life, the unfolding path of your life. What is it worth to you to fix that problem and have the life you've always wanted?

PROSPECT: A lot.

VICTOR: On a scale of 1 to 10, with 1 being not important at all, and 10 being extremely important, immediately, where are you?

PROSPECT: 9.5.

As we went more into this sales demonstration, Victor commented to us: "You see, I haven't 'sold' anything. All I've done is ask questions. But the questions go beyond the superficial. They go into the deepest levels of why they want this change in their life.

"The reason this method works is that people's underlying motivations are very different. Two people could walk into your business wanting to lose twenty pounds, but for very different reasons, at either the conscious level or the unconscious level. If you say, 'I can help you lose twenty pounds,' without going into why they want it, then you're no different from anybody else. But if you can get into the underlying motivations—they're not buying the twenty-pound weight-loss coaching. They're buying a new career. Or a shot at having a great relationship. Or a shot at being a mother, with kids.

"And if you can talk with them about *that*, and help them solve *that* problem—the underlying motivation—then they'll want to do business with you. Because they can tell you actually get what's going on inside of them, you care about what they care about, and you're helping them with something that is actually very deep to them, not a superficial problem. If you try to sell a solution before you've mutually agreed on the problem you're trying to solve—which is what most salespeople do—people mostly aren't interested."

What I learned from Victor, and from reading *SPIN Selling*, is this: if you're talking with someone about their innermost needs and desires, the *last* thing you want to do is throw a bunch of manipulative pressure on them. All that's called for is: get to the heart of the matter. Why do they *really* want this change in their life? What's *really* behind the desire for this change?

And, once you've inquired thoroughly with your prospect about what's going on at that core emotional level, if it turns out that what you're offering honestly and effectively addresses that, then great—you're a match, and it's likely you'll do business together. And if not, then you refer them to someone who *can* help them with that. At no point would you ever try to manipulate or pressure someone into buying something that is not a great match for their deepest desires and needs.

After Victor's demonstration, both Jena and I bought *SPIN Selling* and read and absorbed every word. This single book obliterates the need for any more sleazy, pushy, aggressive, annoying sales tactics on the planet. And sales becomes—breathe a sigh of relief—an honest conversation between two authentic human beings.

Once Jena and I began honestly talking with and listening to our prospects, on an emotional level, about their deepest wants, needs, fears, and desires, rather than subjecting them to some sales "pitch" about our services, our businesses began flourishing. It turns out—surprise, surprise—people don't really want to be "pitched" at. They want you to listen to them; they want you to hear them; they want you to *get* them; and they want to trust your integrity that you will only sell them something they'll end up being happy with, so that you can continue to do business together in the future. And if you can communicate all of these, authentically, they'll want to do business with you.

Of course, I never learned any of this in college. In fact, I never learned *anything* in college about how to get people to want to hire me or do business with me. Which, if you think about it, is kinda strange. Selling a kid an expensive, potentially debt-laden investment in human capital, so that he may increase the value of his labor in the marketplace, without being sure he knows how to *sell* that labor to the marketplace, is sort of like selling a kid an expensive, debt-laden car, without being sure he knows how to drive.

Victor says: "The most useful class I took in college was public speaking. I use it a surprising amount. The second most useful class I took in college was how to be a listener—I took a peer counselor class for suicide prevention, which was all about how to listen without judgments. Thus, the most useful classes I took in college were not part of the main academic experience. A lot of the skills you need to be successful—and I mean, you *need* them if you want to be successful—they're just not taught in college. Even in most business schools.

"I remember one year, I looked at the course curriculum for Harvard Business School, Wharton Business School, and Stanford Business School. Between them, they offered somewhere around four hundred classes. Out of those four hundred classes, there was not *one* class on sales. Wharton had one class on sales force management, but there was no class on sales.

"If you talk to billionaires and millionaires, and you ask them, 'How important was sales to building your business?' you'll find out, it's like *half* the business. And none of the top schools teach it. Yet it's essential. So there's an obvious disconnect there.

"It's a huge problem, when people don't know how to sell. Formal schools teach skills, but they don't teach how to *sell* or *market* those skills. So, the graphic designer says, 'I design great graphics.

I ought to go in business myself.' Or the medical doctor who works for a practice says, 'I'm good at helping patients. I ought to have my own practice.'

"These people are frustrated. They want control over their own work and destiny. They think, 'I'm working for the man, and he's paying me twenty bucks an hour to do whatever work. And he's charging eighty dollars an hour to the client.' They see that, and they think, 'That guy's making sixty bucks an hour off of me! He's taking me for a ride! I'm fed up with this, I'm going to go into business for myself, so instead of making the twenty dollars an hour, I'm gonna make the eighty!'

"So the person sets up shop, they get their business cards printed up, they open for business, and what happens on the first day? Absolutely nothing.

"What they took for granted was the business owner developed the process for getting clients. Without that, you get no money. It was worth the sixty dollars. They don't realize why the sixty dollars was earned by the business owner. The practitioner just sees it as someone stealing their money. Until they try to go into business for themselves, and then they suffer for a couple of years, and they don't try to learn those skills of sales and marketing, and can only tolerate it for so long, and then they give up and go back working for someone else.

"Most people who are successful in their field, you'll find, are very good at selling. Either selling their ideas, selling to get customers, or selling to recruit people to support their vision. Most colleges don't teach that. But it's very hard to imagine a business being successful without somebody being good at selling. It's a *crucial* skill to develop, through either direct experience, or mentorship, or training, or workshops.

"Read about it, study it, and frankly, just do it. A lot of it is trial and error. All experience comes from mistakes. Either making them yourself, or learning from someone else who has. It all counts. But unfortunately, experience is not something you get in college. Mastery comes from doing. Either do it yourself, or learn it from someone who did."

Victor's point about learning from other people's experience is crucial. The book *SPIN Selling* summarizes the research and experience of one hundred researchers who spent a million bucks and twelve years trying to figure out a kind of sales that both makes the customer happy and closes the deal. The fruits of this effort are available at your local bookstore, or online, for around *thirty bucks.*

The originators of *SPIN Selling* (http://www.huthwaite.com) also offer two-day sales trainings all around the country for around $1,600. I haven't attended one personally, but just their book alone had such a profound impact on my life and business, that would be the first place I'd look if I wanted a more intensive in-person study of sales.

My point is not necessarily that you should go out and plunk down $1,600 on a sales training right away (though I'll bet it would be worth every penny). My point is, the information and training to learn this stuff is available to you, at a price within reach for most people reading this book.

Think about it. A typical college course costs between $500 and $5,000, depending on the overall tuition for the semester and how much grant aid you're getting. What do you think, in the long run, is going to have a bigger impact on your life? A $1,600 training, from one of the top sales experts in the world, about how you sell your ideas, projects, and services in the real world? Or a couple of courses of your typical college fare?

Here are some courses available today on campuses across America:

- The Vampire in Literature and Film, at the University of Wisconsin at Madison. From the course description: "Since the problematic image of the vampire vacillates between the real and the imaginary, this will be a truly interdisciplinary course, spanning analysis drawn from medical anthropology to the discussions on literary and cinematic representations of the ancient creature of horror."[2]

- Color Me Cool: A Survey of Contemporary Graphic Novels, at my alma mater, Brown. From the course catalog: "Surveys a variety of comic books and graphic novels, both mainstream and independent. The emphasis, however, will be on the independent graphic novel. Students will also read history and criticism to understand better the context from which the books emerge and to grasp more firmly their visual and textual aesthetics."[3]

- Topics in Comparative Media: American Pro Wrestling, at MIT. From the course description: "This class will explore the cultural history and media industry surrounding the masculine drama of professional wrestling. Beginning with wrestling's roots in sport and carnival, the class examines how new technologies and changes in the television industry led to evolution for pro wrestling style and promotion and how shifts in wrestling characters demonstrate changes in the depiction of American masculinity. . . . Students may have previous knowledge of wrestling but are not required to, nor are they required to be a fan." The MIT webpage for the course proudly links to PDF files of term papers written by previous students, including the paper "Women's Roles in Professional Wrestling, Examined through the Lita-Trish Rivalry."[4]

What's actually happening at colleges across America, among professors, students, and college administrators, is an elaborate game of "Let's Pretend." Professors and administrators pretend that bullshit courses like these might be vaguely related to something valuable to a student's later life. And students pretend that, by taking these courses for easy As, they're getting an "education." For four years, all goes well with the game, and all groups are happy with it, none more so than on graduation day, when the proud student gets a piece of paper from the professors and administrators certifying to the world that she is now "educated."

However, the whole charade implodes when the student goes out into the real world, thinking that the marketplace will value her acuity in vampire-ology or wrestling analysis. It reminds me of a T-shirt I saw once: "I have a liberal arts degree. Would you like fries with that?"

But having a degree in marketing, economics, or business, or even an MBA, isn't much better. As we've seen, even in business schools, you don't tend to get the reality-based skills and experience that will actually lead you to success in your career.

Jena and I spent the equivalent of one college course at a private college, $4,000, to hire Victor for a half-day of private coaching. That half-day, including the referral to read *SPIN Selling*, helped double both of our businesses in the middle of a nasty recession. In the spirit of Victor's admonition to learn from other people's experiences, you don't even need to spend the $4,000 to get that particular piece of advice now—you can get it right here. Spend $30 on *SPIN Selling* by Neil Rackham. It will be worth entire *years* of today's college education.

■ IF YOU WANT TO HELP PEOPLE, LEARN HOW TO SELL

David Ash has spent a great deal of time in the Downtown Eastside of Vancouver, one of the poorest and most crime-ridden neighborhoods in North America. There, he has helped chronically homeless women get back on their feet. Most of the women have been homeless for years or even decades on end. Most have been victims of severe sexual or physical abuse and have struggled with serious mental illness and/or substance addiction (heroin, crack, cocaine, crystal meth). And many of them either are or have been active in the city's sex trade; most are HIV-positive.

David has helped them get off the streets, start eating square meals, clean up off drugs, find appropriate help for their emotional and mental health issues, and get treatment for their illnesses. He is not, however, a social worker; at least that's not his main gig. He's a real estate investor. He owns a 135,000-square-foot hockey arena and sports center for kids in his community, along with many other commercial and residential properties in a large portfolio. With his winnings from his career success, he bought what is now perhaps the property nearest to his heart: a run-down boardinghouse in the Downtown Eastside, which he has turned into the Vivian, a minimum-barrier transitional house for women who get kicked out of every other shelter in town.

But David, fifty-one, was not always so successful, nor so philanthropically oriented. In fact, for many years in his childhood and teens, it looked like his life was heading in the wrong direction.

David grew up in working-class West End of Montreal, part of the English-speaking section of town. "I hung out with the wrong guys, I didn't do well in school, I was high-strung, probably ADHD. Both my parents left school after seventh grade, so education wasn't a major emphasis in my life.

"My mother grew up a ward of the court—at age two, in the midst of the Great Depression, she was taken from her single mother, who was a teenage orphan. She moved from foster home to foster home, where she sometimes suffered physical and sexual abuse. When I was about twelve, she collapsed under the burden of these painful experiences. She had a major nervous breakdown and was hospitalized. For the rest of my childhood, she was in and out of psychiatric wards, coming home heavily medicated, attempting suicide, then starting the whole cycle again. Unfortunately, she eventually left our home and went on her own. She refused hospitalization and other attempts at help, and ended up on the streets.

"School was a gong show for me. My educational career started off with a bang. I failed grade one. It went downhill from there. In grade seven, I had skipped 264 periods, they told me when I came back for grade eight. I was having fun with my friends on the streets, with virtually no supervision at home. I finally dropped out in grade eleven."

David moved to Ottawa to live with his brother, and took on a job as a pot scrubber at a YMCA. For most people who hear this kind of story, that's the end: kid drops out of high school, gets a dead-end job, doesn't go anywhere in life, becomes another high school dropout statistic.

Yet, here's where those stories go wrong. If you have the *will* and the *drive* to better yourself, you usually can, no matter how much (or little) formal education you have. There's no doubt that, on average, dropouts do worse in life than people who complete their formal education. This is probably because people who drop out—on average—have either a lower will to succeed or have faced exceptional personal challenges at a very young age.

But averages always belie a great deal of variation within. If you happen to have or develop the will to succeed—or are lucky enough to find a person who inspires it within you—you can learn everything you need, with or without formal education.

"If there's one thing I had a lot of, it was street smarts," David continues. "At one point, I met a real estate salesman in Ottawa who saw something in me, and he said, 'You should become a real estate salesman.' Keep in mind, my parents had never owned a home. I didn't even know what the word 'mortgage' meant. But something about me respected this man, and I decided to take a six-week, full-time real estate license course he told me about.

"I decided I had to do something with my life, and sales seemed like a natural fit, since you don't need much formal training, and the upside was significant. I'd gotten messages my whole life that I wasn't going to amount to anything, but I had a strong sense of self, and I knew I wanted this. I never connected the stuff they were trying to get me to study in high school to any kind of career benefit, but the connection here was very clear."

David committed totally to passing the course—the first time he ever really committed to any educational endeavor in his life.

Each day, he would head straight home to the apartment he shared with his brother after class ended at three, sit at a little desk, crack open his binder, and start reading a page. If he didn't understand it, he'd read it again. And again. Sometimes he'd spend half an hour on one page. He'd then rewrite each page in his own shorter version. Every night until he went to bed, all day Saturday, and all day Sunday, with Friday nights off. "I studied four times harder than most of my classmates who were mature adults. Many were educated professionals with university degrees."

David passed the course—he passed one crucial test by a single point—and got an entry-level sales job at Century 21. They started sending him to motivational seminars available to all the sales reps. "There was a guy at the front of the room giving a motivational talk on positive mental attitude. And of course, coming from where I'd come from, from the home I'd come from, and my educational experience—I had never heard those three words, 'positive mental attitude,' put together before in the same phrase. So you've got this guy in the front of the room saying that, with a positive mental attitude, you can achieve anything you want in life. He's saying that, no matter where you come from, no matter what your background, if you work hard, if you do this, if you do that, you can achieve great things in life.

"I'm sitting there, and it was like a religious revival meeting for me. My soul swelled. I felt like I was the only guy in the room, and he was speaking directly to me. It was the first time anyone in my life had said, 'You can do something with your life, no matter who you are, no matter where you're from.' I bought what he was selling, I went out the door, and I believed it, and I started consuming any and all motivational material I could get my hands on. *Think and Grow Rich* by Napoleon Hill. For all the guys I know that have started with nothing, that book has probably led to more people becoming financially independent than any other book.

"I became a committed self-studier in motivation and success for the rest of my life. Books, seminars, workshops. In my parents' view, life was basically a burden and challenge, to be survived at best. The stuff I was studying now knocked me out of that mentality. As a mature adult, I now see that much of this thinking, which is powerful and practical, is actually incomplete." David has since given his life deeper meaning and direction with a strong personal faith, as a Christian. "However, I really do credit these investments in motivational and self-help psychology with helping me realize I could achieve what I wanted to achieve in life. It broke down some major mental barriers created in my childhood." (See Success Skill #5, on investing in your own human capital and earning power.)

David began learning the craft of sales, first in real estate, then in life insurance sales. Soon he was earning upward of $100,000 per year, in his twenties, with no high school diploma. If you get good at sales, following all the steps I describe in this chapter, six figures is absolutely within your reach. Sales is the magic skill that opens doors and fills bank accounts.

However, David's path to success was not free and clear yet; he still had a major roadblock. "As is common for sales guys," David says, "I was looking at the top line, not the bottom line." He was enjoying the money that was coming in, living a high-rolling life, and not really paying attention to where it went. Soon he was bankrupt.

"I was twenty-nine, and I said, 'OK, I've got to get my act together.' That's when I read *The Richest Man in Babylon* by George Clason, a classic book on the importance of financial discipline and savings. I had no system, I had no planning, no structure, I was just this guy making money and spending it, figuring it would all work out in the end. I had no real discipline. I figured, I've got to get some process here, because I had too much money come and go as a young man."

His wife, Lise, read the book at the same time he did, and they started instituting some very basic principles outlined in that book: saving 10 percent of all they earned, investing it for the future. That was the beginning of the transformation toward financial responsibility in their lives. They'd save up, buy a little rental property. Then they'd save the income from that, buy another one, exercise strict financial discipline, until they built up to buy bigger properties. He now owns office buildings, retail centers, and a huge hockey arena in his community, employing about thirty-five full- and part-time people. He currently owns and manages a quarter-million square feet of commercial real estate.

Eventually, with his newfound wealth, David decided to come full circle. He spent $1.2 million to buy a twenty-four-room boardinghouse in the middle of Downtown Eastside Vancouver, renovate it, and convert it into the Vivian, named in honor of his mother.

The Vivian is what's known as a "minimum barrier" environment. The women who live there have typically failed out of other rooming houses and shelters. They become locked in a cycle of jails, psychiatric wards, and the streets. The aim of the Vivian is to get them out of this cycle. (See http://www.thedagroup.ca for a moving video about the project.)

David says in the video, "Eventually my mother's mental illness overwhelmed her, and she digressed to a life on the streets—a life very much like the life that these women here lead. In 1999 she died, alone, on the streets, in Halifax, Nova Scotia. These experiences tore us apart as a family. We loved her dearly, we wanted to help her, but we couldn't help her. Now that I have the capacity to help women like her, of course I'm deeply committed to doing that."

David is making a massive positive impact on these women's lives—in many cases *saving* their lives—and he would not have been able to do it had he not learned the art of sales at a young age.

With sales, you can achieve just about anything you want in life. The tougher the challenge you face, the bigger the change you want to make, the better sales skills you'll need to develop!

What impact are *you* going to make with your newfound sales skills?

∎ MARIJO'S STORY

A young single mother of three invested almost one fifth of her entire remaining savings in an urgent bid to provide a better future for her children.

The investment was $0.25, out of $1.35 remaining in her checking account.

It was 1965, and Marijo had been asked to leave her Catholic high school just after she turned seventeen, her senior year, when a bump started to show on her belly. She married the father that year, and went on to be a stay-at-home mom of three for eight years.

When she turned twenty-five, Marijo and her husband divorced, but her ex did not keep current on his child support payments, paying a sporadic $50 here and $20 there. As a previous full-time homemaker, without a high school diploma, she had never held a paying job before. Her parents were shocked and embarrassed by her behavior. ("First, Catholic girls don't get pregnant at sixteen. And second, if they do, they don't get divorced," Marijo explained.) Her two sisters, high school students, spent most of their free time helping with the kids.

She was surviving. Still, her life savings were about to hit zero, and she decided to do something about it, fast, so she could support her children.

Marijo told me what happened next, as we sipped tea in the comfort of her well-appointed living room. The conversation was enhanced by the soundtrack of the mast of her own sailboat clanging lazily in the breeze, just beneath her living room window, opening directly over the exclusive marina in the San Francisco Bay, which houses her sailboat.

I took a quarter out of the remaining money in my checking account, got on the L in Chicago, and went downtown. You could get a transfer and come back for twenty-five cents. That was just within my budget. . . . [Laughing.]

I got off, and walked into the first door off the train stop. It happened to be a charter bus company. I walked through the rows of buses in the garage, into the office, and said, "I'd like to talk to the person who hires salespeople."

And the guy behind the counter said, "We don't have any salespeople."

"Well, how do you get customers?" I asked.

"They call us up."

And I said, perfectly innocently, like it just popped out of my mouth, "So *that's* why there are so many busses parked in the garage!"

He was taken aback. He didn't laugh, for sure. He didn't like it. But there was something about that comment that rang true.

I said, "OK, how about this. Why don't you make a list of the ten people you *wish* would call you up, who have never called. Your dream customers. If I can bring you three of them as customers, will you hire me?"

He laughed, and he said, "Sure." He wrote down the Chicago Blackhawks, the Board of Education, a ski club, and some other names.

The next day, I called and found out who does field trips for the Board of Education. I took another quarter, went into town, and met with the woman. I told her my sob story. I said, "Please, just one field trip. I don't care where it is, what it's for. I just need *something*."

She said, "Oh, *honey*." She reached over her desk, and handed me a stack of files, which contained field trips for the next year. She gave me orders for every day for literally months to come.

My dad drove me to the Blackhawks office. I used my sob story mercilessly, and I got an order. The ski club was easier. I just talked to someone on the phone, and within a week I had agreements from all three.

I got the job. Seventy-five dollars a week. No commission at first. I was terrified of commission. I just wanted a paycheck. I knew if I got seventy dollars a week, I could live. That's what I asked for, and he gave me seventy-five.

In the three years I was there as their full-time salesperson, the profit of each single year exceeded the *revenues* of the owner's entire ten years in business before I got there. In my last year there, I arranged a deal where I got one dollar for every kid that took a tour I sold to the schools. Had he kept his word, that year I would have made $300,000. This was in the sixties, so that was like $2 million in today's dollars.

He said, "You don't really expect me to give you that kind of money, do you?" I think he gave me a $10,000 bonus or something. I was such a wimp then. I was grateful.

When I was ready to leave the company and move on to new things, he begged me to stay. He offered me 51 percent of the company if I would stay. I said no.

Marijo Franklin got married again. Her husband adopted her three children, and with him she had a fourth child—Bryan Franklin. With her finely developed sales skills, she took a job with the Chamber of Commerce, selling memberships. Soon she became one of the top-grossing representatives, among a pool of around eight hundred salespeople. With that record, she decided to walk into the national office. "I introduced myself to the vice president of sales and said, 'I think the way you're teaching people how to sell is really wrong, and if you wanted to get everybody to sell more, I could help you with that." (We need to come up with a female-centric equivalent phrase to "massive balls". . . Massive ovaries? She's got 'em!)

She got the job developing the national sales team. This is in the early '70s, when women just didn't do that kind of thing in corporations. On her first day on the job, on the executive floor, she asked where the ladies' room was. There was no ladies' room. ("We never thought we'd need a ladies' room on this floor," someone said to her.)

Marijo went on to hold a number of high-level sales positions, and then in the early eighties became one of the first executive coaches in the nation, pioneering the field. "At that time, when I said I was a 'coach,' people said, 'Oh, what team?'" Most women in daily contact with high-level executives were *secretaries*; certainly, most executives weren't asking (or paying) women for advice! In the late eighties she founded the California Leadership Center (http://www.california-leadership.com), and has built long-term client relationships with some of the most powerful leaders in Silicon Valley. She's earned millions of dollars throughout her career—and now spends time teaching real-world skills to at-risk youth and their parents, as part of a program she founded to help them create futures they can't even imagine.

One of the most powerful things about learning sales well, as Marijo did when she finally decided to take full responsibility for her young children, is that it knocks down nearly all traditional barriers around formal credentials, stereotypes, hiring protocols, and prejudices. Learn how to sell by creating trusting relationships, and everything else falls into place. The tools are readily available to you. All you need is the will.

HOW TO INVEST FOR SUCCESS

(The Art of Bootstrapping)

■ FROM HOMELESS TO BILLIONAIRE

At age twenty-three, John Paul DeJoria fit whatever stereotypes you might have about people who only have a high school diploma, with no college. He was earning very little money, his wife had just left him and his two-and-a-half-year-old son, he had been evicted from his apartment for lack of payments, and he moved with his son into a borrowed car. He drove around at night, homeless, collecting soda pop bottles for the recycling reward of $.05 for large and $.02 for small bottles, just to get by another day.

But John Paul was determined not to let his son starve. "We were down and out," he told one interviewer. "I had a child to feed. . . . There wasn't any time for poor me."[1]

Fortunately, John Paul had two things going for him: a strong work ethic and a street-smart education in how to get on his feet after being knocked down—often literally. He had received this education thanks to his hardscrabble upbringing on the streets. His immigrant parents divorced when he was two, and he was raised by his single mother in the barrios of Echo Park and East LA. He briefly flirted with gang life in the barrio, but soon he decided to stay on the right side of the law. He was certainly not a favorite with his teachers, however. When a teacher caught him passing notes with a friend, she castigated them in front of the

class: "These two people will never, ever succeed at anything in
life."[2] (His note-passing friend, Michelle Gilliam, later Michelle
Phillips, went on to become a founding member of the Mamas and
the Papas, which has sold over 100 million copies of its albums,
and she starred in the TV show *Knots Landing*.)

But, in this rough-and-tumble life, one thing John Paul learned
from a young age was how to hustle and generate cash for himself.
"My brother and I started selling Christmas cards and newspapers
when I was nine years old. I'd get up at four-thirty in the morning
with my brother, to fold and deliver papers every morning just
so we could live a little better," he told an interviewer.[3]

Now a single, homeless father, John Paul drew on this reserve
of ingenuity, resourcefulness, and enterprise—gained on the streets
as a kid—to pull himself up by his bootstraps and provide for his son.

"I had probably ten different jobs during that period," John
Paul told me. "Everything from selling insurance—I worked for
Connecticut General and John Hancock both. I drove a linen truck
around. My God, I worked for Dictaphone! I worked for A. B. Dick,
which is a photocopy company. I ended up working for *Time* as a
circulation manager, at twenty-six."

Things had stabilized to a certain degree for John Paul and his
son, but life wasn't rosy yet. They were living in a biker friend's
house, eating a very lean diet. "We lived on a very simple diet of
rice, potatoes, lettuce, cereal, canned soup, and macaroni and
cheese, but we managed."[4]

However, John Paul told me, at a certain point he began to hunger for a better future for himself and his son. "I asked my boss
what it takes to be a vice president, and he said, 'Well, you are
twenty-six years old, you are a high school graduate, but no college. Come back and ask me in ten years when you are around
thirty-five.' I thought, 'I don't want to do this when I am thirty-five
years old.'"

A friend connected John Paul to a job in sales in the hair care
products industry. He had developed sales skills during a brief
period selling encyclopedias door-to-door (long before the age of
Wikipedia!). "It's one of the greatest experiences of a lifetime. It
teaches you how to overcome rejection. No matter what you do,
whether it's a service, whether it's a product, whether you work
for someone else—you need to have some kind of experience
where you learn to overcome rejection and don't let it get you

down. Basically, you knock on a hundred doors and they all turn you away. Well, door number one hundred and one, you are just as enthusiastic as you were on door number one. That was a great experience."

John Paul and a friend named Paul Mitchell, a hairdresser, had an idea to start a hair products company. They thought they had a backer, but when the backer changed his mind, John Paul asked Paul what he could spare. Paul Mitchell came up with $350, and John Paul matched it. With $700, they started John Paul Mitchell Systems hair care products (http://www.paulmitchell.com).

The duo focused on two things: creating a great product and selling it well. "You don't want to be in the order business. You want to be in the reorder business. Big difference. My goal was not to sell something to somebody. My goal was to sell something that was so good, they want to reorder it again. And that's the idea that we came up with," John Paul told me.

They spent their $700 on designing the bottles in the company's now-iconic black-and-white—because it was cheaper to print than color. The rest of the materials were purchased on thirty-day terms, which gave them a very short window to make the company work. John Paul and Paul believed in their products and—using John Paul's sales skills—hustled the hell out of them. "I went knocking on doors, beauty salon doors, door-to-door selling our product and Paul did the same thing off the stage when he did beauty shows. And we kind of worked together as grass roots on. . . . [F]inally when the bill was due . . . [w]e didn't have enough to pay the bill, so it was, 'The check's in the mail.' Five days later, we had just enough to pay the bill."[5] John Paul told me, "No one wanted to invest in us. But once we were under way, it did grow organically. It took us about two years to pay our bills on time and have two thousand dollars left in the bank for my partner and me. Initially, that's how we knew we were successful at John Paul Mitchell Systems." The company kept growing organically, and growing, and growing. It now does over a billion dollars in annual sales, its products are sold in over one hundred thousand salons in nearly a hundred different countries, and the company employs thousands of people.

John Paul Mitchell, now a billionaire, has since diversified into many different businesses, including Patrón, now the world's top-selling brand of ultra-premium tequila (and one of my own favorite libations). He devotes a lot of his time to philanthropy. His favorite charities tend to focus on providing food and shelter to impoverished people in the United States and around the globe, including Africa and Thailand.

But, unlike most wealthy people who donate to help feed and house the poor, John Paul is one of the few who has himself been homeless, and on the brink of starvation, barely able to provide for his son at that time. Fortunately for him, his family, his customers, his thousands of employees, and all the people he helps around the world, John Paul learned in the school of hard knocks an important skill: how to pull himself up by his bootstraps. This is the topic of this chapter.

■ THE FINANCIAL LIFE OF A COLLEGE DROPOUT VERSUS AN IVY LEAGUE GRAD—MY WIFE VERSUS ME

Mating wisdom of times past—and still proffered by some with old-fashioned values today—holds that a woman should have slightly less educational attainment than the man she marries, and certainly less wealth.

In the education department, my wife and I followed the traditional script. I obtained one of the finest and most elite private college educations money can buy. My wife, Jena, dropped out of college during her junior year.

In terms of wealth, however . . . well, knowing this book, you can guess what's coming next.

My wife's net worth is roughly $500,000. In turn—while I'm proud of the earnings growth I've achieved over the last four years—I have only recently dug myself out of the debt I accumulated during my profligate and underearning twenties.

How does a college dropout amass a net worth of $500,000 by the time she's thirty-two? It has to do with how she invested.

No, I am *not* going to tell you some amazing trading secret or magic stock portfolio—because that's not how she did it. She did it by investing—and continually reinvesting—her time and money into her own earning power, a strategy I call Bootstrapping Your Own Education and Success. (I'll explain much more about the term "bootstrapping" shortly.)

Let's look into this story in more detail because it contains clues to one of the most important courses you'll ever take in your life: how to invest your time, money, and other resources for success. This is one of the key secrets that have allowed all the self-educated people I interview in this book, including John Paul and Jena, to become successful.

In 2001, at the age of twenty-two, Jena was living near an ashram in Pune, India, and studying yoga there. She had dropped out of college three years earlier, during her junior year, to follow a passion for yoga. She had been living in India for the previous two years, traveling around on $6,000 she had saved from teaching English in Martinique for nine months right after dropping out. She had been visiting ashrams and meditation centers, and even lived in nature for six months, barefoot. She lived in hammocks, in tents, even in caves.

So far, this does not sound like the story of a woman who was about to amass half a million dollars of net worth over the next decade.

At a certain point, however, Jena woke up to her financial situation. She had been living as a more or less penniless nomadic spiritual seeker in India, and she realized that—while this was cool for her early twenties—the penniless part wasn't going to stay cool for much longer. (I also spent my early twenties pursuing existential rather than financial rewards, before I realized that the piper had to be paid. Big difference between Jena and me, though: she wised up financially in her early twenties, whereas I remained in my state of denial about money throughout the rest of my twenties.)

"I was very scared," she says. "I remember, many times in India, thinking, 'Oh my God, I've gotten myself completely out of the system.' It was like the truism of women who give up their careers for the kids, and then the fear is, every year, they're that much less employable, that much more out of the system of money and career. In that spirit, I was concerned that I was screwing myself in terms of my career."

One of Jena's neighbors in Pune, who was visiting from New York, frequently smelled the food Jena was cooking, and they struck up a friendship, sharing many meals together.

It turned out that this man, Joshua Rosenthal, ran a nutrition school in New York called the Institute for Integrative Nutrition (http://www.integrativenutrition.com), licensed by New York State as a vocational school to train people to become health coaches.

Joshua said to her at one point, "Jena, I see how passionate you are about good food. You should come to my school in New York." Sensing her time in India was complete, Jena decided this was the perfect next step in her journey. She flew to New York at age twenty-three, landing one month after 9/11. Jena's family and friends thought she was crazy traveling to New York at that time, but she was determined to make a change in her life.

She stayed initially with her aunt in Jamaica, Queens. A serious violinist since she was a little girl, Jena supported herself in those early days by playing violin for tips during her hour-long trip each way into Manhattan and back. She'd make $50 during each direction in rush hour.

Jena got her first health-coaching client while playing violin in the subway. A man walked up to her, asked her if she was a student, and she replied yes. He asked her what she was studying. When she said, "I'm studying to be a health coach," he said, "I need to be your client!"

(What is a health coach? They are like personal trainers for healthy eating. They provide a level of week-to-week, even day-to-day, attention and encouragement to eat healthier food and make other healthy lifestyle changes; such attention and encouragement would be prohibitively expensive for doctors to provide.)

With her certification from IIN (and no college degree), Jena began seeing clients first in cafés and in her living room. As her practice grew, her rates began to go up, first from $97 per month of coaching, to $150, to $200, to $250, to $300 and up. Within two years, her practice had expanded to the point where she was renting a private office near Union Square three days a week.

"My work ethic was in full drive. My goal initially was to have ten billable hours each of those office days, thirty hours a week total, at an average of one hundred dollars per hour. I did health coaching and private yoga instruction. I found clients through networking on my off days and weekends, through morning Business Network International meetings that started at seven-fifteen in the morning, by doing little lectures here and there, on Craigslist, and on Quentin's Friends."

(Michael's note to readers: Quentin's Friends, http://www .quentinsfriends.com, is one of the best personal and professional networking resources I know of. I've been an avid member since

2003. I am not personally involved with Business Network International, http://www.bni.com, but it also has an excellent reputation, with chapters worldwide. These are two examples of the many low-cost ways now available to increase your business network. High-quality business networking is no longer only for graduates of expensive alma maters.)

As a result of all this hard work, Jena was bringing in about $3,000 in revenues per week, with business expenses of only the $1,500 monthly room rental. Her annual net before taxes, then, was around $130,000.

I have seen this again and again and again. If you can help someone achieve something that is valuable to them, such as losing weight, having a healthier relationship, meeting a life partner, expanding their business—or many other valuable things you can learn from life experience and self-study rather than from an academic degree—and if you're willing to learn some high-integrity marketing and sales around your skill set (see Success Skills #3 and #4), it's really not out of reach to earn $100,000 per year. It just isn't.

Jena was married, at that time, to a self-educated circus arts performer and entrepreneur she met in New York who had started an extremely successful aerial arts school in Brooklyn. He began earning six figures as well during their marriage. But the two both had a voracious instinct for bootstrapping their businesses and keeping personal costs low. (Bootstrapping is a concept crucial to this book, which we'll be learning a lot more about in this chapter. It involves keeping costs low while you generate revenue.) They once split a tiny windowless room in a shared apartment in Brooklyn, for $275 each. "Being consumers wasn't our focus, it was being creators."

Earning six figures and living extremely frugally meant Jena had a lot of cash left over each month. After a brief but serious scare in her business when the 2008 recession first hit, she discovered the power of marketing and sales to get her income back on track. (I tell this story in Success Skill #3, on how to learn marketing.)

At that point, she began plowing her savings heavily, not into stocks and real estate, but into *learning how to increase her own earning power*. She invested in studying with all the marketing and sales teachers I mentioned in Success Skills #3 and #4. And *that* is when her own earnings—and net worth—took off.

After the initial scare in 2008, during the worst recession in a generation, in 2009–10, while everyone else was running for cover, she expanded her business by close to 30 percent. (This shows the power of learning the skills for success.) She clocked over $230,000 in sales in her private coaching, group coaching programs, teleseminar series, and virtual programs in 2010—and this part of her business has almost no overhead.

The vast majority of college graduates would envy the position in life Jena has created for herself through her hard work and self-study: earning great money on a flexible schedule, while making a positive impact on many people's lives and being able to treat the recession as an afterthought.

So, in sum, how did Jena amass a formidable net worth during her twenties without a college education, while I amassed a formidable Ivy League education during my twenties without much net worth?

The answer is simple. Jena bootstrapped her education and her earning power. I didn't.

Bootstrapping is a concept central to the themes in this book. In the world of business, it's a strategy that involves getting to the point of profitability as quickly as possible—even if the profits are small—and then continually reinvesting profits to fuel growth. This is how John Paul DeJoria, Jena, and nearly all the others we've met so far in this book, including Bryan Franklin, Anthony Sandberg, Elliott Bisnow, Eben Pagan, Frank Kern, David Ash, and Marijo Franklin, built their initial success. In order to take this tack, the emphasis from the get-go has to be on frugality and on generating revenue right away. It derives its name from the phrase "pulling yourself up by your own bootstraps."

And, while the concept of bootstrapping is usually applied to business strategy, it can also be applied to your own life. That's where the real relevance to this book comes in. You can bootstrap your own education (including your continuing and professional education as an adult), and you can bootstrap your personal investments of time and money in your own career, just as you can bootstrap a business.

The essence of bootstrapping is keeping expenses low, generating income right away (even if it's just a little bit), and continually reinvesting as much of that income as effectively as possible into expanding your future income.

Jena was a model bootstrapper from the start. She had a strong cash-generation ethic from a young age. (I call it a "cash-generation ethic," rather than a "work ethic," because many people have a work ethic while toiling away at low-leverage jobs, thus not generating much cash.) She started working a paper route at twelve, then at a series of retail and waiter jobs starting at fifteen. She began supporting herself fully (including rent and food) at eighteen, and developed a formidable penchant for frugality, for savings, and for always keeping her net worth positive and growing, from a young age. She got her education inexpensively, through life experiences (you learn a lot traveling through India for two years on $6,000 you earned yourself) and through low-cost vocational training.

In her early twenties, with no college debt, she busted ass networking and prospecting, got thirty client-hours a week as a freelance yoga instructor and holistic health coach at $100/hour, kept business expenses very low, and lived frugally, cooking her own food, paying $275 a month in rent for a shared room in New York City, and choosing to take the building up of her business as her main form of recreation, over passive consumption. She was often saving $40,000 a year or more, the majority of her net income, year after year—which is more than many people with $500,000 or more of income save. You start to build up a significant nut pretty quickly if you keep doing that. Around three years ago she then began investing those savings in high-quality business, sales, and marketing trainings that she had strong reason to believe would lead to an immediate increase in her income. And they did. Voilà.

To get a better sense of what bootstrapping your *own* continuing education and personal investments might mean for you going forward, let's look at the opposite of bootstrapping—lots of up-front expenditures and debt, with little up-front income generation. This is how a great deal of Americans "invest" in their human capital, and it's how I myself lived during my twenties. Rather than bootstrapping, it might be called "charging the boots on credit card."

Hey, I've got an investment opportunity for you. It's going to require an investment of about $45,000 to $200,000 on your part over several years. Given your current finances, you're going to need to borrow a large part of that amount, that is, invest on margin, but that's OK, the rates are pretty low. (One thing you should

know, though, is that if the investment goes under, you're personally on the hook for that money, until you pay it down, for the rest
of your life. There is no way to discharge the debt in bankruptcy,
and your future wages and social security benefits could be gar-
nished if you can't pay.)

The business I'd like you to invest in is, well, sort of in the
exploratory/development phase. It doesn't really know what business it's in, to be frank, or what product or service it sells. In fact,
it may not even know that for a few years. The chief executive in
the business may have to move back in with her parents at some
point during this time—before she figures out the business's mission, revenue model, or core competency. (Oh, and by the way, the
CEO is quite immature. She is often irresponsible and from time to
time becomes distracted by side projects, like partying.)

The business you're about to invest in has absolutely no knowledge or experience in sales or marketing. It doesn't even really
know how to keep its own books or balance a budget, and often
runs up a lot of credit card debt. It's not even sure it wants to be a
business; the CEO may want to start a nonprofit, pursue a passion
in acting, or go help orphans in Botswana. The chief executive has
no business network or contacts to speak of, and in fact has no
experience whatsoever running a business.

Wanna invest?

Unfortunately, this is precisely the way many people in America go about investing in themselves today. It's the opposite of
bootstrapping. It's high-expenditure, high-debt up front now, and
revenue (if at all) much later.

Think about it. Most investments in human capital (i.e., education) are made four, five, or even seven years before the "business"
being invested in (you) will produce any additional revenue from
the investment in capital.

From a bootstrapper's perspective, that's an incredibly fool-
ish investment. If you want to take the bootstrapping approach to
self-investment and development of your human capital—the way
the people in this book did—the way to do it is incrementally,
step-by-step.

Make small, incremental investments in your human capital
and earning power. Buy some of the books I recommend. Take workshops or online training programs to learn different success skills.
Invest in your network of connections and mentors by going to
high-quality conferences, workshops, expos, trade shows, meet ups,

and retreats related to your field and to the success skills in this book. Find a high-quality business or career coach. Then, when these investments pay off in a year or two, use the increased earnings from these investments to make even more investments in your earning power and human capital, again and again, in a snowball effect.

This is how most of the people I interviewed in this book went from "rags to riches." It's an approach to investing in your human capital so different from the approach most people take. Which is why they get such different—and far superior—results than most people get.

■ CYAN BANISTER—BOOTSTRAPPING YOUR EDUCATION

WARNING! Do not do this from your work computer:

When you are at home, go to the Web and type in http://www.zivity.com.

There, you will find the world's first Web 2.0 adult photography social network devoted to appreciating the nude female form in a respectful way. Don't worry, it's all very tasteful; it was started by a classy woman named Cyan Banister, whom we'll meet in a moment, and it's designed to be friendly to women, both as models and as users of the site. Dubbed as "*Playboy* meets MySpace meets *American Idol*," Zivity allows paid subscribers to vote on their favorite models, who get a large share of proceeds. The emphasis is on artistic values, respectful interaction between fans and models, and elegant self-expression rather than sleazy exploitation.

How does one start a world-famous social network for adult-themed art? Not by following the traditional educational and career paths prescribed by society, to be sure.

Cyan Banister, who happens to be five days older than I, dropped out of high school in Flagstaff, Arizona, at age sixteen. "My grandfather told me I'd be a huge failure if I didn't go to college. My mother was very concerned that I'd live in a Dumpster in Flagstaff."

But Cyan never lived in a Dumpster. She had already moved out of her home at fifteen, and has supported herself fully and comfortably since that time. "I figured that most of what I wanted to accomplish in life started with a job. I didn't know exactly what I wanted to do, but I knew that it all started with getting in there and working. My first job, I started in retail and food service. I figured out pretty quickly, in a period of three years, that my future wasn't in retail or food service. [Laughing.] Then I started doing construction work, and figured out that that's also not what I wanted to do.

"A friend of mine that I met at a coffee shop got a laptop,' and showed it to me one day over a cup of coffee. I knew instantly' that that was what I wanted to do. It was like a bit flip. It was over. That was my calling; that was what I had to do. Nothing else mattered to me at that point.

"I started reading books, going out to coffee shops and hanging out with people who were into computers. I got a job at an ISP [Internet service provider] doing dial-up tech support, and slowly worked my way up to a sysadmin [systems administrator], worked my way up to a manager, and just continued on that path for at least ten years." (For tips on how to work your way up a career ladder within a company, read Success Skill #7.)

While Cyan was not gaining a *formal* education during all of this time, it's a huge mistake to say she wasn't gaining *any* education. She was obviously learning a lot during this whole period—and a lot of it was more useful and ultimately more lucrative than anything she would have learned in a formal environment. She was defining and learning about what her passions and interests were, trying out different career paths to see what suited her (a lot easier to do when you don't have student debt yet), learning about computers, about how to do job interviews, about how to work her way up a corporate hierarchy and play office politics, about how to lead and manage others.

One of the key things she was also learning—and this is crucial to our discussion—was how to support herself, to manage her finances, and the simple details of living in society as a self-supporting, independent adult.

"When I first began living on my own and supporting myself at age fifteen, I spent a lot of my time figuring out things like, 'Who takes your trash away?' 'How do you get electricity?' I had my electricity shut off, my trash was piling up outside. I couldn't figure out how these things worked. I had to go ask my neighbor: 'OK, so I've noticed your trash disappears, but mine stays. What's the deal with that?' And she said, 'Well, you kind of have to pay the city . . .' And I was like, 'Really? You have to *pay* people to take away trash!?' The whole learning process of how to live life as an adult, they don't teach you that in school. There was nothing in school that taught me how to pay bills, how to be a responsible adult. I was learning that stuff at sixteen. My friends who went to college started learning that stuff at twenty-two, if then."

In an age when 40 percent of American twentysomethings move back with their parents at least once, this is something many people in our society now don't begin learning in earnest until their early *thirties*. By having learned how to support herself in the real world, Cyan bought herself a crucial ingredient for investing in her own career success and earning power: a buffer that allowed her to experiment with entrepreneurial career paths, without having to worry about "living in Dumpsters."

Most significantly for her later life trajectory, during this time Cyan was also learning a great deal about starting her own business, and made quite a bit of money on the side, beyond her day jobs. "Sometime in between all of this, I started my first business. It was a T-shirt company. Even though my path in life was not to become a T-shirt maker, that venture got me exposed to ideas of entrepreneurialism. That was my first time learning about distribution, marketing, sales. I was nineteen years old. This was before it would have been possible to sell on the Internet, so most of my sales were local. But I got to the point where I had to buy my own printing press, with friends. It was wildly profitable."

While Cyan did later start a venture, Zivity, which received venture funding, her story before that point is a perfect example of what I call "bootstrapping your education." Bootstrapping your education involves getting on solid footing financially, and *then* making incremental investments in your earning power, over time, out of the cash flow—so you're constantly learning and never going into debt.

Here are some key points that all the people featured in this book, who bootstrapped their own self-education and self-investment as Cyan did, addressed early on in their lives:

- Assuming you want to earn more than you currently do, will it be in the *same* field that you're currently working in, or in a new field?
- If you want to earn more in the *same* field that you're currently working in, are there ways you can inexpensively learn about how to market and sell more effectively within this field?

(Learning more about effective marketing and sales as they apply to the organizations/fields you work in is almost always the best and fastest way to earn more money in your career. See Success Skills #3 and #4.)

◼ If you want to earn more money in a different field or industry than you currently work in, how can you gain the experience you need in your new chosen field without abandoning your current cash flow? Perhaps you could learn at night or on weekends, or start small and moonlight in the new business. Perhaps you can "learn while you earn" in some way. Maybe you can find people out there who are already successful in that field, who can mentor you for free, or with whom you can apprentice for free. (See Success Skill #2 on finding a mentor.)

◼ What are your specific life goals and dreams? (See Success Skill #1.) Figure out the most *laser-targeted, lean, focused, efficient, cost-effective, well-researched* educational investments you could make to put yourself on the path of reaching those goals and dreams. (My guess is, unless you want to go into a traditional profession, which requires a formal credential, such investments probably lie outside of formal academic institutions and instead will involve self-education.)

◼ If you wanted to get the education you needed to reach your dreams without going into debt, what would you do? The point is not that debt is always bad—it's that the decisions you make when you're spending your own hard-earned money now, rather than spending "play money" on credit, tend to be more realistic, focused, and reasoned, and less risky and speculative.

◼ PHILLIP RUFFIN—BOOTSTRAPPING YOUR CAPITAL

Phillip Ruffin's first paid employment after dropping out of college—on his way to becoming a billionaire—involved *repossessing a pet monkey.*

In the fifties, Ruffin told me, "I began working as an assistant manager at a department store. Which means you work for a buck an hour, for a hundred hours per week. They had a pet store inside the store: birds, monkeys. I realized my life had to change, when I got the assignment to repossess a monkey. This guy had bought a monkey on credit, and he owed twenty-nine dollars or something. I had to go to the house. The kids were crying as I picked up the monkey and took him back to the store; the monkey bit me on the way back, but I had gloves on. I decided, 'I really don't like this job—I have to do something different.'"

During his first year at Washburn University in Topeka, Kansas, a few years earlier, Ruffin had started a hamburger stand, to help pay his tuition. Pretty soon the stand was making solid money. "So I put the second hamburger stand in," Ruffin told me, "and I kind of forgot about college for a little bit." He soon dropped out of Washburn to focus on growing the hamburger chain. (This was in the mid-fifties, right around the time Ray Kroc, a high school dropout, started building a hamburger franchise called McDonald's.)

Ruffin continued to build the chain up, and soon sold his interest for $29,000, which in 1955 was around $230,000 in today's dollars. "I immediately lost all the money in an oil deal," he told me. So he took the job as the assistant manager—a career he didn't stay in much longer after the monkey bite.

"I started back in college at Wichita State University. I studied business and didn't like it. It was not interesting to me. I couldn't concentrate. The professor kept telling me all this abstract stuff about economics, but it was clear he'd never built a business up from the ground as I already had. I kept thinking about business. I went two years there and quit.

"I found a little convenience store. It was called 11-to-11 Market. I had managed to scrape up fifteen hundred dollars. I borrowed the balance from the bank. I worked from nine in the morning to midnight every day, seven days a week myself. I started expanding in the convenience store business—this was when people didn't even know what convenience stores were. I put one in and another and another.

"In 1968, we put our first self-service gasoline station in Blackwell, Oklahoma. We were pioneers in self-service gasoline. It was a very good business for a long time. We were making a lot of money. In the meantime, I bought a bank, some shopping centers, strip mall centers. We were financing mostly through profit, plus bank loans. I purchased a lot of real estate. I purchased a dairy, which supplied milk to my stores. In 1987, I built a Wichita Marriott, my first entry into the hotel business. We started picking up a few hotels here and there."

At this point in Ruffin's story, I had to ask him: "It seems like everything you touch turns to profit. You just buy a business, profit from it, buy some more, and they do well. What's your secret?"

He replied, in classic bootstrapper form: "We watched our pennies and didn't do anything extravagant. These were real businesses, earning real dollars, not a bunch of risky hype. It was a lot of work. We were working twelve, fourteen, fifteen hours a day.

"We reinvested profits, plus borrowed money from the banks, and paid them back and then expanded to more hotels and stores. That's just the way we operated. We never had a lot of debt."

After many more hotel deals, and a deal to lease out his convenience stores, which netted him $2.2 million in cash each year, Ruffin heard that the Frontier hotel on the Vegas Strip—the second hotel ever on the Strip, built in 1942—was for sale. But no one was buying. "The reason no one would buy it was the longest union strike in history—six and a half years. Nobody in Vegas wanted to buy it because they had union problems of their own. But I wasn't in Vegas. All I did was meet with the president of the union, and we cut a deal. Of course, the deal cost money. We had to bring back those employees that had been laid off for six and a half years. Everybody tried to solve the problem, even Congress tried to solve the problem. It just took money. We had to bring the people back in, pay them back wages, and give them seniority. I didn't buy the hotel until after I had the meeting. We solved it before we bought it. Once the strikers were gone, the Frontier did more business. People didn't want to walk through those lines. That is what gave me the opportunity to fix it.

"In 2007, El-Ad out of New York offered me $1.2 billion, which is the highest per-square-foot offer ever in Vegas. So from nothing, to a billion. That's how it happened. When they wired that money into my bank, Bank of America, I don't think they'd ever seen that kind of a wire into a private account before."

For a while, Ruffin just watched his billion-plus in cash sit there and grow. In a problem many people—including most college graduates—would like to have, he got bored of this. "Frankly, we didn't know what the hell to do with the money. I'd never been a big buyer of stocks. I don't like to invest in other guys' businesses. You know what they do—they have big bonuses, they have all kinds of stock options for themselves. We sat on that money for a while. I didn't like just sitting on money. That kind of money will make you very good money. Eighty-nine million a year, we did. But I didn't like the business. I didn't even care about going to work. I just sat there and watched the screen, watched the money come in."

Ruffin soon found himself back in the action. "A friend of mine said he thought MGM might be having some cash problems and might want to sell a property. I had always looked at Treasure Island. Once I heard it was for sale, I got a meeting with Kirk Kerkorian," Ruffin told me.

(Kerkorian is another famous Las Vegas casino magnate billionaire. Kerkorian dropped out of eighth grade, became an amateur boxer, then got a pilot's license. At the outbreak of World War II, he started flying combat aircraft across the Atlantic for delivery to the British Royal Air Force. This was extremely risky, because the aircraft barely had enough fuel capacity to fly these long flights. He later went into the airline business, and then the hotel business, becoming a multibillionaire.)

"He said he was at $850 million," Ruffin told me. "Of course, I was sitting on that cash. I said, 'Well, I'm at $700 million.' He said no. I said, 'Let's split the difference, 750.' He said, 'That's not splitting the difference, 775 is!' We ended up shaking hands at 750."

I paid for my few nights in Ruffin's lovely Treasure Island Hotel and Casino (http://www.treasureisland.com), when I flew into town to interview him, to see the fruits of his labor firsthand. Ruffin, who once worked repossessing monkeys as a college dropout, now owns the sprawling hotel and entertainment complex. A few weeks before I arrived there, another non–college graduate billionaire, Guy Laliberté, was there, celebrating the record-breaking eight thousandth performance of *Mystère*, the first Vegas production put on by Laliberté's Cirque du Soleil; the show is on permanent residence at Treasure Island.

Ruffin enjoys a long-standing spot on the Forbes 400, with a net worth of several billion. He is happily married to former Miss Ukraine, model Oleksandra Nikolayenko-Ruffin, with whom he has a son. In his office behind the casino, I asked him what words of advice he has for young people seeking success in life.

"The advice I would give to young people? Quit your job. Don't work for anybody. You really can't make any money working for someone else. Maybe it's a hamburger stand. Maybe it's a coffee shop. You can do that. It's very risky to quit your job and start on your own. You have to be committed to it and you have to be willing to work the hours, because you can't have a lot of labor. You can start almost any kind of business yourself. It doesn't take a lot of capital. It's very doable. You have to work your ass off. Be willing to work yourself."

I think Ruffin's advice applies, even for those who are not ready to start their own business or who wish to stay with a career as an employee. These days, *all* employees are entrepreneurs—entrepreneurs in the business of *you*. We all know the days of thinking your employer will provide for you until you retire and beyond are gone, along with the days of pay phones and handwritten letters. So, if you can't rely on your employer for security, what can you rely on?

Your own human capital. This is your greatest investment, and if you are savvy about investing in it—as the people in this book have been—it will never let you down and will keep providing value and cash for the rest of your life. The value of bootstrapping, saving, and building up capital—whether it's financial capital or human capital—is that it keeps on giving, year after year, without being depleted. Once you own it, it keeps on paying in one way or another.

I asked Ruffin, "Have you ever thought of writing a book yourself? You have such a fascinating story. I think it would make a great book."

He replied, "Why would I want to write a book?"

"Well, there are a lot of reasons to write a book."

He said, with a smile and a chuckle, in his charming Southern drawl, "Michael, I'm going to make more from this casino today than you'll make from your book." He looked down at a neat sheet of figures on his clean, nearly empty desk. "I made $820,000 yesterday. Not a bad day of business."

That, friends, is the power of building up capital. You may not become a billionaire casino magnate, but you can always invest in your own human capital. If you invest in building up the *right* kind of human capital—the success skills described in this book— it will keep paying you dividends for the rest of your life.

■ **MARC ECKO, MATT MULLENWEG, AND LIFELONG LEARNING AS AN ADULT**

In high school in New Jersey, Marc Ecko routinely carried around $600 or more in cash in his pocket and had weeks when he was clearing $1,000 in business. No, he was not a rich kid (he lived on the "wrong" side of the train tracks, where the lower-middle-class and working-class families lived). Nor was he a drug dealer, nor was he stealing the money.

Marc had learned how to airbrush graffiti-style illustrations onto people's hats, jackets, shirts, and even their cars. His services were in high demand. "My neighborhood in Lakewood, New Jersey, was very diverse—lots of working-class Jews, blacks, and Latinos. Hip-hop was the emerging cultural trend, and the cultural narrative was driven by black popular culture. Here was a Jewish kid growing up among all this diversity, not religious, reconciling my own identity. I was a fat white kid—too fat to break-dance, and I definitely wasn't going to rap.

"But I was into art. Because graffiti was the aesthetic that young people were talking to each other through if you were into hip-hop, I figured I'd connect with my art. I was a decent artist. Grandma got me a book called *Subway Art* [by Martha Cooper and Henry Chalfant]. I got my airbrush in eighth grade. Once you got the compressor and the paints, it was like a hundred and fifty dollars, which was a lot of money for an eighth grader in the eighties. My parents were like, 'You better make good on the investment.' I was just an artist—but it was a gateway to business.

"My public school education is where I learned a lot of my marketing prowess. I started a business called Ecko Airbrushing. Either it was my stoner friends who wanted me to paint their car, or my hood friends that wanted me to paint pictures of their baby on their jacket. Not to be vulgar or anything, but I was doing better than most drug dealers in my school.

"That, for me, became my school. That was my business school. To be a fifteen-year-old kid standing in line at the Sears service center whenever the compressor would break down, not being taken seriously, having to negotiate my way to get my stuff fixed so I could fulfill my orders. Ordering paint. Hunting down the best how-to videos—there wasn't the Internet then. I followed the thread of that airbrush, and that air compressor, to learning a tremendous amount about business—management of my time, commitment, communication, information, and technology.

"I was making really good money. Come senior year, I'd have some weeks when I'd do a couple of thousand dollars. I had respectable savings, everything I wanted." What did Marc do with that savings? Did he put it in the stock market or a CD account? In classic bootstrapper form, he put his earnings right back into his business and his earning power. "Marketing tools, taking slides and photos. Getting hats embroidered and giving them away to my clients. Going to local town fairs and setting up a booth. I was always reinvesting in my business."

Even though Marc was making serious money for a high school kid in the eighties, and was learning more about running his own business than most people ever do, a counselor got the better of him. "My guidance counselors at school were like, 'It's really cute, these T-shirts, but you really think you're going to feed the mouths of your babies doing this?' At family events, people would be saying, 'You could earn seventy-five, eighty K if you go to college, and if you get a law degree, you might be able to earn six figures!'"

Marc paid heed to this advice and decided to follow his father's footsteps into the Rutgers College of Pharmacy. He kept his business going on the side, however. In 1992, Marc decided to create a customized airbrushed jacket for Michael Bivins, of the R & B group Bell Biv DeVoe, who was appearing at a local concert. Marc could barely move due to shoulder surgery, but his sister hopped onstage and hand-delivered the jacket directly to Bivins, with a handwritten note in the pocket. "I get a call at three in the morning, he wants more custom work. Soon I'm nineteen years old, getting backstage access to concerts, hanging out with all these hip-hop artists, doing art for them, and then I would go back to pharmacy school in the day. There was no passion there. I couldn't get past the periodic table. It didn't make sense to me. There was something in me that was beating about art, some energy that was dominating me."

Failing at classes as he focused on his art and business, Marc had a meeting with the dean of the school, Dr. John Colaizzi. He saw Marc's passion for art and his real-world success, and he was remarkably understanding. "He said to me, 'You don't ever want to be in the place where you coulda, shoulda, woulda. You're young now. Go do it while you're young, and you've got the parachute of youth. You can come back if it doesn't work out for you.' I left school and never looked back."

A family friend introduced Marc to a man named Seth Gerszberg. The New York Times says, "Gerszberg radiates hustle. Spend five minutes with him, and you won't be surprised to learn that he dropped out of college because he was making $5,000 a week selling salvaged architectural ornaments, of all things."[6] Gerszberg invested $5,000 cash for a 50 percent stake in the company, and remains Marc's business partner to this day. Through many twists and turns (and a flirtation with bankruptcy), the duo pioneered the category of "urban wear," turning Marc Ecko Enterprises (http://www.marceckoenterprises.com) into one of the most recognized brands in global fashion, with annual revenues of over $1 billion.

Marc did not graduate from college, but he now has a PhD. In 2009, he was invited back to Rutgers to receive an honorary doctorate, and delivered that year's commencement speech, with Dean Colaizzi proudly looking on.

I interviewed Marc in his impressive offices on Twenty-third Street in Manhattan. Education is one of the topics he's most passionate about, and in an eloquent riff on the subject, he introduced me to a word I'd never heard before. I've been an avid reader of serious nonfiction since fifteen, so it's not that often I get introduced to new words, but this one couldn't be more relevant: "andragogy." Its literal meaning, I found out, is "man-leading," and is contrasted with "pedagogy," which means "child-leading." I Googled it, and in the Wikipedia entry for the concept I found a pitch-perfect description of the way all the self-educated millionaires I'd been interviewing educated themselves. Even from a young age, they educated themselves as adults, not as children:

> Adults need to know the reason for learning something . . .

> Experience (including error) provides the basis for learning activities . . .

> Adults need to be responsible for their decisions on education; involvement in the planning and evaluation of their instruction . . .

> Adults are most interested in learning subjects having immediate relevance to their work and/or personal lives . . .

> Adult learning is problem-centered rather than content-oriented . . .

> Adults respond better to internal versus external motivators . . .

> The term has been used by some to allow discussion of contrast between self-directed and 'taught' education.[7]

It turns out that the millionaires I've been talking to who did not complete their formal education didn't forsake education at all. They were simply following *andragogy* rather than pedagogy.

Think of the opposite of the above description of andragogy: Few reasons ever given to learn something, other than "You need to learn this to get a good grade and graduate." Conditioning kids to be averse to making mistakes, rather than teaching kids that going out, trying lots of ambitious stuff, making a ton of mistakes in the process, and learning from those mistakes is the *essence of how you become good at something*. Forcing a bunch of content down kids' throats that has little relevance to their life goals and thus bears little interest to them, rather than teaching them how to solve problems they care about. And of course, lots and lots of external motivators. This is pedagogy—teaching for children. It is characterized, in essence, by beating education into mostly unwilling kids.

(Sometimes literally. Marc has just become involved in a national movement to end corporal punishment in American schools. He informed me, to my shock, that corporal punishment in schools is legal in *twenty states*, that over 222,000 students are physically disciplined each year by an educator, and that over 20,000 need to seek medical attention because of it. "You can't hit a prisoner in all fifty states in the Union. But you can hit students, as discipline, in twenty states," he told me. Anthony Adams, Elliott Bisnow's dorm adviser from Success Skill #2, is also a leading voice in this movement. The startling anachronism of legalized state corporal punishment belies the century-old roots of our educational system—turning kids into compliant factory workers upon graduation. It also shows how irrelevant pedagogy has become to current economic realities. Could you imagine trying to *beat* someone— literally or figuratively—into starting a company or coming up with a brilliant technological innovation?)

Thank goodness the people in this book started treating *themselves* as adults early on—because few people in the educational system ever will. Though I doubt many of the self-educated people in this book have heard of the term "andragogy," they are all masters of it. That's why they're rich and successful, while most people—who have had their instinct for creative self-education beaten out of them by sixteen years of pedagogy—are not.

———

It turns out that nearly *everyone* I spoke to for this book has this in common: a serious passion for lifelong learning. Put another way, they do not front-load their education early on with pedagogy rammed down their throats, removing themselves from the workforce and taking on lots of debt to do so. Rather, they follow lifelong learning through continual, steady, gradual investment in themselves over time as adults.

Matt Mullenweg is passionate about the importance of developing a habit of lifelong learning and reading, both professionally and personally. During the time he was studying at the University of Houston, in the early 2000s, he began to teach himself to program in a language called PHP, through free online tutorials. He didn't have a particularly technical background—his passion in high school had been jazz saxophone—but soon he started doing simple tasks in PHP from this self-teaching. "'Oh, I can put a hit counter on my little website.' Some stupid little thing like that," he told me. "The PHP Manual online, and comments under it. That had everything I possibly needed. You can learn practically anything you want in the world online."

But soon his programming got more sophisticated, and went way beyond hit counters. In fact, it went on to revolutionize the Internet. This was the very early days of blogging, and Matt decided to create a blogging platform in PHP, called WordPress.

As more and more people starting using the platform across the Web, his notoriety rose, and CNET contacted him with a job offer. "This was the kind of job I hoped to have when I graduated— great salary, great everything. So I asked myself, 'What am I waiting for?'" Matt dropped out of the University of Houston after his sophomore year to take the job at CNET.

However, Matt says, "One characteristic of a lot of entrepreneurs is that they're relatively unemployable. I don't think I was the best employee at CNET, honestly. I was really focused on my own projects, really into WordPress." The blogging platform was starting to take off, and Matt decided to leave CNET to focus on his creation exclusively. Now, WordPress (http://wordpress.org) is the largest content-management system and blogging platform in the world; somewhere around 13 percent of all websites in the *world* run on WordPress, and as of this writing its latest version has been downloaded 27 million times. Many publishing commentators have blamed the Net in general, and blogging in particular, for the decline of interest in serious long-form reading—that is, books—

in favor of more superficial, bite-sized "multitasking-friendly" blips online. Yet Matt Mullenweg, a major player in the blogging revolution, couldn't be more passionate about the importance of long-form reading and writing.

At a café near the WordPress office, in the San Francisco Embarcadero area, Matt told me: "A common quality I see of people who are successful is that they are voracious readers. The book as a format is underrated in the digital age. I'm the first one to say blogs are fantastic, obviously. But they tend to be shorter form. Longer-form works stretch my mind more. When you write a book, it consumes you. What you get when you read that book, then, is someone's entire life for several years or more, distilled into one work. That's really powerful.

"I feel like these things have super-cycles, and I think we're at the nadir of long-form writing. I think we might have just passed it, and it will rise again. The e-book revolution puts an entire library into something as small as a paperback. For me, as I stopped reading books in favor of Internet content, I felt myself getting dumber. Several years ago, I thought, 'Man, I don't think I'm as smart as I used to be.' I just felt a little duller. So I realized I had to start reading again. When I was starting [my company] Automattic, I realized, 'I have no idea what I'm doing, so I need to read as much as possible.' An e-book is ten dollars these days. Anyone can afford a book. Take some of the best books on entrepreneurship. Maybe *Innovation and Entrepreneurship* by Peter Drucker. Or *The Art of the Start* by Guy Kawasaki, which I was really inspired by when I was first starting out. What's holding you back? It's your time and a few dollars. Or go to the library if you don't have a few dollars. And you can have access to the world's greatest wisdom on any topic."

BUILD THE BRAND OF YOU

(or, To Hell with Resumes!)

In August 2009, I saw a tweet from a famous publishing industry exec I'd been following, Debbie Stier (http://debbiestier.com), then senior vice president of digital marketing at HarperCollins, which read, "Will Somebody in Publishing Please Hire This Woman?"

Intrigued, I clicked through the link, where I read about a recent college graduate named Marian Schembari, who had just done something remarkable.

Like many recent liberal arts graduates, Schembari dreamed of working in a major publishing house. And like many recent graduates, she was not having much luck. "I graduated from college in May, and by mid-August, I was ready to slit my wrists, because nothing was happening. I had applied for jobs with all the major publishing houses and even the not-so-major publishing houses in New York. Basically, I was just doing what my college career center told me to do. I had a really great resume. I would spend two hours trying to personalize a cover letter and make it perfect, then send it out, and then hear nothing. All of the things that people told me to do in order to find a job didn't work; no one called me back. I was just getting lost in the abyss of thousands of desperate job seekers. I applied for a job in a small publishing house and the guy told me they got five hundred applications. It was not the greatest job, it didn't pay anything and he had people trampling over each other to get it," she told me.

Marian tried to take a different tack.

She spent $100 on Facebook ads, with the headline "I want to work for HarperCollins" where the company name mentioned was custom-targeted to people who had listed one of the six major New York publishers as their place of employment.

I Want to Work for Harper

I'm Marian. I recently graduated from Davidson College. My dream is to work for HarperCollins. Can you help? Click to see my resumé.

Debbie Stier, who worked at HarperCollins at the time, saw one of Marian's ads pop up in her own Facebook page and wrote a post praising Marian for her initiative and ingenuity. Now this fresh college grad had one of the most respected names in U.S. publishing openly urging her colleagues in the industry to hire her. Word of her employment campaign went viral within the publishing industry. Marian later wrote on her blog, "At least one person from every publisher I focused on e-mailed me to tell me they passed my resume on to HR, wanted to meet, or even just to say they liked my idea."

Impressed with this young woman's initiative and creativity, I wrote an unsolicited e-mail to her:

I have a suggestion for you that will probably be the only piece of advice along these lines you will get:

Why seek an employer? With your drive, initiative, and talent, you could make a successful go as a freelance publishing consultant.

I've been happily self-employed for 3 years now, and I currently make much more than I would be making if I had spent that time trying to rise up from an entry-level publishing position.

I do all this while working my own hours in NYC, living comfortably in Brooklyn, choosing projects that interest me, and from my laptop so I can do it anywhere (I spent 5 months in 2007 doing this work while sipping lattes in Wi-Fi cafes in Buenos Aires!).

You've got the drive. You've got the talent. You could make this happen for yourself. I say, think outside of the box. You don't need some publisher to pay you $35K when you could make much more than that on your own, with your talents.

It's rare that someone has the go-getter attitude that you do and you will go far whatever you choose.

Marian wrote back to me, thanking me for my suggestions but saying that she was going to take an entry-level job that came her way through all the viral hullabaloo around her Facebook campaign. This was a position with a major literary PR firm in the city (a job almost any recent liberal arts graduate wanting to break into the New York City publishing world would have envied).

A few months into nine-to-five life, however, the self-employment bug bit her. She wanted to break out on her own, and she wrote me again, asking for advice. I started mentoring her on how to make the transition to being a freelance consultant. She made the leap, leaving the comfort and safety of the job, and starting with a few freelance social media consulting gigs she got through Debbie Stier.

In the year and a half since she struck out on her own as a freelancer—and just two years out of college at the time I'm writing this—Schembari has created a lively and popular publishing industry blog for herself that routinely gets fifty or more comments every time she posts (http://marianlibrarian.com, powered, of course, by Matt Mullenweg's WordPress); has attracted thousands of Twitter followers who retweet her material constantly; has been quoted on ABC News, CNN, and *Time*; has been cited as an expert on networking on MSN; and has even appeared on a list of "the next generation of publishing leaders" (http://www.digitalbookworld .com). (Think she'd have any chance of getting that kind of recognition within one year of taking the entry-level jobs at a publisher, which she was seeking but never got offered?)

As a result of all this name recognition, demand for her services is booming, and she is now charging $100/hour for her consulting (any recent liberal arts grads out there like that figure?). All of this smack-dab in the middle of the worst economic downturn since the Great Depression.

Marian is certainly doing a lot better than her fellow classmates. "I think one person whom I graduated with has a full-time job; everyone else is struggling or has taken a bunch of part-time jobs. This guy I graduated with had a bunch of honors and fancy awards—he was very, very smart. He's working at Starbucks because he can't get a job anywhere else."

In addition to her lucrative freelancing over the Internet and Skype, which allows her to divide her time between London, New Zealand, and New York, Marian also now sells a course she's created online, called the "Pajama Job Hunt," so that others can have the same success she's had in using social media and personal branding to get jobs.

Marian's advice to recent grads? She told me: "Every industry, from what I've found, has the top 20 blogs and people who are the online influencers. You need to get online and make friends with them, and read everything you can and comment on those blogs. Let's say you want to get into nonprofit, you would Google 'nonprofits on Twitter' and you'll almost certainly find that someone has written a list of the 'Top 25 Non-Profits on Twitter,' or the top hospitals or ad agencies or whatever. Literally, it does not matter what industry you want to be in, there is a community of those people on Twitter. Network where those people are and make friends with them. I mean it's really not that difficult. Get a Twitter profile and just start engaging with that community around your desired industry and profession; you then become known in that community and then it becomes easier to get a job.

"Ignore your career counselor and don't even stress about your resume—have a good one because people will ask for it, but don't put too much emphasis on it. Build an online presence. In my generation, the whole Facebook social media thing is for connecting with your friends and posting pictures of you doing Jell-O shots. But you can do so much more with it."

In short, none of Marian's success depended in the slightest on the fact that she had a college degree and a polished resume, or on anything she studied in school. It depended on her being savvy about building a brand for herself.

■ THE CONCEPT OF "BRAND" EXPLAINED IN ONE SENTENCE

Perhaps no single word in the English language has more overblown puffery, smoke and mirrors, and verbal diarrhea written around it than the word "brand." If you wanted to, you could spend a small fortune on a library full of books about the concept, and you could go drop twenty-five grand, a hundred grand, or even a million bucks on some corporate consultant to "brand" you, the word having become a verb as well as a noun.

I'm about to cut through all the bullshit and give you a one-sentence definition of the word:

Your brand is what people think about when they hear your name.

Voilà, I've just saved you tens of thousands of dollars in hiring "brand consultants," and years wading through books full of trendy, semimystical corporate-speak about "brand leverage."

If people think "trustworthy, confident, intelligent, funny, hip, savvy, and up-and-coming" when they hear your name, then that is your brand.

If people think "wannabe loser" when they hear your name, then that is your brand.

And if people think absolutely nothing when they hear your name, then you have no brand.

And that, friends, is a big problem. Because your brand is one of your biggest assets—far more important, in most cases, than your resume. Great brand, no resume—no problem. Great resume, no brand? Welcome to position #347 of the stack of five hundred equally great resumes.

Your brand—a "reputation that precedes you"—will allow you to command big bucks for your time and insight, as it has for

Marian. It will open doors for you in your career unimaginable if you don't have a brand (i.e., if people don't think much of anything when they hear your name or look you up on Google). People go to college in large part to build up a resume, and then spend years and years adding to that resume. But they spend zero time building up their reputation. That's a huge, huge mistake, and a huge misallocation of time, money, and attention.

On this theme, Seth Godin told me: "If you decided to go out, and instead of finishing school, decided to learn things on your own that you thought were important—then that's your *story*. Everyone needs a story to get a job. On the back of your first book [pointing to my book *The Power of Eye Contact*], it says you went to Brown. That's your story. Your story could be that you have the most popular blog on airline safety. And if you really have the most popular blog in the world on airline safety, and you're looking for a job doing PR on airline safety, that's a really good story. That's better than the story that you went to Brown."

When Seth said this last remark, about airline safety, my jaw hit the floor. I actually *know the author of the most popular blog on airline safety*. She is the senior aviation correspondent for the *New York Times*. She has written one book on aviation safety for Harper-Collins and is at work on another book on the topic. She was director of investigations for Kreindler & Kreindler, a leading transportation law firm, from 2001 until 2008.

She is Marian Schembari's mom, Christine Negroni (http://www.christinenegroni.com). And guess what? She doesn't have a college degree. She attended a small college for three years, got a job at a television station the summer after her junior year, and loved her work so much she did not return. She cut her chops reporting on aviation for CNN, eventually became their chief aviation correspondent, and took off from there.

I asked Seth if he knew of Christine, and he didn't. But in coming up with his example, he essentially conjured her real-life story out of thin air. She built up an amazing *brand* for herself as an expert in aviation safety, from the ground up, with few formal credentials. Looks like Marian took a play from Mom's playbook!

Seth continued on his riff: "Let's say you got into Harvard and didn't go. That's a *better* story than you got into Harvard and you *did* go. And a much cheaper story. And it takes four less years!" I imagine some kid sending a copy of her acceptance letter to Harvard, along with a copy of her letter declining it, and saying to a potential employer, 'Here's what I did with the four years instead. I have the brains to get into Harvard, and I have the initiative to get a Harvard-quality education on my own, and I think outside the box. Hire me." Think more than a few forward-thinking employers might be intrigued?

"There are all these stories available to people," Seth continued. "There just happens to be this one particularly easy/expensive one, which is 'You heard of this college because it has a football team, therefore you should hire me.'

"We're afraid, ashamed—when we don't have that story—to tell the other one, the one which is more unique and shows more personality. I have a very controversial post I wrote, called, 'Why bother having a resume?' The reason you shouldn't have a resume is that any job you can get because you have a resume probably isn't a job you want."

In the blog post Godin references, he writes:

> I think if you're remarkable, amazing or just plain spectacular, you probably shouldn't have a resume at all. . . .
>
> If you don't have a resume, what do you have?
>
> How about three extraordinary letters of recommendation from people the employer knows or respects?
>
> Or a sophisticated project they can see or touch?
>
> Or a reputation that precedes you?
>
> Or a blog that is so compelling and insightful that they have no choice but to follow up?
>
> Some say, "well, that's fine, but I don't have those."
>
> Yeah, that's my point. If you don't have those, why do you think you are remarkable, amazing or just plain spectacular? It sounds to me like if you don't have those, you've been brainwashed into acting like you're sort of ordinary.
>
> Great jobs, world class jobs, jobs people kill for . . . those jobs don't get filled by people e-mailing in resumes. Ever.[1]

In my own case, I will leave it for others to decide if they think I'm "remarkable." But one thing I know for sure is, since the beginning of 2007, not one penny of my income has come from any source that has had anything to do with my having shown a resume to anyone. All my work for the past four years, as a freelancer and author, has come through personal referrals, and a growing track record of demonstrable results and projects if you

Google my name, all of which are aspects of my own personal brand I've been cultivating.

You don't develop those things in college or grad school, you develop them by *doing stuff* in the real world. And then making sure there's a Google trail related to what you've been doing. That's your brand. Create stuff. Sell stuff. Market stuff. Lead stuff. Make sure it's good stuff, then make sure there's a good Google trail about it, so when potential employers or clients Google you (as they all will), the brand impression they come away with (the thoughts that come to mind when they hear your name again) are, "This person gets shit done." Or simply, "Wow."

■ MARIA ANDROS—THE IMPORTANCE OF BUILDING YOUR OWN NAME AS A BRAND

Maria Andros—who does not have a college degree—started out her professional life as a makeup artist. She began working for some of the big makeup companies in Vancouver, doing makeup on high-profile shoots and campaigns for them. She eventually networked her way into the corporate side of the companies, and then into a position as a corporate buyer for a large clothing retailer. Despite this rise through the corporate ladders, she began to feel that familiar feeling among so many who work for large companies: being an anonymous cog in a machine.

"I was working ten- to twelve-hour days and I was only making approximately fifty thousand dollars Canadian. I remember I was exhausted and it was really frustrating for me because I just didn't feel that I was valued there. I hit a place where I had really lost my passion. I felt very stuck. I felt that every single day was *Groundhog Day*.

"You wake up in the morning, you go brush your teeth. You walk to the kitchen, you make your breakfast. You get ready for work, you drive to work. You get to work. You count the hours until your first coffee break, then its lunchtime. And then you get home from work. You're exhausted. You don't even want to talk to your spouse or your friends because you are so tired. You get on the computer and you just numb out and you surf the Internet. Then you go to bed and repeat. That was how my life felt. I knew I had to make a change. I knew I had to do something. I didn't know how I was going to do it or what it was going to be, but I had to do something."

In 2006, Maria went online to see if she could get some ideas for some alternative to her *Groundhog Day* corporate life. She saw on YouTube that many people were building their own followings by making low-cost videos of themselves, almost like their own TV station about them. She had been on TV before for makeup-related stories and felt intuitively that her future lay in building a brand for herself online.

With the video function of her digital camera, she began uploading simple videos about her quest to learn about business, video, and creating a new life for herself—"vlogging" about her journey as she went, and sharing the tips and tricks she was learning. She created a YouTube channel for herself and a blog (powered, of course, by Matt's WordPress), and started getting the word out through blogging and Facebook. She started learning about search engine optimization (SEO) and began optimizing her titles and descriptions for her videos to get traffic from people searching for topics related to entrepreneurialism, self-employment, career development, and social media.

Soon she found herself with a small but growing and devoted following online. Some people started asking her to coach them on their own video marketing efforts, and like that, she had clients, and money started coming in.

Maria started to gain the attention of some bigger bloggers and websites. "I started going to live events and conferences, showing up everywhere, and the people there, including the speakers onstage, would have heard of my social media and video presence. A lot of them knew who I was before I even met them."

That's the essence of building your own brand. People having heard of you—and having a positive impression—before you've even met them. If you can create that effect, doors open for you. A close second, if that's not possible, is people getting a good impression of you *very quickly* when they Google you.

Maria Andros is now widely considered one of the top experts about building one's brand and business through online video. She left her job, markets her services under her own name now (http://mariaandros.com), and has broken well into six figures of earnings, on a completely flexible, boss-free schedule.

A huge question many people have, when they venture into building a brand for themselves, is whether the brand should be their own name or whether they should come up with some name that caters to the industry/niche/market they work in. Maria is adamant that, even if you work for or own another company, you should always build up branding around your own name as well. "No matter what you're up to, you need to market yourself and your name. Make sure you get YourName.com. If it's already taken, put some creative twist on it, but make sure you have your own home for your own brand on the Internet, which serves as the meeting place for blogging, YouTube, Twitter, Facebook, and LinkedIn."

I've seen many people make the mistake of trying to "brand" some kind of concept or niche rather than their own name. If they're building a career in the telecommunications industry, for example, they'll try to build their brand using some generic-sounding site like "Telecom Insider," thinking that it sounds more professional or that it offers better keywords and SEO.

Unless you come up with some *insanely* catchy brand other than your own name, or you are planning to build up a business that you eventually want to sell, this is usually a mistake. People care much more about other people than they do about companies or keyword-laden URLs. Even if you work for another company or are building a company totally separate from your own identity, you should separately and simultaneously build up your online brand around you as a *person*, not around a concept, a company, or a niche. Companies, niches, and keywords come and go. Your own personal brand stays with you for life.

The single best passage I've ever read about branding, from the countless books on branding I've read, comes from the book *The Brand Called You: Make Your Business Stand Out in a Crowded Marketplace* by Peter Montoya. It relates directly to Maria's point:

> If you've given in to the temptation to name your [personal brand] Alliance Capital Investment or Thinkwell Marketing and Design or some other dreadful thing, stop what you're doing and pay attention.
>
> You must name your [brand] after yourself. Period. No one calls to talk to Alliance Capital; they call to talk to you. No one refers Thinkwell; they give your name and number to their colleague who needs advertising. You create the value, not your company name. Let's face it, the only reason you chose that silly

name was so that people would think you're larger than you are. But trust me, you're not fooling anyone. . . .

Still doubtful? . . . [L]et's try an exercise. On a piece of paper, write down 15 to 20 luxury brand names. . . . If you're like me, you have a list that looks something like this:

> Ferragamo
> Versace
> Mercedes-Benz
> Dom Pérignon
> Rolex
> Rolls-Royce
> Prada
> Riedel
> Kohler
> Lauren
> Bang & Olufsen
> BMW
> Bentley
> Yves Saint Laurent
> L'Oréal
> Cartier
> Armani

Take a look at your list. How many of the luxury brands you listed are someone's name? On my list, the only ones that aren't are Rolex and BMW. Every other one began as a person who started a company, built it over time, developed a reputation for excellence, and along the way crafted a stellar Personal Brand.[2]

Maria Andros's name opens doors on the Internet, and in business and career opportunities for herself. She is no longer anonymous, or a cog. She is a brand. And she did it by doing amazing things in her field, and then creating a highly visible Google trail of all these accomplishments, across multiple social media communities. All instead of building up a formal resume.

Google is the new resume for the twenty-first century. How does your resume look?

■ ROBERT SCOBLE AND
THE WORLD'S GREATEST JOB

Robert Scoble has one Shakespeare paper left to write—seventeen years tardy—if he wants to complete his college degree in journalism.

Robert graduated from high school in the early eighties and began working retail in a camera and consumer electronic store. "I was taking one class a semester at West Valley College in Saratoga [Silicon Valley], trying to figure out what I wanted to do with the rest of my life," he told me. Like most of the people in this book, he started supporting himself very early, earning $27,000, which was livable middle-class money back then.

After kicking around like this for many years, in 1991 Robert started a photojournalism degree at San José State. He started writing a column called the "Spartan Nerd" in the school paper, which got noticed by a Valley computer programming magazine. In his senior year, in 1994, the magazine offered him a job. Like Matt Mullenweg, due to his own initiative, Robert had essentially been offered the job he wanted upon graduation, before graduation. He left college for the job. "Within a year, I was sitting in the front row of Bill Gates's keynotes, meeting all kinds of interesting people, organizing conferences."

Flash-forward to December 2000. "I was trying to find new things for the conference to do—new sessions. I was talking to fifty or sixty speakers. 'What should we do this year that we didn't do last year? What's new?' Two of the speakers said, 'Blogging.' I didn't think it was important to do a session on it. I used this new thing called Google, and it said there are only two hundred blogs in the world. But I got curious myself, and started one! What I didn't realize was, this was a disruptive technology that was riding on the back of another disruptive technology, Google—and as Google got bigger, blogging got bigger. I got more into it, started getting more and more traffic to my blog and my boss was pissed that I was doing this blogging thing—he almost fired me. I finally quit my job in 2001, because I got sick of my boss giving me so much trouble for my blogging."

It was a lot easier for Robert to quit and find another job easily because he already had an online reputation by this point at his blog, http://scobleizer.com (now powered by—you guessed it—WordPress). "NEC hired me for the sales department, mostly because of my blog. When I went into the interview, they had a stack of my blog posts printed out right there."

From his job at NEC, Robert got invited to a "Most Valuable Professional" meeting at Microsoft of the top corporate customers. At that meeting, someone confronted CEO Steve Ballmer publicly, saying, "You need to create a better image for Microsoft."

Ballmer responded, "OK, I'll give a dollar to anyone in this room who comes up with a good idea right here."

Robert stood up and said, "Put a more public face on the company." He explained how, outlining what amounted to a strategy for corporate blogging—long before the concept of "corporate blogging" existed.

Ballmer said, "That's a great idea," pulled out a dollar from his wallet, signed it, and gave it to Robert. But Robert eventually got much more than a dollar and an autograph out of that interaction.

A few months later, Robert got a call from a Microsoft executive who had been at that meeting. He said to him, "You're doing something at NEC that I've never seen anyone from a manufacturer do—you're out talking to everyone, blogging, connecting. I want you to come to Microsoft and teach us how to do that."

Scoble interviewed over five hundred people at Microsoft, everyone from the janitor to fellow non-college-graduate Bill Gates, and blogged about what was going on at the company, from an insider perspective. Eventually he got tired of restrictions on his blogging, so he quit in 2006. Not too many people who have such comparatively free-ranging corporate jobs choose to quit, but such is the power of having an incredible personal brand—you can write your own ticket. He quickly found a job at a podcasting start-up, then was wooed by *Fast Company*, and now works for Rackspace (http://www.rackspace.com), the world's largest Web hosting company.

I asked him what his job duties are. "I'm the public face of Rackspace in the Valley. The company is in Texas, so the executives can't be here every night. I'm an ambassador and connector for them. I go to a lot of events, conferences, parties. I also know every tech journalist in the world. I build relationships with press people. If we have a press event, I know whom to invite—and I have their business card. I also travel around the world and interview the leading-edge start-ups. I understand what's going on in the industry, and if I see something happening, I tell the executives, 'You better kick into gear in this area.'" If Robert wants to travel somewhere to pursue a hot lead for the company, he just goes. "I don't even ask anymore. I'm going to Davos next week."

Sounds like one of the greatest jobs anyone could wish for. Not too many people have corporate jobs like Robert does—complete freedom to travel when he wants, go to which events he wants, and talk to whomever he wants, whenever he wants. And the reason is, not too many people have been as passionate, savvy, and persistent about building up their personal brand and network of connections as Robert has. He's become one of the most influential tech bloggers in the world, and lives life completely on his own terms.

I asked Robert if he ever considered writing that last Shakespeare paper, seventeen years late, and get his BA. He burst out laughing. "I have always joked around that if I actually got my journalism degree, my salary would go *down*. Because a journalism degree is not worth anything."

His career advice? Build up your presence as much as possible on new platforms, media, and communities as they arise—the ones that already exist, and the ones we can't even imagine yet, that will no doubt burst onto the scene. "HuffingtonPost.com didn't exist five years ago. TechCrunch didn't exist five years ago. YouTube didn't exist six years ago. Facebook didn't exist six years ago. Twitter didn't exist five years ago. That's the world we're living in now. Why don't you build a LinkedIn page instead of watching TV all night long? The savviest kids today already know how to build networks that work for them." Robert believes that time spent building your presence and network of connections online—your personal brand—is one of the most important things you can do, because it will open doors for you that simply wouldn't open otherwise.

He said he Googled me right after I e-mailed him for the interview request. "Within minutes, I knew something about you. I knew how to plug you into my world. I knew what size influence you had, and in which spheres. I knew your network and whom you were connected to." Luckily, I had already been taking my own advice and building up my online bio on my own site (using WordPress), plus Facebook, Twitter, and LinkedIn.

■ DANIELLE LAPORTE— RADIATING HER WAY TO SUCCESS

In her late twenties, Danielle LaPorte found herself in the position many twentysomethings with college degrees now find themselves: broke and depressed. She had moved back to Canada, after a stint working in the United States flamed out due to the dot-com crash. "I was totally lost. I had a fucked-up identity. I wore pajamas for six months." (Note: This was long before Marian's "Pajama Job Hunt"!)

So she did what many twentysomethings in this position do: she decided to go to graduate school. Art school, to be exact. "I remember sitting in one of my first classes—it was like an intro class, I hadn't been accepted or rejected yet. And I just thought, 'This is the most pedantic, wanking, navel-gazing *crap*.' I had this moment where I looked at everyone and I thought, 'You are going to *pay* for this?' Which is good, because I got rejected from art school. I saved the letter."

Danielle had a few things going for her, however. She didn't have a lot of debt from her undergraduate education. (In fact, she didn't *have* an undergraduate education.) She had ventured into working straight out of high school. Bartending. ("Everyone should bartend at some point. It's Psychology 101.") Then a job at The Body Shop.

She started out pumping peppermint foot cream at a retail store. She asked for and got a series of promotions, all the way up to assistant manager, then a job on the corporate side of the company, in their Department of Social Inventions. Then a job in the United States at a high-profile Washington nonprofit think tank.

How did she get all these promotions? Read the next chapter, on the entrepreneurial mind-set—her strategy was straight out of that mentality. She always looked for the highest-leverage thing that could be accomplished in that moment, and then got it done, never waiting for "permission" or "instructions" to make things better. She just did it. "I just kept doing big things, then asking for promotions once I did them. Doing, asking, doing, asking."

This points to the second thing Danielle had going for her now that she was looking for her next turn in life: audacity. Her own personal style radiated charming, seductive audacity.

She had always gotten where she wanted to go by *cultivating* her own personal quirks, charms, and unique personality, rather than fitting herself into some socially expected corporate box and fitting in. "I was so grateful that I never went to a university. I never had a box to get out of."

She decided she wanted to spread this message—the importance of cultivating, rather than suppressing, your own individual style and expression (your "personal brand," to use the language of this chapter) in the professional realm. She wanted to write a book on the topic.

Problem was, she had never written a book, and had little formal authority to do so. All she had was her own moxie, and her outsized personality. "I'd never even taken a writing course. I'm not even sure about my grammar sometimes. 'Should that be *I* or *me*?' [Laughing.] But I wrote the proposal, and I can sell ice to Eskimos, dirt to farmers. This is the other thing about naïveté. I was like, 'I'll just call.' Just pick up the phone. I landed one of the top agents in the business. It's easy to sell when you believe in stuff. I call it 'Radiate and State the Facts.' You just pound out your devotion, your commitment to what you're doing. Then state the facts in a very measured way about what you're doing. That's it. I am going to radiate and state the facts and if you get it, great. If you don't, then we're not right for each other." Danielle, a master of radiating her infectious personality, got the deal, and her first book came out in 2008.

Soon she decided to build up her brand around herself instead, her own place on the Internet. She started her own blog (http://whitehottruth.com), dishing out her own blend of business and marketing advice. If you check out her writing, it's *dripping* in her own personality. Not too many business consultants write blog posts with titles like "My Dominatrix of Decision Rides a Hedgehog" and "Why Self-Improvement Makes You Neurotic." But Danielle LaPorte does. Which is why, I believe, people are drawn to her writing in droves, and line up to consult with her—rather than lining up for the masses of businesses out there that "play it safe," hide their personalities out of fear, and end up with zero personality (and few customers) at all.

Danielle held "Fire Starter Groups" in sixteen cities to help teach budding entrepreneurs to start the fires of their own creativity. "I held groups in pole-dancing studios and in boardrooms. Whatever it takes! I did hundreds of one-on-one sessions to develop fresh teaching material." She then parlayed this material into an e-program, "The Fire Starter Sessions," which grossed $170,000 in the first year.

She currently charges $1,000 for a one-hour consulting session, and you'll have to wait several months if you want to book one. She's just sold her next book project, based on the Fire Starter Sessions, to Random House for a quarter of a million dollars. I bet a lot of people who got accepted to grad school—rather than rejected, as she was—would envy *that*. Let's face it. A little line on your resume saying you went to grad school doesn't have much personality. A thriving, high-traffic blog, oozing with personality and brilliance, a full $1,000 per hour consulting practice, an online e-course, and a book deal with Random House does.

Much of the success of the people in this chapter—from Marian Schembari to Maria Andros to Robert Scoble to Danielle LaPorte—stems from their fearlessness in cultivating and expressing their original, authentic personal brand.

Of course, in order to *express* your originality, you have to *be* original—and it's an oxymoron to teach someone to be original. But one thing that helps is removing from your mind the decades of programming we've received in school to play it safe, conform, fit in, stick to the crowd, don't stand out. That's a ticket straight to the purgatory of the center of a foot-high resume stack, right where most recent college grads end up. I hope the stories in this chapter have provided inspiration and examples of how to escape the stack—indeed, how to escape the tyranny of the entire resume format—and make your presence known.

THE ENTREPRENEURIAL MIND-SET VERSUS
THE EMPLOYEE MIND-SET

Become the Author of Your Own Life

Ten years ago, Hal Elrod was driving home on the freeway to Fresno, California, with his girlfriend, after speaking at a motivational conference related to his work. A budding public speaker, he had just received the first standing ovation of his life, and he was thrilled. In fact, he was so excited by his triumph that he wanted to call his mother and father and share the news with them. But he looked down at his clock and saw that it was 11:34 P.M. He remembered thinking he didn't want to wake them.

That was the last thought he remembered for two weeks.

He woke up from a coma in the hospital six days later, though he has no recollection of the week following the coma either.

That night, a man had been hanging out at a bar near where Hal spoke, drinking. He'd only had a few beers, but he was intoxicated enough that, when he entered the highway, the man didn't realize he was entering on the *off ramp*.

The man "merged" right, into what he thought was the slow lane, not realizing that he was now driving at 70 miles per hour headlong into the fast lane of oncoming traffic. Straight toward Hal.

Hal's two-door Mustang collided with the man's Chevy truck head-on, each going 70 miles per hour, with no brakes before impact.

Hal's airbag engaged, protecting him from the initial impact. But the worst was still to come.

The Mustang spun out, ending up perpendicular to the road, with Hal's door facing oncoming traffic. The car behind Hal's didn't even have time to brake before hitting Hal's door directly.

Hal's femur suddenly snapped and was sticking out of his thigh. His pelvis was smashed between the oncoming car and the center console of his own car. All the bones in his left elbow were crushed, he severed the radial nerve in his left arm, all the bones in his left eye were crushed, and his eyeball was basically dangling. His ear was hanging on to his skin by a quarter of an inch. The ceiling of the car buckled and sliced a V from the front of his skull to the back of his head.

Hal was the only person who suffered any major injuries in the accident; the drunk driver, Hal's girlfriend, and all other drivers involved in the accident were safe.

When emergency services used a Jaws of Life tool to pull the roof back, Hal started spewing blood. It turned out that the car had been keeping him alive—he had such a large hole where his femur had pierced through that the pressure from the door was keeping his blood inside his body, preventing him from bleeding out.

When emergency services pulled Hal out of the car, the blood came out with such fury that he flatlined—his heart stopped beating—making him, by some definitions, clinically dead for the next six minutes; with chest decompressions, they were eventually able to resuscitate him.

Six days later, Hal came out of his coma in the hospital; he had flatlined two more times during that period.

He was twenty at the time of the accident. A C student throughout high school, he had been a student for a year at the College of the Sequoias, a community college in Visalia, in Central California. He left after his first year to go into sales, found he had a knack for it, and within a year was earning six figures at an annualized rate.

At some point in his sales career, he had learned about a concept called "the five-minute rule" from one of his sales mentors. This mentor, a high school dropout and now a successful sales manager, had told Hal: "You're going to have customers who aren't going to buy from you. Some might be rude to you or cut your appointment short. You're going to have days when you don't reach your goals. And it's OK to be negative sometimes. But not for more than five minutes. You've got to live by the five-minute rule. Bitch, moan, complain, vent, get it out of your system, whatever you've got to do. But just for five minutes. Beyond that, there's no benefit to dwelling on it. Instead, focus 100 percent of your energy on what's in your control. What can you do now? How can you learn and benefit from the experience? How can you move forward?"

Once he regained consciousness and memory in the hospital, two weeks after the accident, the disfigured Hal remembers calling upon this advice and experience, gained during his sales training, to help him cope with his accident.

"I very quickly came to the realization that I had to accept what had happened to me. And while I felt plenty of negative emotion about the accident before that realization, after I had that thought, my negative feelings around it disappeared almost overnight.

"At one point, unbeknownst to me, my doctors called in my parents—both my physician and my psychologist, who was helping me deal with the trauma. They said to my parents, 'We're very concerned with Hal. We believe he's in denial. This is very common with accident victims that have been through such a horrific accident, and sustained so much damage. They go into a state of denial, in which they can't face what happened. Every time we see Hal, he's always laughing and smiling, he's telling jokes and making us laugh. That's not normal, not for someone who's been through what he's been through. We need you to talk to him and sit down and find out how he's really feeling. Because until he accepts what's happened to him, and faces it, the emotional healing can't begin.'" Hal continued:

> My dad came in one night, sat next to me, and got real serious. He said, "Hal, I want to talk to you. Turn the TV off, I want your attention. How are you feeling?"
>
> "Uh . . . great, Dad, why?"
>
> "Well, I know you have friends here, you're laughing, you're joking, you're reminiscing, telling stories. But when you don't have people around to distract you, when you're not watching TV, when it's late at night and you're falling asleep and you're by yourself, and you're thinking about what happened to you, how are you feeling? Are you sad? Are you angry with this drunk driver for doing this to you? God knows your mom and I want to kill this guy! Are you depressed? The doctor says all these things are normal, but it's important that we talk about it."

I really thought about it. Am I depressed, am I sad, am I angry? I looked into myself. Then I looked at him, and I said, "Dad, I thought you knew me better than this. I'm great! In fact, I'm *grateful*. I can't change what happened to me. There's no point in feeling bad about it. If I feel down on myself, or sad or depressed, that doesn't change anything, it just makes me miserable." I told him about the five-minute rule. "It's been weeks since the accident. I'm way past my five minutes."

I realized that there was literally zero benefit to focusing my emotion or energy on things that have already happened in the past, so I'm totally focused on how I can turn this into a positive experience, and what I can learn from it.

I told my dad: "I'm already seeing how I can turn this into a positive experience. There are two things I've always wanted to do. I've always wanted to write a book. Maybe I could write a book about this someday. And, the last year since I've been giving speeches at sales conferences, my dream has been to become a motivational speaker. Well, up until now, I really didn't have that amazing of a story to tell anyone. You and Mom were pretty good to me, I had a good childhood, I didn't have any drama to speak about! [Laughing.] But this is something I could share with people. I see it's my responsibility to overcome this in the best possible way, and have the best possible attitude, so that one day I can teach other people how to do the same thing with their challenges."

The doctors said Hal would never walk again.

Hal has since recovered fully, has written a book called *Taking Life Head On!*, and now makes his living traveling as a motivational keynote speaker (http://www.YoPalHal.com), sharing his message—about taking responsibility for your challenges and creating the life of your dreams—with high school and college students around the nation.

None of us would choose to undergo the ordeal Hal underwent, nor would we wish it upon anyone else.

Yet, here's a remarkable fact about Hal's story. *Hal Elrod probably got more out of a life-threatening accident, which smashed him to bits, than most people get out of their entire formal education.*

That's not to say that car accidents are *good* things—of course I'm not saying that. May neither you nor I ever be injured like that.

But Hal Elrod *chose* to turn this immensely challenging event into something that ultimately had a profound positive impact on the rest of his life for the better. Thus, by his own volition, he got far more value out of this *horrific* experience than most people ever do by passively following whatever predetermined path society had laid out for them. The turn of events that occurred around that accident may have been one of the most positive things that ever happened in his life—because he *chose* to make it so.

We don't get to choose what happens to us. But we get to choose what it means. And in that choice is a tremendous power. This chapter, the final, longest, and most important chapter in the book, is about that choice: the choice to become the active ingredient in your own life. It's called "The Entrepreneurial Mind-set"—and you can exercise it whether you're an entrepreneur, an employee, or still a student.

■ FROM F IN BUSINESS CLASS TO A MULTIMILLION-DOLLAR BUSINESS—HOW TO ESCAPE VICTIMIZATION AND ENTITLEMENT, AND STOP MAKING EXCUSES

In his early twenties, Joe Polish got invited by an old high school buddy to join him on a weekend Jet Ski trip with a multimillionaire self-made entrepreneur. Joe jumped at the opportunity, as he was extremely down-and-out at that time in his life—running a small carpet-cleaning business that was perpetually on the verge of bankruptcy—and he needed a change in his life. Joe told me:

> I figured I would go and pick this guy's brain. At the end of the day, we were sitting on the tailgate of a pickup truck at a lake in Arizona. This was my chance. I said to the guy, "I hear you do real well in business, and I have a carpet-cleaning company which isn't doing as well as I'd like it to. I'd like to go into another business where I can make some real money. I hear that you do pretty well, so I was wondering if you had any recommendations of what sort of business I could go into where I can do really well."

He said, "There are other people in your business that are making a lot of money?"

"There's a couple of cleaning companies in Phoenix that make over a million dollars a year," I said to him. "But they've been around a long time, they've got good name recognition, they're established. Where's with me, it's almost impossible to make this business work, and all people care about is price . . ." and blah blah blah. I was making all these excuses.

I thought these excuses were legitimate. I had been working really hard. I was not ripping people off. I was doing the right thing—I delivered good work. I truly cared about my clients. I explained to him how I'd gotten certified, I'd gotten training, I'd learned this craft over the last year and half or two years since I dropped out. I couldn't figure out why I wasn't successful.

After I made all these excuses to this guy as to why I wasn't successful, he said, "Well, if there are other people doing well in your industry, and you're not, there's nothing wrong with the business you're in, there's something wrong with you."

And I said, "Well, no, no, no, you don't understand . . ." and I went through a whole other list of excuses as to why the business wasn't working. "I'm good at what I do. It's just a really tough business. I want to get into a different, better business, which will be easier."

He said, "Look, young man. You're like most people. You think the grass is greener on the other side. What's going to happen if you go into another business is you're going to spend another six months, another year, another two years, learning the technical skills of another industry, so you can go out and repeat the same bad business habits that have caused you to be a failure in this business.

"What you need to do, young man, is learn fundamental business skills. Because once you do, you can apply those to any industry. But until you learn how to make a business work, it doesn't matter what industry you go into, you're still going to fail at it."

That was probably the most profound advice ever given to me, at a time in my life when I was willing to hear it, and have it sink in.

Joe had gone to college for two years at New Mexico State University. He then left to go to Chandler-Gilbert Community College in Arizona. He got an F in the course "Owning and Operating a Small Business" while there. And a C in the course Principles of Marketing. But a friend told him that another guy was making oodles of money in the carpet-cleaning business. He hated school— he found the classes too abstract and removed from day-to-day realities and concerns—and decided to leave and see if he could support himself in this new business.

For the first two years, the business was a complete failure. Part of this stemmed from some serious personal problems. He had a difficult upbringing. His mother died when he was four, and he moved around a lot as a child, often living in trailer parks, in circumstances that involved physical and sexual abuse. "I had zero memories of anything positive in my childhood. By high school, I was very messed up. I was pretty much a drug addict. In my worst possible state, I weighed a hundred and five pounds, from freebasing cocaine for three months straight. I was completely lost."

By the time of the lake trip, however, Joe had gone past rock bottom, had cleaned up from drugs, and now was ready for change in his economic life as well. Which was why he was ready to take this wealthy man's advice:

He didn't give me a solution to my how-to-make-money problem. (The solution, it turned out, was simply learning marketing. I was good at the technical skills of the business—I could deliver the jobs. I just simply didn't have enough people hiring my services. I didn't know how to market and position myself. I didn't even know what marketing was.)

No, the guy never gave me the answers. But what he gave me was a huge paradigm shift. I left that Jet Ski trip, and I remember driving back to my home. I remember thinking to myself, "I live in America—this is one of the greatest countries in the world, in my opinion *the* greatest country in the world. I'm young. I've got full use of my limbs. I abused myself with drugs early on in my life, but my brain still seems to work pretty well. And I've got access to a lot of stuff. If there's other people having success in business, and I'm not, they know something that I don't. So I actually have to learn what it is other people know.

What I did—thanks to this man's inspiration—was get rid of an entitlement attitude and get rid of a victim mentality. I decided, "I'm going to figure out how to do this." I made a pact to myself that I would not get out of the carpet-cleaning business until I figured out how to make it successful.

Joe decided he would do *whatever* it takes to succeed. Which meant, of course, education. But not bullshit, abstract, theoretical education. *Useful, relevant* education. Self-education. He immersed himself completely in learning direct-response marketing—largely the kinds of materials I described in Success Skill #3. He studied copywriters such as Gary Halbert, and fellow college-nongraduates Claude Hopkins, David Ogilvy, and Dan Kennedy, and started implementing what he was learning into his business. Within a year, Joe had turned his carpet-cleaning business into a six-figure business. Soon, so many other carpet-cleaning proprietors wanted to know his secrets that he began a second business teaching them marketing skills. He eventually sold the carpet-cleaning business itself, and now his marketing training business has generated *millions* in revenue. He's also become one of the most respected teachers of marketing skills to small entrepreneurs, and hosts the #1 most popular marketing podcast on iTunes (http://ilovemarketing.com).

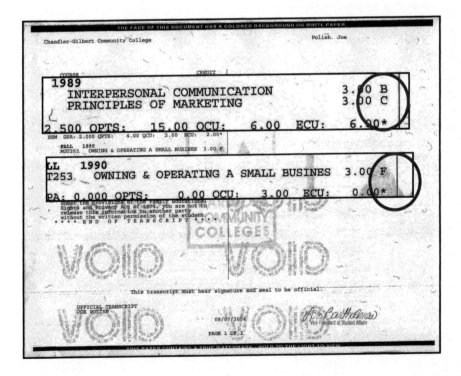

Now a self-made multi-deca-millionaire, Joe Polish shared with me a piece of wisdom he himself gained from one of his best friends, business author and mentor Dan Sullivan. Joe told me: "There are two decisions you need to come to in order to be free, and to be more effective. First is that you are not entitled to *anything* in the world, until you create value for another human being first. Second, you are 100 percent responsible for producing results. No one else. If you adopt those two views, you will go far."

■ THE ENTREPRENEURIAL MIND-SET VERSUS THE EMPLOYEE MIND-SET EXPLAINED

What is the main difference between the self-educated people I've featured all throughout the book—who have enjoyed massive success in their lives—and the majority of other people, who are wondering how to bring more success, happiness, and achievement into their lives?

It all boils down to one thing. They've chosen to do *whatever it takes* to create the lives that they want, including exercising the effort and initiative to figure out what "whatever it takes" is. What they didn't do is sit around, waiting for someone else to feed them the answer, give them the right opportunity, make things safe or easy for them, give them some "Fail-Safe, Guaranteed Plan of Action," or give them permission or authorization or the right credentials to get started figuring what needs to get done, and getting it done.

Bryan Franklin and his partner in business and life Jennifer Russell have called this shift—toward taking your success in your own hands—"The Entrepreneurial Mind-set versus the Employee Mind-set."

I believe that this mind-set shift is the single key distinction that separates the self-made success—on ample display in the stories of this book—from the passivity, feelings of victimization and helplessness, and "quiet desperation" (to use a famous phrase from Thoreau) in which most people sadly find themselves.

Keep in mind, this distinction has nothing to do with whether you're actually an entrepreneur or an employee. It's about *mind-set*. Many employees display the entrepreneurial mind-set (they're usually the ones who get promoted and promoted again and again), and many entrepreneurs display the employee mind-set (they're the ones who typically go out of business).

The entrepreneurial mind-set, according to Bryan and Jennifer (who codeveloped this concept), involves six key distinctions. Most people in this book have never heard of either of them, yet nearly everyone in this book—indeed, nearly everyone who creates success for themselves in their careers—intuitively follows these distinctions. It is, perhaps, the DNA of career success.

The Entrepreneurial Mind-set versus the Employee Mind-set
(courtesy of Jennifer Russell and self-educated millionaire Bryan Franklin)

ENTREPRENEURIAL MIND-SET	EMPLOYEE MIND-SET
Focus on contribution	Focus on entitlement
Focus on outcome	Focus on output
Sort for what's needed	Sort for what's requested
Work yourself out of a job	Work to protect your job
Go toward big decisions, even without authority	Turn away from even the small decisions you have the authority to make
See your circumstances as illusory and temporary	See your circumstances as fixed and permanent

If you want to be an entrepreneur, I have found, these distinctions contain the key tools for creating your own entrepreneurial success. If you want to have a kick-ass career in a corporation as an employee, these distinctions contain the key tools for distinguishing yourself from the cubicle herd and getting on the radar of people who make promotions and look for leadership talent in your organization, fast.

One key: rather than looking at this chart to determine "where you fit," and sitting back with smug satisfaction if you think you already fall on the left side, the person with the true entrepreneurial mind-set is always on the lookout for ways in which the employee mind-set might have grown back into her consciousness. She roots it out again and again as though it is a noxious weed the moment she spots any trace of it.

■ Focusing on Contribution versus Focusing on Entitlement

Focusing your life around contribution means paying great attention to what *you* can contribute to any given person or situation you care about, banishing all sense of being entitled or "deserving" of one outcome or another entitlement from your mind. It's the "give, give, give" philosophy espoused by Elliott Bisnow, Eben Pagan, Seth Godin, Russell Simmons, and others in Success Skill #2 about connecting with powerful mentors and influencers.

Bryan says: "Contribution is an acquired taste. If you look in your life right now, I'm sure you'll find places where you are very solidly in an entitlement mind-set—where you believe that just by sucking in air and then blowing it out again, you deserve to be given benefits and rewards, without any reference to the actual contribution you've made and its results.

"Anything you believe you can *count on* to be there, without regard for what you yourself are doing to *ensure* it's there—that's entitlement. When you lose a job, or a client, do you have the sense that you *lost* something that you *had*? (That's entitlement.) Or, do you immediately think, 'Wow, I needed to contribute more there. How can I contribute more in the future?'

"I can't express enough how many people there are with an entitlement mind-set, up and down corporate hierarchies. It's so rampant. For example, there's a certain *'How dare they!'* attitude many employees have after being laid off. That's entitlement. The employee assumes that because the company hired them, they're entitled to a job.

"That attitude, that you're entitled to a job, even a promotion, no matter what results you produce there, is a death sentence for doing the kinds of things that actually lead to your getting promoted and becoming indispensable in the organization; it is itself a leading risk factor in getting laid off."

■ Focusing on Outcome versus Focusing on Output

The people in this book did not assume that, by going to class five days a week and dutifully doing homework and papers and studying for tests, some wonderful outcome was going to arise from all this diligent output of work, just like parents and teachers and society said it would. Rather, they engaged in deep inquiry about what outcomes they specifically wanted to create in their lives, and then *relentlessly* engaged in *only* the activities directly related to producing those outcomes in their lives.

Self-educated serial entrepreneur Scott Banister, who sold his IronPort Web security appliance company to Cisco in 2007 for $830 million, is a living example of focusing on outcome instead of output. Scott was studying at the University of Illinois at Urbana-Champaign in the late nineties, with the intention of becoming a professor of computer science. On the side of his studies, he began teaching himself HTML (hypertext markup language). He soon applied for and got a job as a webmaster, and then started various Web companies, including a banner ad company with college buddy Max Levchin (who later went on to cofound PayPal).

"We tell kids school is important, and most kids, including myself, believe that, and keep going further and further into formal education, with the attitude that 'this is what's important in the world.'

"Well, the problem with that is that that's just a cliff that just ends at some point. It's like 'Do well in school! Do well in school! Do well in school!' And then, once you're out, you realize: oops, actually, this is not how the world works, you don't earn any money directly from doing well in school, and you can't even support yourself! It's a road that might go somewhere, but it might not. For a lot of people, that's a really disappointing thing. They dutifully go through the process, and they finish high school, and they go to college, and they finish college, and they're like, 'Great, where's my red carpet to financial security!'

"That's just not how the world works. I found quickly that, by day, I was going to class, learning a bunch of abstract, theoretical stuff, whereas by night, I was working on a business. I could see that business is how things actually get done in the world, and how people make money in the world: you build stuff, things that consumers want." See how Scott is focusing on contribution and outcome here, rather than on entitlement and output? This is pure entrepreneurial mind-set at work.

"I realized that was how I would achieve my goals—through business. For a while, I kept those goals going simultaneously—I was like, 'Oh, I have this set of goals around going to school, which I was ingrained with as a child, and then I have these goals related to creating new products and businesses.' But very quickly it became clear, business is where I'm learning all the real skills that are going to help me for the rest of my life. And this stuff in class, I didn't even know when it is going to help me or anyone else, ever. I realized, getting involved with business sooner rather than later, as opposed to being off in this education bubble, which is very different from the way the work world works, was incredibly important for me.

"There's this really weird notion out there. All the way up through college, we assume we're learning a vocation, separate from business, such as being a doctor, or a lawyer, or an engineer, or a nurse, or a computer programmer. And then, alongside all these vocations, there's this other vocation over here called 'business.' And that's for some small number of people, who go learn about 'business.' And the rest of us will become doctors, lawyers, engineers, nurses, computer programmers. The reality is, no matter what vocation you're in, you end up working for a business of one kind or another. Thus, everyone's vocation is business. No matter what you're doing, your vocation is business. The more you can understand the machinery that you're working in, the better off you're going to be."

Scott Banister, and other self-educated success stories featured in this book, relentlessly look at the *outcome* they want to produce in the world and in their lives, and relentlessly focus on how to achieve that, cutting out all extraneous crap not relevant to that outcome. It's one of the key factors that distinguishes those with the entrepreneurial mind-set from those with the employee mind-set.

Those in the employee mind-set, in turn, feel satisfied if they just work harder and harder and harder—in school, at a workplace, in a business—without paying much attention to whether all that effort is directly producing the specific outcomes they want.

In many ways, our modern school-to-workplace system was *specifically designed* to be populated with people exhibiting the employee mind-set of cranking out more and more output without focusing on real-world outcomes.

Many people spend four years soaking up bullshit in academia, then go to work for consulting firms, which peddle bullshit to bloated corporate bureaucracies already full of bullshit.

You can always make a fast buck peddling bullshit—that is, peddling output unrelated to outcome. But if you want real financial security—comfort in the knowledge that you will always be able to generate resources for yourself and your family—then develop a keen nose for any situation in which you are expected to drone away at lots and lots of hard-work output, without any regard for the value of the real-world outcome all this work produces. Run away from these situations as soon as you get the first whiff.

Instead, run always toward creating real-world results for people who are willing to pay for these results, and you'll never have to worry about money; it will always be there for you in sufficient supply. Exchanging your cash for bullshit (which is mostly what happens in higher education these days), or exchanging your bullshit for other people's cash (which is mostly what happens these days in the bloated corporate, government, and nonprofit bureaucracies for which college serves as a job credential and training ground), is never a recipe for long-term financial security. The entrepreneurial mind-set, which involves focusing on outcome rather than output and contribution rather than entitlement, applied in your own ongoing self-education, your own business, or in your place of work, is the recipe.

■ Sorting for What's Needed versus Sorting for What's Requested

If you look for and take care of what's *needed* in a situation, rather than what's requested by your boss, your teammates, or your clients, you'll always be the first one up for promotions, the first one to win new business, and the last one laid off.

Multi-entrepreneur Russell Simmons told me, "Find out what people in your organization need, and give them that service. That is the way entrepreneurs think—'I'm going to fix the problem.' You get paid by how many problems you solve, and people will gravitate toward you. If you know your boss's job better than your boss, your boss is going to count on you for more things. You can begin to learn different parts of the job more than the boss knows them— you can't start anywhere, it doesn't make a difference. The person who can start solving problems and exercising initiative and leadership at the bottom certainly won't be able to at the top, either—and in fact, that person won't even get to the top."

Sadly, our education system, in its current form, is essentially

one long series of contrived classroom situations in which the purpose is essentially to do what has been requested by an authority
figure. This is the *opposite* of how success occurs in the real world.

The late Wharton management professor Russell Ackoff writes,
"Every child learns at a very early stage that when they're asked a
question in school they must first ask themselves a question: What
answer does the asker expect? That's the way you get through
school, by providing people with the answers they expect. Now,
one thing about an answer that somebody else expects is it can't be
creative because it's already known. What we ought to be trying
to do with children is get them to give us answers that we don't
expect—to stimulate creativity. We kill it in school."[1]

To be successful in the twenty-first century, when all the
factory-style jobs are being shipped offshore, you need to train
yourself out of the habit—drummed into you from a young age in
school—of simply responding to the requests of authority figures,
hoping that collecting their little gold stars of approval will get
you ahead.

■ Work Yourself Out of a Job—Don't Work to Protect Your Job

What's the best way to ensure you never climb to the next rung on
the ladder in your workplace or business? By clinging desperately
to the lower rung as if it were your salvation in life.

How do you become a leader in your workplace or your business? By making yourself obsolete in your current role and finding
a higher-leverage role to play. And then making yourself obsolete
in that and finding a higher-leverage role to play. And on and on.

Celebrated business author Guy Kawasaki—who holds an undergraduate degree from Stanford and an MBA from UCLA—
expresses this sentiment cogently in the *New York Times*: the "ideal
goal would be to make yourself dispensable—what greater accom-
plishment is there than the organization running well without
you? It means you picked great people, prepared them and inspired
them. And if executives did this, the world would be a better
place."[2]

This notion of making your job obsolete, of making yourself
"dispensable" in this way, would seem to fly in the face of Seth Godin's notion of a "Linchpin," or an indispensible employee, which

I cite widely in this book. Actually, someone who continuously makes themselves "dispensable" and "redundant" at their lower-leverage roles in the organization—through good hiring, outsourcing, delegation, automation, systematization, whatever—and at the same time continuously seeks roles of greater and greater leverage and leadership, *is* indispensible to the organization. That's a linch-pin in action.

■ Go Toward Big Decisions, Even Without Authority

The people in this book are successful because they didn't wait around for someone to tell them to be successful. They didn't wait around for someone to tell them they could make big decisions in their lives, and have a big impact.

Could there be anything more audacious than deigning to have a big impact on society, without jumping through all the hoops and checking off all the checkmarks society tells you that you need to check off before you can do so?

Bryan explains: "If I work in a retail store, and I don't have any training, tools, power, or budget, and I believe I can make a positive impact on sales, I'm going to start just making those decisions. I don't need the authority. I'm trying to make a contribution and have the outcome be good for the store. I might make a mistake, and I'll accept the consequences, but any smart boss will see that my intentions are to make him more money and will soon start to see me as an indispensable employee, ready for promotion.

"People with an employee mind-set don't want to be the one responsible for making a bad decision, so they move away from re-sponsibility for all decisions. It's part of protecting their job. But they didn't get the message that, in this economy, such behavior is the *opposite* of ensuring your future employment. Because they're not making any real decisions, which means they're not having any real impact. They'll be the first to go when leaders start look-ing to trim fat."

■ See Your Circumstances as Illusory and Temporary, Not Real and Permanent

This last point might risk getting too philosophical for some readers. But I think it's important.

A key aspect of the entrepreneurial mind-set is seeing the world around you as largely made up. Sure, there are societal rules, but those rules are often arbitrary and outdated, and can therefore frequently be broken, bent, bypassed, or just plain ignored, to good effect.

The people we've met in this book, with the entrepreneurial mind-set, look out at the world and see malleability, elasticity, plasticity, flexibility. They see how they can bend currently accepted "reality" toward the reality they would prefer.

Those with the employee mind-set, in turn, look out and see a world full of protocols, rules, regulations, fixed hierarchies, established orders. They bow their head down and "stick with the program," hoping that if they just do what they're told and what's expected of them, it will turn out all right, just as Mom or Dad or Teacher or Professor or Boss said it would.

Seth Godin said to me: "Most people don't see that they have options beyond what society tells them to do. That's the biggest problem. They honestly believe that compliance is the shortcut to success. If you go to any newspaper in America—the newspapers are all dying. What better business landscape is there to do groundbreaking, innovative work? And yet, there are all these people who work in newspapers who think that they can comply their way to success. It's insane."

One of my main motivations for writing this book is encouraging you, my readers, to see the world as less fixed—a little more open to creative molding and shaping—than you thought it was when you first started reading the book.

There's more wiggle room, more flexibility at the joints of society, than you might have imagined. You just have to look for it. This is the essence of the entrepreneurial mind-set, which all the people I've featured in this book share in one fashion or another.

"A reasonable man adapts himself to his environment," George Bernard Shaw tells us. "An unreasonable man persists in attempting to adapt his environment to suit himself. Therefore, all progress depends on the unreasonable man."

Hal Elrod did not "make up" the fact that his body was crushed in a near-fatal car accident. That was a hard, brutal, inescapable reality, over which he had no choice. But nearly everything after his accident he created himself. He literally made up the story as he went along. Whereas most people would view his accident as a defeat that would radically lower the quality of their experience for the rest of their lives, Hal chose to view it as an opportunity to grow, to develop a deeper relationship with life, to become a stronger man, and to reach even higher for his dreams. After the accident, he got right back into the driver's seat of his own reality.

This is a skill at which nearly everyone interviewed in this book excels—writing their own script in life.

What script would *you* write if you were the author of your experience—the active ingredient of your life—rather than the passive receptacle of society's program?

■ THE MILLIONAIRE JUNK MAN AND THE MYTH OF THE DEAD-END JOB

Once, in the middle of a three a.m. bull session at my high school, Deerfield Academy boarding school, I took a break from another all-night paper-writing marathon and asked one of my dorm buddies why we were all working so damn hard. The answer was forthcoming: "to get into a top college." (For the tone of this answer, think *"Duh?"*)

We were obsessed with college—which college we would get into, how high on the pecking order it would be. Of course, Harvard, Yale, Princeton, Columbia, Brown, Stanford, MIT, Penn, and Duke were at the top, or Williams, Dartmouth, Middlebury, or Amherst for those who wanted a smaller school. Other name-brand schools such as Georgetown, Cornell, Johns Hopkins, Tufts, and NYU would also do. The terrible fear was not getting into any brand-name school, and being relegated to some middling no-name college.

That night, I decided to push the line of questioning a little further. I wouldn't normally have asked these questions, as the answers were so taken-for-granted at Deerfield. Perhaps I was just overly sleep-deprived and not thinking straight.

"And why, exactly, is it so important to get into a good college?"

"To get a good job."

"And why, again, is it so important to have a good job?"

"To make tons of money."

"And why do we want to make so much money?"

"*Dude*, shut up—to buy shit with. To have a nice car, nice clothes, a nice house, to eat in nice restaurants, to go on ski vacations. To have a hot wife. Dude, you don't want to end up as a *garbageman,* do you?"

"Oh yeah," I muttered, and went back to my paper-writing.

Thus, these were the main motivators that would get us, sixteen- and seventeen-year-olds, to do four or five hours of homework a night in high school (plus application-worthy extracurriculars), and spend our Friday and Saturday nights in studying or writing papers: first, the fear of failing a given test or project. Few of us ever failed, but the fear was ever present. Next, the fear that such a failure would bring our grade for that class down. Next, the fear that the lower grade would somehow contribute to our failing to get into one of the elite schools. And finally, the fear that failing to attend one of the elite schools would lead to our being garbagemen. Deerfield was a place full of bright, talented kids from wealthy backgrounds scared to death they were all going to become garbagemen.

Indeed, when I interviewed the self-educated subjects of this book, I started all the interviews in the same way: "Most people, including parents, teachers, and politicians, will tell you that if you don't get your college degree, you're going to end up as a garbageman. How did you avoid buying into that viewpoint and having faith in yourself that you could go out and succeed by educating yourself instead?"

Yet, when I began interviewing Brian Scudamore, I had to stop myself as soon as I was about to utter the word "garbageman" in my little opening spiel. Because Brian is a junk man, of sorts. A very, very wealthy junk man.

He's not literally a garbageman, in the traditional sense. But as founder and CEO of 1-800-GOT-JUNK? (http://www.1800gotjunk .com), he probably created more wealth via hauling junk than just about anyone on the planet.

One day in 1989, as a freshman in college, Brian found himself wondering how the heck he was going to pay for his college education. He was standing in a McDonald's parking lot in Vancouver, and he saw a truck go by, which said "Mark's Hauling."

"When I saw that pickup truck," Brian told me, "I thought, 'Uh-huh, there's the idea. I'm going to go buy a beat-up pickup truck and I'm going to start hauling junk.'"

He went ahead and bought an old truck for $700 and started the business. Soon, through a lot of hustle, he had money coming in. Yet as quickly as he started the business, he began to feel a tension between what he was learning in class and what he was learning on the streets (literally!). "I was learning hands-on how to do things. I was solving my own problems rather than saying, 'Coca-Cola had this problem with marketing and distribution and this is how they solved it.' That is a completely different scale, and it's one that most people won't be able to relate to. My self-made education was practical, and I felt that I was learning by making mistakes rather than reading about someone else's mistakes. I got to make mistakes firsthand and say, 'Okay. Congratulations! Another screw-up!'"

Brian finally decided he was learning more about life through his real-world business than in his classes. He decided to leave school and focus entirely on his business, which was already profitable. "My father is a liver transplant surgeon. He had expectations that I was going to follow in his footsteps, or at least do something academic, something respectable. When I told him I was dropping out of school to become a full-time junkman, he was pretty freaked out. But in the end, he said, 'Okay, you know what, I've got to trust you. You're an adult. You're responsible for making your own decisions.'"

That is really the message of this entire chapter. People with the entrepreneurial mind-set take responsibility for making sure that every experience they have, no matter how challenging, is an opportunity for expanding their learning and their capacity for leadership. They don't shield themselves from responsibility; they take responsibility for seeking out roles of greater responsibility.

Brian kept making mistakes in his business and learning from them, kept growing as a businessperson and a leader, growing step-by-step. "I was dealing with the responsibility of having a business to run and customers to serve. I was learning how to hire and fire people when I made mistakes and brought the wrong people on board. I was learning the logistics of managing a business, of making phone calls, doing jobs, and learning about customer service. I was learning how to market the business and take responsibility for my own actions, saying, 'Okay, I've got a business to grow here and there are no phone calls coming in. What am I going to do?'"

With all this learning and growth, Brian had four trucks under operation within a year, then five the next year. Within five years of leaving college, through good hard bootstrapping (see Success Skill #5) his rubbish-hauling business was doing $1 million in revenue. He bought his first home at age twenty-four.

The business has since exploded. (There's a lot of junk out there that needs to be hauled! Leave it to a self-educated entrepreneur to see that as an opportunity rather than a fate to be avoided at all costs.) The company now has over two hundred locations across Canada, the U.S., and Australia, with U.K. operations opening soon. It does well over $100 million in junk-hauling business per year.

Looking back on all the fear and frenzy my Deerfield classmates and I experienced at the prospect of not getting our proper credentials to become a middle manager in a "good" job, I'm now tempted to ask, "And what if I did become a garbageman?" This might sound naively romantic for someone who has never done any real manual labor (except in volunteer programs). But in light of the work histories of the people profiled in this book, I believe it's a fair question

The fear my Deerfield classmates and I felt of becoming garbagemen—and the specter of "dead-end jobs" used by general culture to terrify kids into college—assumes that such jobs are static, like a low caste in ancient India: once a garbageman, always a garbageman.

Yet, even a cursory read of the lives of the people we've met in this book shows that, for all of them, "dead-end jobs" in their youth were anything but. Rather, such jobs provided valuable exposure to the values of work and industry, opportunities for meeting mentors and others who could advance their career prospects, and a stream of income and savings that helped them live independently, which often became initial capital for ventures that eventually made them affluent. Nearly every person I feature in this book started out their working lives in low-status "dead-end" jobs, from fast food to waiting tables to door-to-door sales and telemarketing to manual labor. But they sure didn't stay there. Why not?

In a wonderful book called *50 Rules Kids Won't Learn in*

School: Real-World Antidotes to Feel-Good Education by Charles Sykes, Rule 15 is: "Flipping burgers is not beneath your dignity. Your grandparents had a different word for burger flipping. They called it opportunity." Sykes writes: "You live in a country with extraordinary opportunity and income mobility: if you start at the bottom, that doesn't mean you will stay there. The important thing is to actually *start*."[3]

If you have the entrepreneurial mind-set, it doesn't matter what job you start out with, even hamburger flipper. You will find a way to become the most valuable damn hamburger flipper in the joint, and then find a way to manage and lead the other hamburger flippers, and then find a way to assume even more responsibility and leadership in some other workplace, and on and on, up and up. Of course, most garbagemen are not going to start multimillion-dollar junk-hauling empires. But it is simply false—almost to the point of propaganda—to assert that starting out in a so-called dead-end job is a condemnation to stay that way for the rest of your life. It is, if you never educate yourself. But the people in this book chose to view such jobs, instead, as expenses-paid laboratories for learning about business, leadership, and the entrepreneurial mind-set.

David Ash, the real estate investor, told me: "I looked at everything I did as an apprenticeship—even low-level sales jobs. I looked at it as something that was going to prepare me for something greater one day. That allows me to embrace whatever menial task or low-level job as simply a necessary stage in the process of becoming successful.

"I was able to characterize myself, in the process, by saying, 'This isn't who I am. I'm this other person meant for much greater success than this—but I know that all greater success has as its seeds these types of activities. I must embrace these fundamental, simplistic activities, which maybe the average person scoffs at, because they are foundational, necessary, in building within me experience and character sufficient for me to be this greater person that I envision myself to be one day.'

"So I saw in all of those experiences, as tough as they were—and don't get me wrong, I didn't like a lot of them—opportunity for learning, growth, and greater leadership. I rejoiced in the challenges I faced, knowing that all the books I'd read, all the autobiographies I'd read by great men, all had this necessary journey of starting at the bottom rung.

"I read about the man who started the Ritz-Carlton hotels,

César Ritz. He started at the lowest rung of the ladder, a high school dropout working as a waiter in a hotel. With time, he was managing hotels, and with more time, he owned them and began a world-class chain.

"What distinguishes the guy who's the waiter, who then goes on to own the hotel, and then a chain of hotels, versus the guy who just remains a waiter and stays bitter and angry about being a waiter for the rest of his life?

"Well, the guy who ends up owning the hotel never sees himself as a waiter, first of all. He only sees himself in the role of the waiter, as a necessary transitional point, to get from being a waiter, to being the manager of a hotel one day, which would give him the necessary knowledge to maybe own a hotel.

"I never saw myself as a salesman, whatever I happened to be selling on the telephone or door-to-door. I always saw myself as the guy who was going to run this place one day, or run some sort of organization like it. As soon as I was running the organization for someone else, I then switched to seeing myself as the guy who owned it. So I just accepted where I was, as a necessary place I had to be, in order to learn what I had to learn, and do what I had to do, to get to the next greater level.

"I was always looking for opportunities for leadership, for opportunities to contribute, for ways to develop relationships with higher-ups, who could help me and whom I could help. My peers typically weren't my coworkers. I wasn't the guy who hung around the coffeepot with everyone else. I was the guy who came in an hour earlier than everyone else. I was friendly, but I wasn't going to work for camaraderie with my coworkers.

"My coworkers were coming twenty minutes late, then they would go to the coffeepot and waste another fifteen or twenty minutes. So I'm working for a full hour and a half before the guys I'm working with are even starting to work. You can imagine the effect of having 20 percent more time in your day has on your work. It wasn't that I was a genius, it's that I worked more effectively than a lot of these other guys.

"I cared. They saw it just as a lousy job that got them to Friday. I saw it as a necessary step to get me from being the guy doing the 'lousy job' to the guy that's running the operation that provides all of these jobs, and then to the guy that owns the business that provides all the jobs. I never thought of them as lousy at any step of the way. I always thought of them as very worthy, and very much a part of the process.

"When I became the manager and then owner of these types of businesses, I tried to encourage my employees to view things this way, so they could rise through the ranks of the company. But very few ears were ready to hear that. Most people saw their jobs from a short-term perspective. They weren't thinking the long game. When you're thinking just in terms of this month or the next six months, it makes sense to see your job as just a lousy source of a paycheck. But not when you're thinking about the next ten years."

Oh how rare is the entrepreneurial mind-set; develop it, and you will go far.

Am I saying that every person born in some god-awful slum in Rio or Nairobi has the opportunity, through the entrepreneurial mind-set, to become a millionaire, and that the people remain poor simply because they've adopted the employee mind-set? Of course not; that's pure propaganda for the status quo of vastly uneven resource distribution in life. People are born with different chances in life, which vastly influence their chances for affluence. The simple fact that I was born learning English in America, versus Swahili in Kenya, gave me a massive leg up in the pursuit of wealth and success in the world, from birth. To suppose otherwise is sheer self-delusion—it's being "born on third base and thinking you hit a triple," as they say.

However, there's not a doubt in my mind that, whatever station you're born into in life, whatever era and whatever country, rich or poor, adopting the entrepreneurial mind-set gives you the *best* chance of raising your station, and the *only* chance at making your biggest dreams come true. Thinking otherwise—for example, thinking that Big Brother government is going to save the poor—is as delusional as thinking that we're all born with equal opportunity.

The entrepreneurial mind-set may not be a *guaranteed* bet, but it's certainly your best bet.

People with the employee mind-set (whether they are actually employees, or whether they are entrepreneurs) may work hard. Very, very hard. But they haul ass along a path others have created for them; they don't create their own path. They are the passive recipients of instructions, orders, and guidance, not the active creators of their own world. They do not have the answers; someone else does. They do what others around them tell them and expect them to do. They hope—indeed, expect and demand—that, if they please the people above them, a steady stream of benefits will flow their way. ("I did what you told me. Now give me my reward!") If the reward is not forthcoming, they complain and get bogged down in bitterness and resentment, like a child who didn't get a candy from Mommy.

To people with the employee mind-set, power resides elsewhere, not within themselves. There may be some safety and security in clinging to the employee mind-set (or at least the comforting illusion of safety) because those with employee mind-set rely on someone more powerful and resourceful than themselves to save them and shield them from risk. But whatever safety there may be—and it diminishes each year forward into the age of outsourcing, offshoring, and downsizing—there's certainly no freedom, no self-determination.

If you always asked yourself how you could make a greater and higher-leveraged contribution to the people you work with and the situations you find yourself in; if you focused like a laser on actual outcome of the projects you're involved with, rather than the output of your time and effort; if you were relentless about taking care of what's actually needed in your workplace or team, rather than just doing what was requested of you; if you started running toward the big decisions in your organization, rather than away from them, whether or not your job description called for it; if you became a diligent student of the ways in which social reality is more flexible and malleable, and less predetermined, than you think it is—if you did all these things, is there any chance you would come out behind?

Of course, there's always a chance of failure no matter what. But that chance is dramatically lower if you adopt an entrepreneurial mind-set in whatever you do (even if it's nine to five), rather than the millions of people who go through life with the passive employee mind-set, consciously choosing (out of fear, lack of imagination, or sheer laziness) to run as fast as they can toward becoming replaceable commodity cogs, with the same generic resume as everyone else, the same paper credentials.

Seth Godin told me: "Safe is the new risky; risky is the new safe. The riskiest thing you can do is play it safe. There are countless examples of people who are now unemployed because they played it safe. All those people who went to Wall Street because it was the safe thing to do, to follow instructions—they all lost their jobs. Go down the list. More and more, if it's a 'safe' job, it's risky."

Those with the employee mind-set have willfully participated in their own corporate dehumanization, by choosing safety in numbers (it's always safer in the middle of a herd) rather than taking risks and adopting an entrepreneurial mind-set in their work. You've heard warnings before about how "the nail that sticks out gets hammered" and how "if you stick your neck out it will get chopped off." Well these days, the guillotines of offshoring and outsourcing, the hammers of downsizing and automation, are waiting to chop off and hammer down all those who *don't* stick their necks out, stand up, and exercise leadership.

If you take on the entrepreneurial mind-set, you see yourself as *responsible* for the impact you have in your business or workplace, and for your own success and advancement in life. You have become the active ingredient in your own life, and in your workplace.

You see a problem in your life or in your surroundings and fix it. You don't count on some higher authority to make things better; you make it better yourself, whether or not you have the authority.

You believe in your own power to blaze your way forward; if someone else was going to blaze the trail, it would have already been blazed.

If you encounter a problem or a roadblock along the way, you figure out how to fix it or bypass it.

You seek help when needed, but you take responsibility for finding the best help, the best answers; you don't just passively accept whatever help or answers are immediately available.

You don't wait around for someone to save you or solve your problems.

You are an active creator of your success, not a passive recipient of instructions, tasks, and rewards.

To a large degree, you create the social and financial reality you live in.

Are you ready to be free?

■ CODA: FROM ERRAND BOY TO EISENHOWER'S BUDDY

At the beginning of the 1900s, a young boy named Louis Marx, born in Brooklyn to Jewish immigrants from Berlin, stays up late on school nights, reading books on "how to become a $5,000-a-year man." At that time, $5,000 was about $113,000 in today's dollars and it was the "magic number," which meant you had made it in your career, much as earning six figures symbolizes a certain arrival today.

Louis graduated high school at age fifteen. Ma and Pa ran, well, a ma-and-pa store, a dry goods retailer that kept closing in one neighborhood of Brooklyn, for lack of business, and reopening in another, with higher hopes. College was out of the question—and the option was scarcely relevant to Louis's life.

Though growing up in relative privation, and bearing the same last name as the most famous revolutionary of all time, Louis didn't harbor any resentment for his lot in life. "The class struggle? Someone sold that idea. We never felt it."[4]

After high school he went to work as an errand boy for Mr. Ferdinand Strauss in New York, a German man who ran a large toy manufacturing and retailing outfit under that name. "Within a few months, the boy was running the factory," Strauss later told *Fortune*.[5]

Louis came up with a toy idea that the old man decided to take a chance on—a paper horn that made sound effects, and could also be worn as a lapel flower. It sold well, and Strauss promoted the teenage Louis to director. He was earning his $5,000 by age twenty.

Louis had strong views about management issues and didn't let his young age deter him from advocating passionately what he thought was best for the company. In an ongoing discussion over whether the company should remain a retailer as well as a manufacturer, Louis stuck his neck out and argued that the company should divest its retail business and become a pure manufacturer. A later *Fortune* profile on him said, "Marx felt that these stores deflected too much working capital and company energy from volume production. The issue came to a vote at the Directors' meeting. Everyone voted against Marx. 'Was my neck down!' he says. 'There I was, still a kid, and out on the street.'"[6]

Marx decided to go into the toy business himself, with his

brother, David. "His working capital consisted of an old table from his Brooklyn home;. . . . the 'office' was a room so small that it was hard to close the door when the table and Dave and Louis were all present.

"Not having the capital to lease or buy factories, he set himself up as a very special sort of middleman. He would find, for example, that a chain store was selling for 10 cents an 'automobile' for which it paid 7 cents. He would study the 7-cent automobile exhaustively with this question in mind: which would be better—to build more automobiles for 7 cents or as good an automobile for 6 cents? When he felt sure of his answer and of a manufacturing solution, he would go to the large chain-store buyers and make his proposition. Having got his order, he would commission a manufacturer to make the goods."[7]

Within years, in the early 1920s, Louis Marx and Company became the largest toy manufacturer in the world, and Louis Marx became a multimillionaire in his twenties—a multi-decamillionaire in today's dollars. Ferdinand Strauss went out of business. Louis bought his old boss's assets and leased manufacturing space in the old Strauss factories.

In the fifties, Louis teamed up with the company of another non–college graduate named Walt. Young Walt had learned about business at age nine by running a paper route. Called "the second dumbest" in class by one teacher, he exhibited no interest in school—and little interest in anything except drawing cartoons. After dropping out, he briefly took a job at the post office to support himself as he drew. Then, in 1918, at age sixteen, he lied about his age so he could enlist in the army, and soon he was shipped off to France to drive an ambulance in World War I.[8]

After returning a year later, the twenty-year-old high school dropout started an animation company called Laugh-O-Gram. "The company had problems making ends meet: by the end of 1922, [he] was living in the office, taking baths once a week at Union Station" in Kansas City.[9] The company went bankrupt a year later. Walt Disney then moved out to Los Angeles to live with his brother, where the two opened Disney Brothers Studios.

In the fifties and beyond, Louis Marx and Company was producing toys based on every Disney-themed character you could imagine, including Mickey, Donald, Pluto, Goofy, Cinderella, and Bambi. The company was the main face of Disney toys throughout that era.

By 1956—keeping the now ten-year-old baby boomers well supplied with their Christmas and birthday presents—Marx and Company was doing $50 million in business, around $390 million in today's dollars. Louis appeared on the cover of *Time* magazine in 1956. In 1972, he sold the company to Quaker Oats for $50 million, about $253 million today.[10]

In his half-century career as a toy manufacturer, starting out as an errand boy, Louis revolutionized the toy business. He was responsible for introducing mass-manufacturing into the industry, employing at peak over eight thousand people in his assembly-line plants in the United States and around the world. For this reason, he was often called by the press "the Henry Ford of toys."

The 1946 *Fortune* profile entitled "Louis Marx: Toy King" says: "The comparison is natural and valid. Both men are completely self-made; both became rich early in life by putting what had been essentially luxury items into the hands of the many; both did it by determinedly lowering prices through their own varieties of mass production and mass selling. Like Ford, Marx developed three things in the process: a vibrant and aggressive interest in general human affairs, an industrial kingdom in which his writ alone runs, and a resolutely individualistic way of doing business with which his rivals, like it or not, are obliged to reckon."[11]

They had another biographical fact in common. Ford didn't have a college degree either. Ford was born on a farm near Dearborn, Michigan, and grew up as a farm boy, with little formal schooling—but a keen interest in tinkering with the machinery on the farm. He left home at sixteen to become an apprentice machinist in Detroit.

Ford writes in his autobiography: "An educated man is not one who is trained to carry a few dates in history—he is one who can accomplish things. . . . A man's real education begins after he has left school. True education is gained through the discipline of life. . . . A man may be very learned and useless. . . . Merely gathering knowledge may be the most useless work a man can do. What can you do to help and heal the world? That is the educational test. If a man could hold up his own end, he counts for one. If he could help ten or a hundred or a thousand other men hold up their ends, he counts for more. He may be quite rusty on many things that inhabit the realm of print, but he is a learned man just the same. When a man is a master of his own sphere, whatever it may be, he has won his degree—he has entered the realm of wisdom."[12]

In the early '30s, Louis helped a young air force colonel locate a hard-to-find toy train switch for the colonel's son's electric train set. The men became friends, and the colonel introduced him to another friend, an air force captain called "Beedle" Smith.

At one point, Louis sent Smith some caviar as a holiday present. "Smith, who had no taste for caviar, passed it on to his next-door neighbor at Fort Myer, Brigadier General [Dwight] Eisenhower. Later, Ike dropped in to thank Marx."[13] The two became lifelong friends, exchanging a glowing correspondence that is housed in the Eisenhower Presidential Library. Louis was a frequent guest of Ike and Mamie at the White House throughout the '50s, personally delivering toys for the White House Christmas tree. The president became godfather to several of Louis's children.

One of those children, Patricia, is my mother. I met my grandfather Louis only once, when I was a baby, too young to remember. I certainly didn't follow his path in life. I went through the highest halls of formal education and spent much of my twenties meandering and lost as a wannabe "avant-garde" literary writer, often living month to month, as I chose to spend my time writing screeds denouncing capitalist materialism, instead of working.

In his twenties, my grandfather had no higher education and lots of street smarts. In my twenties, I had lots of higher education and no street smarts; I didn't begin thinking seriously about money and career until age thirty.

Now in my thirties, I can see that the old man also had a lot of wisdom. I am glad a bit of his spirit has rubbed off on me.

May the spirit of all the bold souls in this book inspire *you*.

THE EDUCATION BUBBLE IS ABOUT TO POP— ARE YOU PREPARED FOR THE AFTERMATH?

In 2005, Cortney Munna graduated from one of the most prestigious universities in the nation, New York University, with a bachelor's degree in women's studies and religion. To pay for this education, she took out two private loans from Sallie Mae of around $20,000, a private loan from Citibank for $40,000, plus federal loans. Five years out of school, in May 2010, she owed $97,000 for her education. At that time, she was living in San Francisco, earning $22 an hour working for a photographer.

Munna's after-tax pay as of May 2010, when I read about her story, was around $2,300 a month. Her rent in San Francisco was $750. Her student loan payments, if she was paying them, would have been around $700, which was 30 percent of her after-tax income. Not many people could sustain $700 monthly debt payments on a $2,300 income, on top of rent and living expenses, for very long. Most people facing such a wall of unsecured debt, relative to income, would probably end up declaring bankruptcy sooner or later. However, student loans are one of the only types of debt not dischargeable in bankruptcy; the only place they get discharged, if not paid down in full, is the grave.

Munna found a temporary solution. She continued her education in night school, which allowed her to defer debt payments. Thus, her loan balance kept compounding upward each month, debt rolling on top of debt. At her hourly earnings at that time, there was no way she would ever race against compounding interest to pay down the debt. At twenty-six, at the outset of her adult life, Munna found herself in a massive financial hole, one that could mar her financial prospects for much of her life—and there was no obvious way for her to get out.

I learned about Munna's story from clicking on a link on the *New York Times* site, which read "Another Debt Crisis Is Brewing, This One in Student Loans." The link led to an article by Ron Lieber entitled "Placing the Blame as Students Are Buried in Debt." The basic premise of the article is the reasonable judgment that, when many people are getting into $100,000 of unsecured debt at the outset of their adult lives, with no easy way to get out relative to their salaries, something has gone terribly wrong. The article sleuths through the story of Munna and essentially asks, "Who's to blame for this mess?" Her parents? The loan providers? The schools? The students who take out the loans?

In a follow-up to the story, Munna states: "I openly acknowledge my responsibility for my current situation, as well as the naïveté in my estimation of the return on investment of a 'high quality' education and a liberal arts degree."[1] This is an honorable acceptance of accountability, and it is fair enough; no one held a gun to Munna's head, forcing her to take those loans out.

Yet simply painting the story as a picture of an adult making poor choices, and who must live with those choices for the rest of her life, seems to me to miss something important. After all, when Munna was originally taking out the loans as she entered college, she was seventeen, at the very cusp of adulthood, not yet old enough to vote, join the military, or legally buy a pack of cigarettes or a beer, or to be tried as an adult in court. Culturally and legally, we acknowledge that people under eighteen should enjoy some amount of protection from the long-term consequences of their decisions.

The civilized world got rid of debtors' prisons a long time ago. The idea is that people make mistakes, and they should be given a second chance in life. Yet we as a society have a strange blind spot around this concept; we (meaning adult society at large, including parents, teachers, politicians, and media pundits) more or less corral our adolescents into taking on massive amounts of unsecured debt to pursue a college education. In the article, Cortney's mother, Cathryn Munna, says, "All I could see was college, and a good college and how proud I was of her. . . . All we needed to do was get this education and get the good job. This is the thing that eats away at me, the naïveté on my part." Cathryn Munna is a grown woman and rightly takes responsibility for her own decisions.

Yet, where did she get this idea that "all we needed to do was get this education and get the good job"? Where did she get the idea that getting a liberal arts degree from NYU would be a good reason for her daughter to go $100,000 into debt? Did these ideas just occur randomly to Cathryn Munna? Were they bizarre, out-of-line, wacky beliefs relative to the culture around her? Where did she get the idea that this was the only way for her daughter to pursue a successful and happy life?

This is the cultural climate in which parents and adolescents are immersed: the myth of higher education. The idea, promulgated in surround sound by other parents, teachers, school administrators, guidance counselors, college brochures, and politicians, is that your only hopes for economic empowerment involve borrowing large sums of money to get a BA degree, and once you have this magic degree, your ticket for life will be written. This is the water we swim in.

An analogy is useful here. The *New York Times* article makes this analogy explicitly: the housing bubble. Sure, the adults who took out ridiculous loans to buy ridiculous houses are responsible. Sure, lenders acted in a predatory way in many cases. Sure, the shenanigans of Wall Street financial engineers played their role. I'm not trying to disavow personal responsibility for any of the players in these messes. But at a certain point, all of these individual factors metastasized into one overarching culture of insanity that spread throughout the nation, in which average, otherwise sensible and sane people found it incredibly difficult to resist making financially disastrous decisions.

In the last year, a number of commentators have picked up the analogy between the housing bubble and the current state of higher education. One of the most strident of these has been Mark Taylor, chair of the Department of Religion at Columbia. In a commentary on the *New York Times* site, entitled "The Education Bubble," he writes, "The next bubble to burst will be the education bubble. Make no mistake about it, education is big business, and like other big business, it is in big trouble."[2]

In a *New York Times* op-ed entitled "End the University as We Know It," Taylor makes a comparison between higher education

and yet another dying, debt-drowned industry: "Graduate education is the Detroit of higher learning. Most graduate programs in
American universities produce a product for which there is no
market (candidates for teaching positions that do not exist) and
develop skills for which there is diminishing demand (research in
subfields within subfields and publication in journals read by no
one other than a few like-minded colleagues), all at a rapidly rising cost (sometimes well over $100,000 in student loans)."[3]

In the *Washington Examiner,* Glenn Reynolds writes, "It's a
story of an industry that may sound familiar. The buyers think
what they're buying will appreciate in value, making them rich in
the future. The product grows more and more elaborate, and more
and more expensive, but the expense is offset by cheap credit provided by sellers eager to encourage buyers to buy.

"Buyers see that everyone else is taking on mounds of debt,
and so are more comfortable when they do so themselves; besides,
for a generation, the value of what they're buying has gone up
steadily. What could go wrong? Everything continues smoothly
until, at some point, it doesn't.

"Yes, this sounds like the housing bubble, but I'm afraid it's
also sounding a lot like a still-inflating higher education bubble. . . .
I think it's better for us to face up to what's going on before the bubble bursts messily."[4]

As stories mount of recent college, professional, and graduate
students gaining diplomas with mountains of debt and few prospects of paying it off, it's more and more difficult to avoid thinking
that we're heading toward some kind of cataclysmic national reck-
oning around higher education. Even the field of law, long considered the safest of the safe choices among professions, is feeling
massive earthquake tremors. Toward the end of my time writing
this book, in January 2011, an article in the *New York Times* appeared, with a Web link leading to it that read, "For Law School
Graduates, Debts If Not Job Offers." The article, by David Segal,
tells the story of Michael Wallerstein, who has amassed around a
quarter of a million dollars in debt by age twenty-seven to attend
bottom-tier Thomas Jefferson Law School.

"Mr. Wallerstein, who can't afford to pay down interest and
thus watches the outstanding loan balance grow, is in roughly the
same financial hell as people who bought more home than they
could afford during the real estate boom. But creditors can't fore-

close on him because he didn't spend the money on a house. He spent it on a law degree. And from every angle, this now looks like a catastrophic investment."[5]

Wallerstein did everything society told him to do to be successful: go to college, get a degree, go to law school, get a law degree. At the time of this writing, he had recently taken a $10-per-hour job as a legal temp.

WHEN ARE WE GOING TO START GIVING OUR YOUNG PEOPLE BETTER CAREER ADVICE?

I hope my book is a step in the right direction.

■ IF YOU'RE UNDER TWENTY, THIS MAN MAY WANT TO PAY YOU $100,000 TO "STOP OUT" OF COLLEGE

Peter Thiel is another person who sees that higher education may be going the way of the housing market. Thiel cofounded PayPal, which sold to eBay for $1.5 billion. In 2004, he famously invested $500,000 in Facebook—the first outside investment in the company—and the stake is now worth billions. As president of Clarium Capital, he oversees over $2 billion in assets.

In January 2011 I met with Peter in his San Francisco mansion— far and away the most stunning piece of real estate in which I have ever stepped foot—which he rents, overlooking the Palace of Fine Arts near the Marina.

Peter gestured toward his majestic rented living room. "The house I'm living in—very nice house. The people who built it spent seven years building it. At the end of the seven years, they decided not to move in. What they had chosen to do with their lives changed during those seven years. I think it's very hard to know what people want to do over twenty years. One of the things that went wrong with housing—when people did the mortgage calculators and compared it to renting—was a big-picture mistake: If you rent, you have options. If you buy, you have fewer options. So buying should be a *lot* cheaper than renting, because of all the options you're giving up."

Peter, who holds undergraduate and law degrees from Stanford, sees an analogy here with investments in formal education. "Take the tracks where one can make a plausible case that formal education is an investible decision. These tend to be the college tracks that are less fun. Premed and engineering: those are the two where college is really not just a high-priced consumption decision. You're spending a lot of Friday nights in the library, memorizing organic chemistry or doing engineering problems.

"But even in these limited cases where college is actually an investment, it only works if you actually do that career. Your premed, plus medical school, plus residency, only is a good investment if you commit to being a doctor for the rest of your life. The challenge with that is that you are constraining the kinds of choices you make when you're just eighteen, starting out.

"You're implicitly giving up on a lot of other things, very early on—so the rewards have to be a *lot* better to make it worth it. It's this piece about flexibility and adaptability that people never think about. One of the things people said during the housing boom, 2005, is 'Yes, this house costs a million dollars, and maybe the price is a little high right now, and it's cheaper to rent, and I might like to spend that down payment on other things—but it will be fine over twenty years.' That may be true. But one of the things that's implicit with that statement is that you know the path your life is going to be on over the next twenty years.

"Similarly, the economics of becoming a doctor or an engineer—the few things where formal education actually makes a lot of sense—should be *insanely* higher than anything else. If they're just close, that's very bad, because there's all this flexibility and adaptability you're giving up."

Partly to combat these problems Peter sees in higher education, he has funded the Thiel Fellowship (http://www.thielfoundation.org), which is awarding twenty budding entrepreneurs under the age of twenty $100,000 each to "stop out" of school and start their business directly. He caused waves around the nation when he announced this program in 2010. The press release says, "From Facebook to SpaceX to Halcyon Molecular, some of the world's most transformational technologies were created by people who stopped out of school because they had ideas that couldn't wait until graduation. This fellowship will encourage the most brilliant and promising young people not to wait on their ideas, either."[6]

In predictable fashion, commentators enthralled by the all-kids-must-go-to-college-or-they'll-end-up-as-janitors ideology reacted in horror. Jacob Weisberg, chairman and editor in chief of the Slate Group unit of the Washington Post Company, said in *Slate* (http://www.slate.com) that the program was "appalling" and "nasty." He accuses Thiel of inciting the young toward "halting their intellectual development around the onset of adulthood" and sees the program as indicative of a trend toward "diverting a generation of young people from the love of knowledge for its own sake and respect for middle-class values."[7]

Weisberg's complaint neatly encompasses nearly all the commonplace assumptions about higher education we've been questioning all along in this book. The most glaring is that college is the only way young people can continue their intellectual development; I believe the stories I've told throughout this book of self-educated people put that belief to rest.

Weisberg also assumes that college is really about "love of knowledge for its own sake." A critic of one of the *New York Times* articles about Cortney Munna, cited earlier, echoes the sentiment in a comment on the *Times* site. "What [Munna] has learned is what a university offers: the tools to understand the world and society. She will do well, even though it'll be tough paying off those [$97,000 in] loans."

I'm all for the love of knowledge for its own sake, and for the tools to understand the world and society. One look at my own bookshelf, full of philosophy, psychology, politics, literature, poetry, spirituality, biography, and popular science, should make that clear. But can Weisberg, and this commenter on the *Times* site, look at me with a straight face and suggest that kids should spend a hundred or two hundred thousand dollars, and rack up a hundred grand in debt, at the outset of their adult lives, to pursue "love of knowledge for its own sake" and "the tools to understand society"? Can't you pursue the love of knowledge throughout your entire lives in less outrageously expensive ways that don't involve crippling debt, such as—gasp!—*reading on your own* after work and on weekends, or taking an online class?

When a respected commentator calls the prospect of a young person *receiving $100,000* to pursue entrepreneurship for a few years—in lieu of *going $100,000 into debt*—"nasty" and "appalling," I cannot help but think we have come into Orwellian times around education, in which "Mountains of Debt Is Freedom."

Finally, the showstopper: Weisberg's suggestion that encouraging entrepreneurship among young people causes them to lose "respect for middle-class values." In American political culture, suggesting that some stance disrespects middle-class values usually ends the discussion right then and there; it's the rhetorical equivalent of farting loudly in the middle of a live television debate. Can we really question *middle-class values*?

Actually, yes, we can. Middle-class values are essentially the stuff of the employee mind-set, the precise values that have led so many young people to be completely fucked in our current economy: follow orders, get all the checkmarks that parents and teachers and society and politicians tell you to get, stick with the herd, don't stick your neck out too much, don't try anything too bold, just do as you're told and there will be a nice cushy job with government- and company-sponsored benefits aplenty waiting for you to guide you through your safe life and your comfortable, secure retirement. This might have been a good set of values to guide young people in 1950, but not in 2011.

I asked Thiel why he wanted to pay promising young people to "stop out" of school. He said: "Some of my friends and I were thinking, 'What can we do to encourage more innovation, more entrepreneurship?' The basic fact is, when you come up with a great idea for something new, the correct thing is to just do it. Because there's no training for it, there's no way you can prepare for being an entrepreneur. By definition, you tend to be doing something new, that's not been done, and so there's no really good tracked training you can get. Even though I think the formal school isn't necessarily *incompatible* with being an entrepreneur, I definitely don't think it prepares people for that in any interesting way. Schooling is important if you want to become a lawyer, a doctor, or a professor. But it's not as critical for being an entrepreneur.

"I'm concerned that schooling has actually changed over the last few decades, in a way where going to school has become much more detrimental than it used to be. The big reason is that it costs so much more, and people accumulate all this debt.

"It costs something like a quarter of a million dollars to go to a good private college. The state schools are not as expensive, but the costs are going up even faster because of all the government cutbacks. If you end up with a hundred thousand dollars of debt, that will powerfully, significantly restrain the kinds of things you can do afterwards. You will have to take high-paying jobs in tracked careers, and you will not be able to do something entrepreneurial. You will not be able to do something in the nonprofit world. There might be things that are just fun, or that are socially useful—there are all sorts of things that are valuable, but do not have a high payoff. And those are all getting really constrained when kids are coming out of school weighed down with all this debt.

"It's significantly different from the seventies and eighties, when it was almost free—it was like a four-year party, and then you could go on to do other things. Maybe you still should have done something right away after high school. But there wasn't that much of a cost to going to college. At this point, there's a much higher cost to it.

"The broader goal of the 20 Under 20 program is to start a conversation about the role of education in our society, and to get people to think more about it. I don't think there's a problem with people going to college. I don't think everyone has to become an entrepreneur. But I think given the costs involved, it's actually important for us to think about this stuff earlier, rather than later.

"One of the strange paradoxes about education is that it's actually become a way to avoid thinking. Speaking about my own example—I did not drop out of college. I grew up in Northern California, I went to Stanford as an undergrad, I went to Stanford Law School—seven years straight through college. I don't have any regrets about having done it—I learned a lot, I met some great friends in the process.

"But I do have regrets about how automatic it was. If I had to do it over again, it would have been good to think about it more. I really didn't think about it at all. Formal education has become a way to be on autopilot, and not to think about what you want to do with your life.

"One skill that is true of nearly all successful people, particularly entrepreneurs, is learning how to build a team and work together with people. This is very removed from what people learn in school.

"Maybe you learn that if you're captain of a sports team or something, but outside of that, most of the things you do in school are competitive in a purely individual way, where it's just you against everybody else. And most successful businesses are not just one person—they are at least a small team of people. People with different backgrounds, different skills. One of the most difficult and key aspects of business is getting people to work together. Not just on a well-defined game, such as in a football team. But on the 'infinite game' of building a business. [Thiel is referring to a book called *Finite and Infinite Games: A Vision of Life as Play and Possibility* by James Carse, which distinguishes between 'finite' games, where the rules are well defined and stay stable, versus 'infinite' games, where the rules keep shifting and changing as you go along. Carse and Thiel suggest that most of the important things you would want to accomplish in life are infinite games, not finite games.]

"It's the kind of thing our supercompetitive school system is not actually very well geared to do. People always have this Darwinist metaphor for business, where you're in this ecosystem, you're fighting other people, you're fighting other animals, you worry about how much space you have, how big your plot of grass is that you're grazing on, and so forth.

"What's very wrong about that metaphor is that companies themselves are not unitary entities. They're complex entities that are made up of many different people, and getting them to work together is a huge part of being successful in business.

"That's not the kind of thing you learn in school—how you work together with people on a project for years at a time. Maybe you do it for a short homework assignment. It's typically not a very functional thing, in an academic context, and people don't work as hard in such things, because they know it's kind of a joke. Group projects tend to be not as serious, and people don't take them as seriously. Well, doing many things that are important in the world is like a group project, but it's actually very serious. That's outside of the standard, hypercompetitive individualistic academic paradigm."

Thiel also sees our current education system as encouraging a kind of conformity that is anathema to innovation, entrepreneurship, and job creation. "There's a degree to which great companies are somewhat contrarian. You have something you're very passionate about, which other people don't necessarily agree with. If you're trying to do something new, that's never been done before—if you're going from 0 to 1 instead of from 1 to N, if you're the first person who's thinking about this, who's working on this project—it will typically not be seen as respectable, reasonable, sane, by everybody else.

"There's something about the education system that is heavily geared toward the sane and the respectable, and away from the first and onetime, and the unique. It's the difference between substance and status. Status comes from a well-defined game that people play, and the status rules are pretty well defined. Get this credential, get this job, do this, this, and that, and you'll have status—it's this well-defined status hierarchy.

"Whereas in things that are substantive, something that makes a difference to people's lives, the meaning doesn't just come from this competitive social dynamic. At its best, education is substantive. At its worst, it's a pure status dynamic. An awful lot of formal education has become extremely status oriented. I was speaking to people who were going to business school a few months ago. I asked them, in a very friendly, neutral way, 'How many of you are doing this because it's a credential, and how many of you are doing this for the learning?' It was basically, everyone, 100 percent credential, only.

"There's something weird about a system where it's all credentials, and everybody knows it's credentials, and it's sort of like the Wizard of Oz who's hiding behind the curtain. I think formal education has become very status oriented, and very far substantively from what people are interested in accomplishing in their lives and the world. And it's gotten worse as our society has become more tracked.

"You have parents sending their kids through age eighteen to piano lessons, and sports, and you do this, and this, and that, and tutoring for the SATs. At its best, education would be much more creative, and much more autodidactic: 'I'm passionate about this area, so I'm going to learn about it intensely.' At their best, companies are also autodidactic. You could envision formal education that's very compatible with entrepreneurship, but that's not where we are as a society, for all sorts of historical reasons.

"The costs of college have been going up extremely quickly, and it's taking more and more years to pay that investment back. And that's *assuming* you want to do the things for which the credential really helps.

"To me, it's highly debatable whether college is an investment decision or a consumption decision. I think for most majors aside from premed, engineering, and the hard sciences, college can best be thought of as a consumption decision. It's like a four-year party. [Note: Actually, a five-year party, as that's the average time it takes now for someone to get through college. Read *The Five-Year Party: How Colleges Have Given Up on Educating Your Child and What You Can Do About It* by Craig Brandon.] And maybe that's fine. If you want to have a four-year party, people should be allowed to do it.

"But it's similar to what happened in the housing insanity in the last decade. People talked about housing as though it's an investment. But really, if you have a huge house, with a huge swimming pool, and lots of extra rooms, and so forth, probably it was just a consumption decision, and a bad one at that. I think formal education in many cases is more consumption than investment."

I interviewed Thiel toward the end of writing this book, and to my surprise, he referenced the very scene from *The Graduate* with which I opened the book. "Nineteen sixty-nine was *The Graduate*. The advice was, 'Plastics.' That was actually really good advice in 1969. If you followed the advice in the movie, you would have done really well in the seventies and eighties. That was the tracked career type thing then.

"Thematically, the United States has been, for many decades, a very stable place, where the right thing to do has been this super-tracked, predictable path. It's worked really well. But that's no longer the case. The kinds of skills you want to have are ones that are better adapted to a more chaotic world.

"The people who did really tracked careers in the late sixties, who didn't drop out of college or go to an ashram in India, who just went straight through and did the tracked things, who went into 'Plastics,' etc., ended up having very successful careers. Because we had this very stable society, there weren't as many people competing in those professional careers, and so forth.

"Today, it's the exact opposite. Everyone is trying to do something that's hyper-tracked, and yet the reality is that we're in this much more chaotic, crazy world in the next few decades. You want to do something where it's not tracked, and you can be adaptable.

"It's this weird generational thing from the baby boomers to the millennials. The baby boomers were too different, at a time when that was the wrong strategy. Now the millennials are too conformist, at a time when that's the wrong strategy. We're now in a chaotic time, where people need to have skills that are adaptable."

Thiel is pointing out something which I think is incredibly important, and cuts to the heart of my whole intention with this book. If we only know one thing for certain about the future of work, business, and careers, it is this: the future is not going to be anything like we predict. The only thing we can be certain of is uncertainty.

I say that, not as some pseudo-spiritual poetic notion, but as a cold, hard, objective fact. Systems theorists have known for decades that the more complex any system gets (whether it's a physical or biological system, a social network, an organization, or an entire economy), the more unpredictable its behavior gets. The more elements of a system there are (people, businesses), and the more interconnections between those elements (cheap global transportation, global media, and the global Internet), the less useful predictions about the future behavior of that system become.

Why does increasing complexity breed increasing unpredictability?

For a very simple reason. The more interconnected a system such as a global economy becomes, the more changes in one part of the system can have effects that cascade throughout the entire system.

Nineteen terrorists armed with box cutters provided the spark to start a bonfire of events that included a major global economic downturn and two massive wars.

In a more positive example, a few kids sitting in their Harvard dorm room (before they dropped out) launched a venture that changed, within a few years, the way much of the world socializes and communicates.

That's the globalized, interconnected world we live in now. Changes in one part of the system impact the entire system. Prepare for many more interruptions, shocks, surprises, global reorganizations, "black swans," and totally unforeseen developments on this scale (both positive and negative). The "left field" out of which random and unpredictable events can come has just gone global.[8]

In this increasingly unpredictable and chaotic world, the wisest choice for thriving and flourishing is to focus your efforts on cultivating skills, habits, and ways of being that will work for you under a wide range of market circumstances and economic realities, and which will allow you to bounce back and adapt to changes, shifts, shocks, crashes, and new opportunities as they arise. This is called cultivating *resilience*.

I predict many of the critics of my book will incorrectly say I reduce education to mere "vocational training." My book, in fact, recommends the *opposite* of vocational training. Vocational training prepares you for a specific job—even though many of the jobs people are now training for may not exist in five or ten years! The courses in this book prepare you for success in any job, including jobs we can't even imagine because they don't exist yet. It is a completely adaptable set of personal and professional skills for life in the real world, applicable under any market conditions, any economic landscape, any personal circumstances.

What I hope I've given you in this book is the keys toward *economic and career resilience.* If one thing is sure, it's that we're all going to need a lot of resilience, flexibility, and adaptability if we want to survive and thrive amid the waves of change (both destructive and constructive) that are coming our way.

Our education system, as it stands, from kindergarten through graduate school, is the opposite of resilience, flexibility, and adaptability. It teaches a narrow set of academic/analytic skills, mostly divorced from the practicalities of life, and drills them into you for hours, days, weeks, months, and years on end. Analytic skills may be valuable to success in a rapidly changing, chaotic world, but they are far, far from the whole picture. Success, happiness, contribution, innovation, and leadership depend on a range of human skills, most of which are not taught in school.

Thiel says: "To question formal education in our society—it's the one thing that's really taboo in our society. And if you want to have a candidate for something that's really a bubble, you need incredible belief. In the nineties, people really believed in technology. This last decade, people really believed in housing. The precondition for a bubble is intense belief without any possibility for questioning it. Our beliefs about education fall under this category right now.

"I worry that our thinking about education has gotten to be 100 percent outsourced. People just follow the tracked programs other people tell them to do, without questioning it at all. I worry that we've forgotten how to think for ourselves about education, and we need to recover that.

"My number-one candidate for a bubble in the United States today is higher education. It is believed incredibly intensely. To question it is to put yourself outside the circle of respectable belief.

"But there's obviously a lot to question. What it comes down to, I believe, is not left versus right, but establishment versus non-establishment. Things that require an established track to enter into, versus things that require a lot of innovation. The tracked establishment in the United States has badly failed. It doesn't work that well anymore, it's not that compelling."

Peter introduced me to Sean Parker, who was the founding president of Facebook when Peter invested in the company. I met with Sean in his new town house in the West Village in Manhattan. (For those who are curious: I personally found Sean to be the direct opposite of the vapid slickster Justin Timberlake portrays him as in *The Social Network*. I found him to be pensive, philosophical, self-aware, and intensely intellectually curious—recommending book after book to me that he felt I needed to read. Out of respect for his time, I kept trying to end the interview, and he kept telling me about one more concept or idea or angle I needed to consider for my book. We rapped philosophical for four hours.)

According to Sean, the decreasing returns to sticking with the establishment in your education, and the increasing returns to choosing the road not taken, stem from the Internet. "When these incredible tools of knowledge and learning are available to the whole world, formal education becomes less and less important. We should expect to see the emergence of a new kind of autodidact/ thinker/entrepreneur/businessperson/leader who has acquired most of their knowledge through self-exploration. Because for the first time in human history, all of the world's knowledge is available at their fingertips. Perhaps more than anything the Internet has given us, this is the most significant discontinuity event.

"My career unfolded along the leading edge of this transformation, so in a sense I was too early to reap all the benefits. But there's a generation of kids coming, who have grown up with Wikipedia, who have grown up with a notion that they're not just a consumer of media, but a participant. They therefore have a deeper and more ingrained skepticism of the media, and therefore have a better capability to distinguish truth from fiction, authority from charlatan. This capability for meta-analysis of information is essential as they wade through the vast sea of information. For the first time in history they have all the world's information at their disposal, accessible from anywhere they want. The result is that this emerging generation no longer has reality dictated to them— they are finally empowered to construct their own unique, and possibly idiosyncratic, perspective on the world, if they so choose.

"Any high school student in the world can get online and dig deeply into anything that interests them. What's changed is that the information is linked in a hypertext manner, so they don't need to learn things linearly. The traditional method of instruction is to create some linear progression of information that can be put into a textbook and can be read one page after another, starting with things that are thought to be foundational, and moving onward. When in fact all human knowledge is massively interconnected in complicated ways and isn't structured linearly at all. That linear structure is something that is necessitated by the medium of a book and the chronological experience of life in a classroom. The potential exists now, with all of this information linked together now in totally arbitrary ways, to follow your own path through that information.

"I think we'll start to realize that the real enemy, in terms of human progress, is social conventionality, in the general sense, and not just via institutionalization and bureaucracy. I think we'll look back at institutionalization and bureaucracy as a problem and artifact of the mid-to-late twentieth century, and we'll start to more clearly see that that was a special case, of this more general case, which has been a part of human history since the beginning: conformity, or a lack of individualism. Bureaucracy and institutionalization are just expressions of that deeper current throughout history."

Sean Parker graduated high school in 1998—and did not move on to college—just at the outset of this "dislocation event" he describes. He was at the crest of the wave. To get a sense of how thoroughly this wave has transformed the way cutting-edge young people are thinking about education now, we can turn to the story of a young man named Max Marmer.

Max entered Stanford as a freshman in the fall of 2010, but he soon felt out of place. "I spent a lot of time thinking about what I wanted my future to be, how can I make a big impact, and what would be my best, most direct route to doing that. Many of my peers had given very little thought to all of that."

During the time he was deciding to leave Stanford, multiple friends and mentors began forwarding to Max a link to Peter Thiel's announcement of the Thiel Fellowship that fall. Thiel's encouragement that young people didn't need to wait to get a paper credential to start doing big things in the world spoke to Max directly. He decided to apply for the fellowship, but (unlike most other applicants) he also made his final decision to leave college and start his own company immediately, whether he received the fellowship or not. He is now the proud founder of The Startup Genome Project (http://www.startupgenome.cc).

The Project is inspired by the work of successful serial entrepreneur Steve Blank, who argues in his books and teachings that a startup is an organization that should be designed specifically to *learn.* "A startup needs to learn about the problem, the solution, who the customers are, the market, and getting all these pieces to fit together. An early-stage startup is a set of assumptions, and you need to test those assumptions systematically," Max told me. His project is designed to help guide startups in going through that learning curve.

Notably, he is walking his talk and learning at a rapid clip through the launch of his company. He has traded theoretical education in college courses, which cost him a fortune, for real-world education in his own startup, in which he's instead *earning money* while he learns. He has simply bypassed the higher education bubble. "I believe the education system as a whole is broken beyond repair, and starting anew via creative destruction is our only hope for system-wide improvement," Max wrote in a blog post announcing his decision to leave Stanford.[9]

This reminded me of a sentiment that Marc Ecko shared with me: "I hate the word 'reform.' You don't 'reform' the iPod into the iPhone! You *change* it! You reimagine it! It's not *reform*, it's reimagination."

(For those who say Max is losing out on gaining "wisdom," "critical thinking skills," "perspective on life," and all the other humanistic value one can undeniably gain from a college education: I can't imagine an educational environment where one can gain more critical thinking skills, perspective, and life wisdom than in an early-stage startup, whether the startup ultimately succeeds or fails. And Max is gaining these now, however this first startup of his turns out. I have many more answers to objections such as these in my companion PDF report *The Dropout Revolution: Why Today's Savviest Kids Are Forsaking Debt and Educating Themselves*, available for free via the note at the beginning of this book.)

I was interviewing Max in the eleventh-floor dining room of the Celebrity Century cruise liner, somewhere in the middle of the Caribbean, in April 2011. The entire boat—normally occupied by retirees and honeymooners—was taken over by a thousand young entrepreneurs, mostly in their twenties, networking, partying, and plotting in various ways to make a massive impact on the world.

It was my first time attending Summit Series, dubbed the "Davos of Generation Y." I had met the founders when I had interviewed them six months earlier for the chapter Success Skill #2; they had upped their game this year and had put the whole conference, previously held in convention centers, on a gargantuan boat. Young people buzzed around, chatting over the music, dancing, trading contact information. As I spoke with Max, overlooking the sea, a friend of Max's spotted him and walked up to us. Max introduced us: "Hey Michael, this is Trevor. He's also an entrepreneur who's leaving school."

"Leaving school?" Trevor cut in as if to correct an insulting slight. "I've already left school!" Trevor Owens had left NYU during his senior year to help build The Lean Startup Machine (http://theleanstartupmachine.com), a series of intensive boot camps designed to promote entrepreneurialism and train entrepreneurs in the business principles of "lean thinking."

I had never been on a cruise before. The series was originally the brainchild of Elliott Bisnow, who had left Wisconsin to pursue his dreams. Three years later he was hosting some of the world's most powerful people at his own cruise liner weekend event/party. Sir Richard Branson—who did not complete high school—opened the event. The next speaker was Blake Mycoskie, founder of TOMS shoes (http://www.toms.com), a company famous for donating one pair of shoes to children in need for every pair it sells. Blake, of course, did not complete college. Peter Thiel (whom I introduced via e-mail to Elliott) spoke to the audience about his fellowship, and received powerful applause for his comments about the failure of higher education today.

A revolution is happening. All of a sudden, I was meeting kids everywhere who were waking up and realizing something profoundly important: they have more power and choice to control their own destiny than most parents, teachers, pundits, and politicians tell them. They don't need to follow the crowd running into a building that's burning down, just because everyone else is running into it. They have choice. They have the tools at their disposal now to create their own path through life.

Peter Thiel continued on this theme: "I was talking with someone here in San Francisco, who was running a foundation to get minority students into college and then into various tracked careers. There's a sense in which that sounds like a very respectable, worthwhile thing to do. But then the man said, very proudly, 'And here's how many of our kids got jobs at Lehman Brothers!' He said that in all seriousness. Well, Lehman Brothers doesn't exist any-more! It imploded along with much of the rest of the financial es-tablishment.

"He said it in the spirit of, 'We got these minority students to enter into this establishment that they normally wouldn't have gotten into.' Four years ago, this would have been a very liberal, progressive thing to do. But is helping minority students—indeed all young people—enter into establishments that are crashing all about them as we speak really the best way to help them anymore? Versus helping young people do something totally outside of the establishment?"

One of my favorite of all TED videos is a segment called "Let's Raise Kids to Be Entrepreneurs" by Cameron Herold.[10] Cameron, a serial entrepreneur, has started numerous highly profitable busi-nesses. He went on to become an early COO of 1-800-GOT-JUNK?, helping it grow from $2 million to $105 million in six years "with no debt and no outside shareholders." He is the author of *Double Double: How to Double Your Revenue and Profit in 3 Years or Less*, of which he has direct experience from his entrepreneurial work (http://www.backpocketcoo.com).

He says in his talk: "Right now we teach our kids to go after really good jobs . . . like being a doctor and being a lawyer and being an accountant and a dentist and a teacher and a pilot. And the media says it's really cool if we could go out and be a model or a singer or a sports hero. . . . [O]ur MBA programs don't teach kids to be entrepreneurs. They teach them to go work in corporations. So who's starting these companies [which employ everyone else]? It's these few random people."

Cameron graduated from university, but he never thought much of formal education. He got a 62 percent average in "the only university in Canada which would accept me" and almost flunked out because he was spending all his time managing and growing a highly profitable house-painting franchise, which he has said was his true education. He told me:

> I called home from the university in the second year. I was really frustrated with my accounting course.
> My dad said, "What are you frustrated about?"
> I said, "I don't understand it. I have now hired a kid to do my assignments for me. I'm paying a guy in beer to do every one of my weekly assignments. First I am ashamed of doing it, and sec-

ondly, I am terrified because I have to write my midterm tomorrow, and I don't understand it."

He said, "What do you need to pass?"

I said, "Probably like 52 percent, because this guy is doing a good job with my assignments."

My dad said two things. He said, "First, do you want to be an accountant when you grow up?"

"No, I want to be an entrepreneur."

"Good," my dad said. "So don't worry about it because when you graduate from the university nobody is going to give a shit what you got on this course."

Then my dad said, "Second, you just learned how to hire your first accountant. You are hiring someone to do the work that entrepreneurs shouldn't be doing."

Now, I don't advocate cheating in college. But I do believe Cameron's story raises an incredibly important point. Our educational system, from kindergarten through college, basically tells kids, "Work hard, do this busywork, do this set of problems, wade through this long text and make notes on it." It completely trains kids to be the doers in business, rather than the people who *hire* doers. We have way too many doers right now relative to the people hiring the doers (a.k.a., high unemployment). This is why. It goes right back to our education system, designed in its current form over a century ago to crank out masses of compliant factory workers and organization men—for which there are no longer jobs.

Which brings us back to Peter Thiel's vision. "We want to help young people create something that totally disrupts the current establishment, the current system. That's entrepreneurialism at its best. I think people are a lot more open to rethinking this today than they were five years ago. You have people who are going to college, they don't get a job, then they have to move back in with their parents. This was not what was expected."

Thiel told me he asks a simple question of people who are seeking employment with him, as well as asking it of the young people applying to his fellowship program. He says that many young people, raised for years and years through the hoop-jumping and conformism of the formal schooling system, have an incredibly hard time answering it. So it weeds out most applicants: "Tell me something that you think is true that very few people agree with."

We've seen that those who have clung to outmoded, rigid, stale, conformist notions of formal higher education are now getting slaughtered economically, as their formerly safe jobs get outsourced, downsized, offshored, and automated, and as once-secure establishments crumble into the wireless, digital, networked ethers.

What do *you* think is true about your own education, and about your own path to success in the real world, which very few people agree with?

I hope this book has inspired at least a few disobedient thoughts.

GRATITUDE

This book would not exist without the encouragement of Marie Forleo. At a small dinner party in the spring of 2009 in New York, just after I handed in my first book to HarperCollins, I decided to test out several book ideas on my guests for my next one.

I mentioned my three top book concepts to the guests. Honestly, I can't even remember what they were, but the response to all of them was lukewarm at best. I felt despairing at this response. Figuring I didn't have much to lose at this point, I decided to try one idea on the group, an idea I'd been thinking about for a while but had always dismissed, as it seemed way too controversial.

"Well, I have one other, really crazy idea," I said to the guests. "I want to write a book about billionaires and millionaires who educated themselves, and didn't finish college."

"THAT'S your next book!" Marie shouted instantly in excitement. "I'd buy that in a second."

Marie's validation was all the encouragement I needed, and I chose that topic. Thank you, Marie!

I am incredibly grateful to all the self-educated people and other experts who shared their stories and opinions for this book. *This book would be nothing without you.* I give all my thanks to the following interviewees:

Maria Andros; David Ash; James Bach; Andy Bailey; Steve Baines; Scott and Cyan Banister; Howard Behar; James Bell; Elliott

Bisnow; Michael Bissonnette; Jeff Black; Opher Brayer; Gurbash Chahal; Rose Cole; Christine Comaford; Richard Cooper; Jade Craven; Decker Cunov; John Paul DeJoria; Felix Dennis; Erica Douglas; Marc Ecko; Hal Elrod; Kent Emmons; Mike Faith; Lauren Frances; Bryan Franklin; Marijo Franklin; David Gilmour; Paul Hawken; Dennis Hoffman; Mike Jagger; Cameron Johnson; Derek Johnson; Jeremy Johnson; Frank Kern; Randy Komisar; Eva Konigsberg; Jena la Flamme; Danielle LaPorte; Max Marmer; Matthias Mazur; Jonathan Mead; Loren Michelle; David Morris; Dustin Moskovitz; Matt Mullenweg; Eben Pagan; Sean Parker; Joe Polish; Lynda Resnick; Gordon Ruddow; Phillip Ruffin; Anthony Sandberg; Jeremy Schwartz; Robert Scoble; Ryan Scott; Brian Scudamore; Russell Simmons; Linda Sivertsen; Spencer Thompson; Tyler Willis; and Woody Woodward.

I am also grateful to the many experts I interviewed who do have college and/or graduate degrees. Many thanks to Gregory Berns, PhD; Chris Brogan; Victor Cheng; Keith Ferrazzi; Seth Godin; Ace Greenberg; Cameron Herold; Josh Kaufman; Robert Kiyosaki; Randy Komisar; John Kremer; Charles Murray, PhD; Kenneth Roman; Marian Schembari; Peter Thiel; and Johnny Truant.

The following people all connected me to one or more interviewees: Elliott Bisnow; Justin Cohen; Adair Curtis; Mike Del Ponte; Mike Faith; Tim Ferriss; Jonathan Fields; Marie Forleo; Sandor Gardos; Adam Gilad; David Hassell; Cameron Herold; Ken Howery; Lisa Kotecki; Jena la Flamme; Tonya Leigh; Justine Musk; Kenneth Roman; Polly Samson; Marian Schembari; Yanik Silver; and Peter Thiel. Thank you so much for your help.

John Kremer's incredible "College Dropouts Hall of Fame" (http://www.collegedropoutshalloffame.com) provided inspiration, and many of my initial ideas about whom to contact for interviews. I learned of self-educated serial entrepreneur Woody Woodward's book *Millionaire Dropouts: Biographies of the World's Most Successful Failures* after I began writing this book. Woody (http://www.millionairedropouts.com) graciously sent me a copy of his book, which contains biographical sketches of one hundred famous people without college degrees. I found his book, and an interview I did with him, highly inspirational, confirming for me that I was on the right path in choosing this topic.

The very dramatic difference in quality between the first draft and the final version is due in great part to the influence of my sharp, insightful, and sensitive editor at Portfolio, Jillian Gray. This is a far, far better book thanks to your help, Jillian—I appreciate it tremendously and it was a joy working with you. Thank you also to all other members of the Portfolio team I worked with, including Adrian Zackheim, Will Weisser, Natalie Horbachevsky, Allison McLean, and Tiffany Liao, for your immediate and unwavering belief in this project. You gave me the opportunity to write this book, helped me make it what it is, and helped get it out into the world with a bang.

David Moldawer also played an important role early on, providing wise guidance in shaping the book at the initial stages.

At the home of Naomi Wolf, I met Erica Jong. Through Erica, I met Sandi Mendelson. Sandi connected me to my amazing agent, Esther Newberg. In this chain of connection, you all played a crucial part in helping my dream come true in this book. Profuse thanks to all of you.

Much of this book was conceived, pitched, and written during the time I was studying under the mentorship of my friend Bryan Franklin. Bryan, you helped me reach big. I will always be grateful. Your guidance and influence are reflected throughout this book.

The manuscript benefited tremendously from the incisive editorial comments of Sandor Gardos; my parents, Daniel and Patricia Ellsberg; and my wife, Jena la Flamme, all of whom read it in draft form. Thank you all so much for your time, and for trusting me with your candid feedback, which I incorporated extensively. Also, eagle-eyed copy editor Muriel Jorgenson made this a far more readable book.

Every book I ever write, I will always express my gratitude to three specific people. First, to my parents, Daniel and Patricia—two of my best friends in the world—for your overwhelming love and support. You both gave me my passion for constant learning—one of the greatest gifts you could ever have given, a gift that will burn in my soul for the rest of my life.

Jena la Flamme became my wife as I was writing this book. Jena, this is the second book I've dedicated to you, the first book of our marriage, and the first book (though surely not the last) inspired by you. This book would not exist without your fearless commitment to self-education. You are my everything.

NOTES

To find full citations to all works cited, as well as Web links to these works, visit http://www.ellsberg.com/education-works-cited.

▌ INTRODUCTION

1 Robinson, accessed March 28, 2010.
2 Murray, locations 986–987 on Kindle edition.
3 Cherry, accessed December 19, 2010.
4 See Gladwell's discussion, in *Outliers*, of the Michigan Law School study, which found that minority students—despite being admitted with lower grades and test scores, as a part of affirmative action, and despite earning lower grades in law school—went on to have law careers every bit as successful as their white peers. (Kindle edition, locations 1050–1059.) "Being a successful lawyer is about a lot more than IQ," Gladwell concludes, to explain the findings of the study. (Kindle edition, locations 1105–1114.)
5 I want to make clear that while I think certain of Gladwell's points in his book support the basic message of my book, I doubt he himself would agree with much in my book overall. Later in his book, he argues that more hours in school training hard in academic subjects, not fewer hours, is essential for inner-city kids' success.
6 Shapiro, p. 782.
7 Williams, accessed January 15, 2010.
8 Kleinfield, accessed October 9, 2009.
9 Pink (2001), locations 197–199 on Kindle edition.

10 Pink, locations 810–819 on Kindle edition.
11 Pink, location 843 on Kindle edition.

■ SUCCESS SKILL #1

1 Johnson, location 1035 on Kindle edition.
2 Johnson, locations 2696–2714 on Kindle edition.
3 Komisar, p. 154
4 Komisar, pp. 65–66.
5 For a detailed and brilliant exposition of survivorship bias, see Taleb.
6 Godin (2010 A), accessed April 3, 2010.
7 Moskovitz, accessed March 22, 2010.

■ SUCCESS SKILL #2

1 Cohen, accessed December 13, 2010.
2 Bertoni, accessed December 13, 2010.
3 One of his product lines, the David DeAngelo series of trainings for men, is quite controversial. The early trainings in the series focus on helping men "pick up" women through pickup lines, tricks, and cocky attitudes. However, later trainings focus on authentic communication, meaningful relationships, and personal transformation. Eben states openly that the sequence is intentional, designed to bring in the vast majority of men who would never go straight for the more touchy-feely stuff first. One of his philosophies is "sell them what they want, and give them what they need." It's like those enterprising churches that, instead of "preaching to the converted," bring in rock bands and cage-fighting matches to lure hormonal teenagers to church, and then give them a dose of spirituality and uplift along with it.
4 Gowen, accessed December 13, 2010.
5 Garland, accessed December 15, 2010.
6 Tracy, accessed December 15, 2010.
7 Pavlina, p. 186.
8 For more discussion of these market failures, including externalities, common-pool-resource problems, and public goods, see, for example, Fox; Hawken, Lovins and Lovins; Kapp; and Ostrom.
9 Quoted in J. Simmons, location 3199 in Kindle edition.
10 Godin (2010 B), locations 2601–2611 in Kindle edition.
11 R. Simmons, locations 3194–3207 in Kindle edition.
12 There is a distinction between giving without an expectation of return and just giving randomly to every stranger you pass. Some people advocate the latter, at least in rhetoric, but it doesn't seem realistic to me, and frankly I don't tend to see the people who preach this practicing what they preach. Energy and attention are limited, and I think most of it should be focused on giving to people with whom you're building long-term, meaningful relationships.

Of course, the network you're building should contain both people who are further along the path to success than you, who are pulling you up from above, and people who are earlier in their development of success, whom you're pulling up even as you are pulled up by others. In other words, this philosophy has all the room in the world for charity for those poorer and less fortunate than ourselves. But if you're giving to poor people with no intention or effort at building a relationship or any human bonds—drive-by charity—it's basically patronizing, it reinforces the divisions that already exist between you, and I don't think that form of charity does them or you much good in the long run.

The best giving, I believe, is giving in the context of building meaningful, long-term human bonds with those we're helping: giving when there is an explicit intention to form a meaningful human connection over time, one in which you both impact, give to, and learn from each other in your own ways, growing and developing together.

■ SUCCESS SKILL #3

1 Kennedy, locations 689–697 in Kindle edition.
2 Kennedy, locations 690–703 in Kindle edition, *emphasis in original.*
3 Johnson, locations 809–830 in Kindle edition.
4 Godin (2009), locations 1132–1140 in Kindle edition.
5 Kennedy, locations 377–386 in Kindle edition.
6 Clark, accessed May 2, 2011.
7 Resnick, p. 23.
8 Ibid.
9 Resnick, p. 41.

■ SUCCESS SKILL #4

1 Kiyosaki, pp. 170–171.
2 Longinovic, accessed May 2, 2011.
3 Rodriguez, accessed May 2, 2011.
4 Ford, Sam, accessed May 2, 2011. Thanks to Meagan Templeton-Lynch for finding this one and the vampire course, in her article "The Craziest College Classes: 2010 Edition." See Templeton-Lynch, accessed May 2, 2011.

■ SUCCESS SKILL #5

1 Success Magazine, accessed May 2, 2011.
2 Krier, accessed March 13, 2011.
3 Morgan, accessed March 13, 2011.
4 Ibid.

5 CNBC, accessed March 13, 2011.

6 Walker, accessed March 17, 2011.

7 Wikipedia contributors, "Kirk Kerkorian," accessed March 17, 2011.

■ SUCCESS SKILL #6

1 Godin (2008), accessed January 3, 2010.

2 Montoya, pp. xi–xii. In brackets, I changed the word "business" to "brand," to expand its relevance to all people, not just those starting businesses.

■ SUCCESS SKILL #7

1 Quoted in Fireside Learning, accessed May 2, 2011.

2 Kawasaki, accessed May 2, 2011.

3 Sykes, p. 57.

4 *Time*, accessed May 2, 2011.

5 *Fortune*, p. 21.

6 *Fortune*, pp. 122–127, 163–164.

7 *Fortune*, p. 127.

8 Stewart, p. 13.

9 Wikipedia contributors, "Walt Disney," accessed December 23, 2010.

10 Pinsky, p. 9.

11 *Fortune,* p. 122.

12 Ford, Henry, pp. 121–123.

13 *Time,* accessed May 2, 2011.

■ EPILOGUE

1 Munna, accessed January 29, 2011.

2 Taylor (2009 A), accessed January 29, 2011.

3 Taylor (2009 B), accessed January 29, 2011.

4 Reynolds, accessed January 31, 2011.

5 Segal, accessed January 31, 2011.

6 Thiel Foundation, accessed January 31, 2011.

7 Weisberg, accessed January 31, 2011.

8 For more on this topic, see Taleb.

9 Marmer, accessed April 12, 2011.

10 Herold, accessed March 17, 2011.

INDEX